A PRACTICAL GUIDE TO
WITCHCRAFT
AND
MAGICK SPELLS

A PRACTICAL GUIDE TO
WITCHCRAFT
AND
MAGICK SPELLS

CASSANDRA EASON

quantum

LONDON • NEW YORK • TORONTO • SYDNEY

quantum

An imprint of W. Foulsham & Co. Ltd
The Publishing House, Bennetts Close,
Cippenham, Slough, Berkshire, SL1 5AP, England

ISBN 0-572-02704-4

Printed in Great Britain by St. Edmundsbury Press, Bury St. Edmunds, Suffolk.

Contents

INTRODUCTION
The Power of White Witchcraft

'Merlin, give me the strength to carry on.'

I found this prayer not in some medieval book or carved on the wall of an ancient castle but written in ballpoint pen on a page torn from a diary and left – along with scores of similar pleas – on an ancient pile of stones in the Forest of Broceliande in Brittany.

Archaeologists say that this is the grave of a Neolithic hunter, but local tradition says that in this forest dwelled Vivien, the Lady of the Lake of Arthurian legend, and that here, having seduced Merlin in order to learn his secrets, she ensnared him with his own spells. The stone pile is known as Merlin's tomb, and each year hundreds visit the site to thank the wizard or to ask for his aid. When I visited the tomb, prayers – written on scraps of paper or card – were squeezed into gaps in the stones or pinned to the tree that shelters the tomb.

Whatever the origins of the tomb, it has been transformed into a source of power. For this badly signposted spot, a short walk up a muddy track from a cramped, rough car park, had a tranquil, spiritual air that you might expect at a great cathedral or far more impressive stone circles. Such spots unleash the magick inside us. But even if you never visit Brittany or Stonehenge at sunrise on Midsummer's Day, you can still make use of your own magick.

This is a book about white magick and witchcraft as sources of wisdom, healing and positivity. Like Native American spirituality, to which true witchcraft is akin (some say both were carried by the people of Atlantis), the practice of white magick is based on the belief that that all life is sacred and interconnected in an unbroken circle. For example, every fully grown birch tree – defined in magick as a tree of new beginnings and regeneration – breathes out enough oxygen for a family of four and absorbs the carbon dioxide that we exhale, transforming it again to life-giving oxygen. And this sacred spark of a common source of divinity is contained not only by trees, but also the stones, the animals, the people and everything else on the Earth and in the waters and the sky.

Our higher selves, our souls, are influenced by the cycles of the Sun, the Moon, the stars and the natural world on a deep spiritual level. We can draw down their energies into ourselves to amplify and replenish our own, like tapping into a cosmic energy supply rather than having to recharge our powers from our own, separate dynamos. Through them and through us courses the universal life force, known as *ch'i* to the Chinese, and *prana* in Hindu philosophy. It is a source upon which we can draw not only nor primarily for specific needs, but also for energy, harmony and connection with others, the world and the cosmos. It is an energy that can permeate every aspect of our being.

A very special spirituality

Witchcraft and Wicca (one of the major forms of witchcraft) both derive their names from the Anglo-Saxon words for wisdom; 'witch' is from the old English word *wita*, meaning 'wise' and the Wicca were the wise ones. Witchcraft is said to be the oldest religion in the world. It is the indigenous shamanistic religion of Europe that has, in spite of ferocious persecution from the fifteenth to the seventeenth centuries, survived in the folk tradition of many lands and through families who kept alive the old beliefs and worship of the Earth and the Moon Mother.

Not so many centuries ago, our ancestors burned yule logs at Christmas as a symbolic gesture to bring light and warmth back to the world on the mid-winter solstice at the darkest time. They danced around the maypole on May morning, the beginning of the old Celtic summer, to stir into life the Earth energies in a sacred spiral pattern. These rituals go back into the mists of time and appear in similar forms in many different cultures and ages. Today, however, too many modern societies have lost the sacred connection and scorn such gestures as superstition, treating the skies, the Earth and the seas merely as a larder, fuel store and garbage can. Once, things were very different, as Black Elk, the Sioux shaman, explained:

> *'In the old days when we were a strong and happy people, all our power came from the sacred hoop of the nation and, so long as the hoop was unbroken, the people flourished. The flowering tree was the living centre of the hoop and the circle of the four quarters nourished it. The East gave peace and light, the South gave warmth; in the West, thunder beings gave rain and the North with its cold and mighty wind gave strength and endurance.'*

And so the Earth was respected as the sacred mother, giver of life and crops, to whose womb the dead returned. It is no accident that the Sioux Medicine Wheel and the Celtic Wheel of the Year are so similar in formation and purpose, linking all life to the cycles of nature. So if we are to use magick in a positive way, we must remember that it brings responsibility along with benefits.

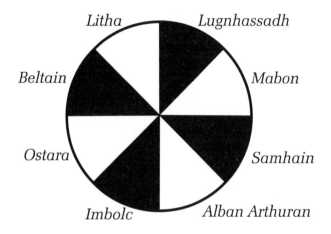

Magick and knowledge

White witchcraft is essentially the process of drawing on ancient wisdom and powers via the collective mind that we as individuals can spontaneously but unconsciously access in our dreams and visions. In magick, we can use rituals and altered states of consciousness to access this cosmic memory bank at will and in doing so, some believe, draw on the accumulated powers of many generations, especially in healing magick. This cosmic consciousness – or Great Mind or akashic record, as theosophists call it – is perhaps what made it possible for pyramids to be built at almost the same time in lands as far apart as Egypt and South America, and for shamanism to follow similar patterns in unconnected continents. By accessing this source of power, we may create a ritual or use certain crystals without consciously knowing their significance, only to find out that our invented spell closely resembles one from another time or culture; we know how to heal without being taught.

Gaining such knowledge has been described as 'inner-plane' teaching and if you can trust your own deep intuitions, you need very little formal teaching about magick. If you scry at the full moon or during one of the ancient festivals, by looking into water and letting images form, this deep wisdom will offer solutions to seemingly impossible dilemmas.

The practice of witchcraft demands great responsibility, for you are handling very potent material when you deal with magick. The benefit is that by focusing and directing your own inner powers and natural energies you can give form to your thoughts and needs and desires and bring them into actuality. The more positive and altruistic these focuses are, the more abundance, joy and harmony will be reflected in your own world.

Magick and giving

It is said that if you smile in London in the morning, the smile will have reached Tokyo by evening. This principle, which lies behind all white magick, has been named morphic resonance, and has been investigated for several years by the Cambridge biologist Dr Rupert Sheldrake, author of a number of excellent books based on his extensive research into psychic phenomena. Dr Sheldrake suggests that as animals of a given species learn a new pattern of behaviour, other similar animals will subsequently tend to learn the same thing more readily all over the world; the more that learn it, the easier it should become for others.

So if we carry out positive magick and spread goodwill, then we really can increase the benign energies of the Earth and cosmos. Even banishing or binding magick can have a creative focus, diverting or transforming redundant or negative energy, for example by burying a symbol of the negativity or casting herbs to the four winds.

Magick and responsibility

True magick is not like a cake in which everybody must vie for a slice or be left with none: it is more akin to a never-emptying pot. Like the legendary Cauldron of Undry in Celtic myth, the more goodness that is put in, the more the mixture increases in richness and quantity. The Cauldron of Undry, one of the four main Celtic treasures, provided an endless supply of nourishment, had great healing powers and could restore the dead to life, in either their former existence or a new life form. Located on the Isle of Arran, it could be accessed by magical means or through spiritual quests, and many scholars believe it was the inspiration for the Holy Grail. But when using magick, you should take only as much as you need and perhaps a little more; you should not demand riches, perfect love, eternal beauty, youth, a fabulous job and a lottery win or two.

So, magick does not provide a help-yourself time in the sweetshop. The results could be like eating three times more chocolate than you really want and then feeling very sick. You cannot give the gods or goddesses your shopping list and then sit back and wait for Christmas: the divinity is within you to be kindled, and so you need to demand of yourself far higher standards than someone who believes in the forgiveness of sins.

If you do wrong, you cannot just say sorry to the godhead and carry on without putting right the mistakes or at least learning from them. Confession may be good for the soul, but magick demands more than that: you've got to live with the consequences of your deeds, words and thoughts because the power of a blessing or curse may be even greater on the sender than on the intended recipient. You must also ensure that you cannot harm anyone in the process of getting what you want. If you do spells for revenge, then the effects will rebound on you threefold.

Effort and will-power

Magick is not like the magic a conjuror uses to bring a rabbit out of a hat: that kind of magic is just a trick, which relies merely on the art of illusion. White magick is much more than that. It is intensely exciting because it means that we can extend the boundaries of possibility, recalling the psychic powers of childhood when we could span dimensions as easily as jumping across a puddle. We can increase our personal magnetism to attract love and luck and regenerate the innate healing abilities both of the human body and the planet. What magick does not do is provide quick fixes with a twinkling of stardust. It does not produce a faerie godmother, who turns up with a shimmering frock and a platinum credit card to pay the taxi fare home if the handsome prince is short of money and the faerie coach has crumpled into a pumpkin.

After the candles and incense have burned through and we sit, exhausted but exhilarated after sending our wishes to the cosmos through dancing or chanting, we then have to use every effort, every talent at our disposal, to make those wishes come true on the earthly plane. The psychic kick-start provided by the magick must be used to translate the magical thoughts into actuality. So we must work overtime with new enthusiasm and inspiration to get that project finished, send off to the publisher that typescript that has been gathering dust, do whatever it takes to help ourselves to get the results we desire. My late mother would always say if I asked for extra funds, 'Money doesn't grow on trees'; and this holds true even in the magical world. Money, success and opportunities have to be generated and earned. We need to add our own will-power to the power we have drawn on.

What is more, under the cosmic profit-and-loss scheme, if we ask for a psychic overdraft, we must give back, if not immediately, then at a later date. So when your finances are better or your immediate troubles are passed, you should make a small donation or give time to a worthwhile cause connected with the area of the spell. This balances up the account whose cosmic energies you tapped into.

Many shamans or witches demand some sort of payment for services, and this is not from avarice, but because all too often if something is not paid for, it is not valued. So be sure that you pay the shaman – especially the cosmic one. This is grass roots magick, but it works.

Magick for your needs

'Enough for my needs and a little more' is another of the maxims of this incredibly moral craft, as I mentioned earlier. You would be amazed the number of times I am asked: 'Okay, if you are a witch, how come you can't predict the lottery numbers?' The answer is that it all comes down to need: and do I *need* a million pounds? True, like any mother of five children I lurch from one financial crisis to the next and when things get really dire, perhaps I could magically bring forward an anticipated payment or attract an unexpected windfall from abroad. But I don't really *need* a million pounds. And what about the negative effects? If I became incredibly rich, I would almost certainly lose the incentive to write. Credit card bills are a powerful focus for creativity. And, of course, my kids would never get out of their satin-sheeted beds.

Lotteries are generated by human hands primarily for the purpose of making money for their creators. They really are random affairs and so it often happens that it is the wealthy people who win even more money – although that does not necessarily bring happiness.

Casting your needs into the cosmos and trusting they will be met does work, but not if you are expecting magick to compensate for an unnecessary shopping binge. Nor, after a period of overeating and no exercise, can you expect a miracle diet to work so that you shed a stone in two days while still eating chocolate. Spells tend to work best when there is a genuine need, generated by real emotion and linked to determination on a practical level.

The rules of magick

Magick is not beyond or above life, but a natural though special part of your world. It is about not leaving fate, your fate, to any guru or deity, but shaping it with your own innate power, the power that emanates from some higher being, goddess or god, energy source, what you will – the divine spark within us all. There are no absolutes in magick, there is only what works for you and enhances your innate wisdom and spirituality. You should use this book as you would any other DIY guide and adapt its suggestions to suit what is right for you. Choose whatever you feel are the most appropriate herbs, crystals or even entire rituals for your specific purpose.

There are provisos, however. You must always remember that the form, the words and even ultimately the associations of particular oils, incenses and planetary hours are not what really matters. The truly important thing is that you should keep to the basic rules of witchcraft that are quite as strict and twice as hard as any conventional religion. These are rooted in wisdom, compassion, honesty, honour and common sense and are summed up in one short phrase: *'An ye harm none, do what ye will'.* Put in modern-day language, this means, quite simply:

'Do whatever you like as long as you don't hurt anyone.'

Simple, did I say? It is in practice incredibly hard to harm none, especially if you are seeking promotion, fighting against an injustice or struggling to survive. But it may help you if you remember the other equally vital law of witchcraft, the Threefold Law. This states that everything you do to others, both good and bad, will be sent back to act on you with three times its intensity and strength. So, if you act always and only with positive intent to help and heal, you will automatically receive all manner of good things and you should become truly wise and happy.

According to the rules of magick, as I said earlier, you cannot be angry, mean or cruel and then expect to say sorry to a deity and have the slate wiped clean. Magick is about taking responsibility for your own actions all the time and that is incredibly onerous. But, on the positive side, the results are equally potent, and if you can learn to tap into the source of light and life and joy, you will amaze yourself and others by what is possible. Thus will your psychic powers also spontaneously unfold and guide you in your everyday world, increasing your spiritual power and wisdom.

The magick is within you, so let it flow and make the world a better place.

CHAPTER 1

The Origins and Practice of Witchcraft

A history of witchcraft

Witchcraft probably originated about 25,000 years ago in the Palaeolithic era. At that time, humankind and nature were seen as inextricably linked. People acknowledged every rock, tree and stream as deities in the life force, and the Earth as mother, offering both womb and tomb.

Prehistoric witchcraft

Early man used sympathetic, or attracting, magick – in the form of dances, chants and cave paintings of animals – to attract the herds of animals that provided for the needs of the group, and to bring fertility to humans and animals alike. Hunters would re-enact the successful outcome of a hunt and would carry these energies into the everyday world. Offerings were made to the Mistress of the Herds and later to the Horned God, who was depicted wearing horns or antlers to display his sovereignty over the herds. Animal bones would be buried so that they, like humankind, would enjoy rebirth from the Earth Mother's womb.

Where hunter–gatherers today continue the unbroken tradition that stretches back thousands of years – for example, among the Lapps in the far North of Scandinavia and the Inuits – these rites continue, led by a shaman, or magick man, who negotiates with the Mistress of the Herds or Fish in a trance for the release of the animals.

One of the earliest recorded examples of shamanism is the Dancing Sorcerer. Painted in black on the cave walls of Les Trois Frères in the French Pyrenees, this shamanic figure, which portrays a man in animal skins, dates from about 14000 BC and stands high above the animals that are depicted on the lower walls. Only his feet are human and he possesses the large, round eyes of an owl, the antlers and ears of a stag, the front paws of a lion or bear, the genitals of a wild cat and the tail of a horse or wolf.

By the Neolithic period, which began around 7500 BC and lasted until about 5500 BC, the hunter–gatherer culture had given way to the development of agriculture, and the god evolved into the son–consort of the Earth Mother. He was the god of vegetation, corn, winter and death, who offered himself as a sacrifice each year with the cutting down of the corn, and was reborn at the mid-winter solstice, as the Sun God.

The Neolithic period also saw the development of shrines to the Triple Goddess who became associated with the three phases of the Moon: waxing, full and waning. The Moon provided one of the earliest ways by which people calculated time. Since its cycles coincided with the female menstrual cycle, which ceased for nine moons if a women was pregnant, the Moon became linked with the mysteries first of birth, then of death as it waned, and finally with new life on the crescent. Because the Moon was reborn each month or, as it was thought, gave birth to her daughter each month, it was assumed that human existence followed the same pattern and that the full moon mirrored the mother with her womb full with child. The full moon was also associated in later ages with romance and passion, originally because this coincided with peak female fertility. Moon magick for the increase of love and fertility is still practised under the auspices of the waxing moon. It was not until about 3,000 years ago that the male role in conception was fully understood in the West, and only then were the Sky Father deities able to usurp the mysteries of the Divine Mother.

A trinity of huge, carved stone goddesses, representing the three main cycles of the Moon, and dating from between 13000 and 11000 BC, was found in France in a cave at the Abri du Roc aux Sorciers at Angles-sur-l'Anglin. This motif continued right through to the Triple Goddess of the Celts, reflecting the lunar cycles as maiden, mother and crone, an image that also appeared throughout the classical world.

Witchcraft and the early Christians

After the formation of the Christian church, the worship of the old deities and the old ways were banned and the nature festivals supplanted by Christian ones. The Christians were pragmatic, however, and Pope Gregory, who sent St Augustine to England in AD 597, acknowledged that it was simpler to graft the Christian festivals on to the existing festivals of the solstices and equinoxes. So, Easter, for example, was celebrated on the first Sunday after the first full moon after the spring equinox, which is where it remains today. In the same way, the crosses on the hot cross buns that we eat on

Good Friday were originally the ancient astrological signs for the Earth, and were eaten to absorb the power and fertility of Mother Earth. Hot cross buns were still thought to retain their magical qualities until the early decades of the nineteenth century and were said to offer protection against drowning. For this reason, hot cross buns were hung from the roofs of coastal churches where their remains can still be seen. The old ways did not die quickly, however, and so for centuries the two religions co-existed as people gradually transferred their allegiance from the Earth Mother, or Mother Goddess, to the Virgin Mary and the female saints.

The persecution of witches

But in medieval times, two largely political issues brought about the persecution of witches, especially women. The religious emphasis on the sin of Eve and the belief in the inferiority of women had existed since the time of St Paul, but with the rise of an organised male medical profession, women healers who had acted as herbalists and midwives became a threat. This was not least because their skills ensured less painful childbirth, which was considered contrary to the curse of God that the daughters of Eve should bear children in sorrow. So midwives were a prime target for the new persecutions and were often accused of sacrificing babies to the Devil. Given the high rate of infant mortality, this allegation was hard to refute, and a grieving mother might easily blame the midwife for the death of her infant.

At a time of appropriation of common land and the enclosure of smallholdings, especially in Europe, such accusations were a popular way of removing peasants, particularly elderly widows or spinsters, reluctant to give up their land rights, since being found guilty of witchcraft carried the penalty of the seizure of land.

Some researchers have suggested that as late as 1693 in Salem, Massachusetts, the desire to appropriate land was behind at least some of the mass accusations of witchcraft made at the time. One landowner, Giles Corey, was apparently an innocent witness at the trials at first. However, he himself was accused of witchcraft and was pressed to death – a torture in which heavy stones were placed on the victim's chest and which took three days to kill them – rather than confess, for if he had, his property would have been taken from his descendants.

High-ranking practitioners of magick who attempted to conjure demons were usually male, and included both popes and royalty. They generally escaped censure, however. The folk religion of the countryside was an easier target.

In December 1484, the Bull of Pope Innocent VII was published, appointing Heinrich Kramer and Jakob Sprenger as inquisitors against witchcraft and heresy. These two clerics wrote the *Malleus Maleficarum,* the notorious *Hammer of the Witches,* which described in lurid detail the tortures that could be used to obtain confessions from suspected witches. In it, they adopted the policy that it was better to kill an innocent person who would be rewarded in heaven by God than to allow a guilty person to remain unpunished. This book became the best-seller of its time and was quoted to justify the atrocities practised against witches in mainland Europe and Scandinavia. Although torture to obtain a confession was not permitted in England except by royal assent, many inquisitors were very cruel even to young victims, who would eventually confess in the hope of having their interrogation brought to an end.

No one really knows how many people have been put to death for witchcraft. The worst period for witch burnings and hangings in Europe was between the mid-fifteenth and late seventeenth centuries, when the number judicially executed as witches during this period is generally accepted to be about a quarter of a million people. In addition, many more were lynched or hanged unofficially by mobs eager to find a scapegoat to blame for bad harvests or dying cattle. This unhappy era came to be known as the Burning Times.

Matthew Hopkins, who died in 1647, brought about the executions of at least 236 accused witches. He styled himself as Witchfinder General and, with four hired assistants, instigated a reign of torture and terror especially in the eastern counties of England, amassing a huge fortune for himself in the process.

In the colonies of America, the most notorious trials were those at Salem, held between 1692 and 1693. During this period of mass hysteria, 141 people from the town and immediate area were arrested, and 19 were hanged. Even a dog was hanged. Dorcas Good, a four-year-old child, was the youngest victim to be accused of witchcraft and imprisoned. She was released on bail after her mother was hanged, but her younger sibling died in prison. Dorcas was driven insane by her experience.

About three-quarters of all those killed as witches in Europe and Scandinavia were women, mainly lower-class older women, female healers, village herbalists, wise women and midwives. With the death of so many experienced healers and wise women, much knowledge was inevitably lost, and for a time infant mortality increased as male physicians took over the roles of the deposed midwives. But anyone who was different in any way – eccentric, senile or physically deformed – could be accused. Any old woman living alone might be blamed for the deaths of animals, the failure of crops and outbreaks of disease that were in reality caused by poor hygiene and diet, bad weather, human neglect or simply blind Fate.

Of course, this occurred to some extent before the Burning Times. The difference was that now the Church and State were legalising and even encouraging this persecution. Even faeries became associated with witchcraft. The Bean-Tighe, a faerie housekeeper, popular in the mythology of Ireland and Scotland, was said to reside with the village wise woman and assist her with chores; in the worst of the wave of hysteria over witchcraft, if an old women had an immaculate house, it was claimed she had faerie help – and so by implication was consorting with the Devil.

Under torture, even the innocent would admit to the vile deeds suggested by their inquisitors. Many of the confessions now appear to be remarkably uniform and come straight from the pages of the works on demonology, with which the members of the Inquisition would be familiar. Simple village circle dances performed at the time of the full moon and the old rituals performed to bring fertility to both fields and people – with a figure dressed as the Horned God and couples making love in the fields or leaping over a bonfire – became all too easily translatable into evidence of satanic covens. Although the last person executed for witchcraft in England was Alice Molland at Exeter in 1712, it was not until 1951 that the Witchcraft Act of 1736 was repealed and replaced with the Fraudulent Mediums Act.

Those who continued to practise the 'old ways' were usually families who could be trusted not to betray the secrets, although the fires of the Lughnassadh (the first corn harvest) continued in remote areas until well into the late nineteenth century and are being revived by pagans as community celebrations, especially in the USA. The secret family covens would pass the traditions down through the matriarchal line, usually by word of mouth. Those who could write, recorded their spells and rituals in 'Books of Shadows' – so-called partly because of the secrecy required to write and protect them. These were usually buried or burned with the witch on her death, or on rare occasions were handed on to the eldest daughter.

Witchcraft in modern times

By the late twentieth century in the USA, witchcraft had been recognised as a valid religion by the American Supreme Court and accepted by the American army, but other countries, including the UK, are not so tolerant. What is more, in many lands, especially among smaller communities, misunderstanding and prejudice still persist. In the UK, for example, Wiccans who practise openly and have children are sometimes regarded with suspicion by some health professionals. My dear friend Lilian, a white witch and healer, recalls how one woman passing her home would always cross herself and walk on the other side of the street. I myself once volunteered to read the runes at the local school fête to raise much-needed funds. I was told in no uncertain terms by a member of the Parents' Committee that the chairman of the school governors would not have any truck with the occult. I was asked to bake Easter rabbit biscuits instead, but since my domestic skills are far behind my divinatory ones, I declined.

My own witchery

People started calling me a witch long before I adopted the title, which I did as a result of a book I wrote in 1996 called *Every Woman a Witch* (though it must be said that men as well as women can harness what are entirely natural powers).

When the book was published, some people in the media joked about my childhood in England's industrial Midlands – not considered a place where magick or spirituality can flourish. It seemed that they could not accept the fact that my spells focused on the mundane issues of how people might obtain the money to mend a leaking roof or find their own inner harmony amidst the clutter and noise of a family, rather than on more ethereal rituals celebrated by fey maidens wafting around in flower-filled gardens.

But, in fact, if I were to make any claim at all to authenticity (not that authenticity matters as much as sincerity of purpose), it would be through those Midland roots, which are connected to what is said to be the most ancient order of witches known. At the turn of the twentieth century, my father's family were canal people and my father grew up at a time when the boats were still a major form of transport for coal and iron. Some of these Midland canal people were known as 'water witches' because they practised a religion based on the sacredness of Water and Earth. Their symbol was the six-spoked Sun wheel, painted on their boats. This sign was once thought to be a ship's wheel, but this is improbable, since canal boats have large rudders.

Unlike the Romany gypsies, the Midland water witches were descended from the Friesian seafarers of the Netherlands and 1876 a book entitled *Oer Linda* was published, named after the family who had been custodians of the wisdom since the sixth century BC. Some insist the manuscript is a forgery and that the existing version dates only from the thirteenth century. But the authentic water gypsies knew their lore by inheritance rather than from a book, and the similarities are remarkable. Ritual was practised by the canal people within a triple magical square, each square joined by four lines and constructed from wood known as 'the mill'. Only the women entered the sacred area, under the leadership of a senior female water witch, though the chief male, known as the Master, summoned the entity to assist in the ritual. If you would like to read more about this, you will find some recommended books listed in Further Reading, page 301.

Certainly, I can recall two terrifyingly swarthy aunts who commanded the family, and my father recounted many superstitions and much canal lore when I was young. This included the tale of a terrifying character called Kit Crewbucket, whose ghostly form would appear on a boat or be seen in the water before it went through a dark tunnel. Canal life has a whole mythology, much now lost as the old working boats have been replaced by weekend leisure traffic. You will find more on the details of these old superstitions in my book *Ghost Encounters* (Blandford, 1998).

Wicca

Wicca, as it is performed today, is not modern witchcraft per se, but a contemporary neo-pagan religion. It is, however, one of the major forms of witchcraft. It began in its modern form with the teachings of Gerald Gardner after the repeal of the Witchcraft Act in 1951, though its descent can be traced to the ancient nature religions. This traditional method of Wicca is quite formal, with covens using ritual tools and learned invocations emphasising the Goddess and her representative, the High Priestess, as their head. The Goddess is the archetype or source energy of the ultimate feminine power or principle. All the named goddesses represent aspects of particular qualities of the Goddess in different cultures. Her consort is the Horned God and his representative in the coven is the High Priest. Though each coven is autonomous, formal Wicca follows a system of degrees of learning and does not permit self-initiation. The High Priest initiates the female members and the High Priestess the male. They celebrate eight sabbats, or seasonal celebrations.

There are, however, numerous forms of Wicca and of witchcraft, many of which draw on ancient traditions. For example, the feminist

Dianic Wicca, founded in the 1970s, is spiritually descended from the nature religion of the Italian witches who worshipped Diana as the Triple Goddess of the Moon from about 500 BC.

Since the 1970s, less formal practices and covens have evolved, which may or may not have a structured learning system, and these create their own spells and ceremonies, rather than using an existing system, such as that recorded in Gardner's own Book of Shadows, revised by his High Priestess Doreen Valiente. These individual ceremonies are recorded in books created to reflect the evolving rituals of each coven and its own emphases. This method is much more conducive to solitary practitioners who can incorporate magick into their domestic and working lives.

Wiccan rituals and ethics

Wiccans believe in polarity rather than a single godhead, both in magick and in life. Evil is therefore not a separate demonic force to be eradicated, and the darker aspects of life emanate as a result of alienation from the natural order of things. However, even those things that are bad can act as catalysts for change; death and endings are as much part of the cycle of life as are birth and beginnings. Dark and light, night and day, positive and negative, destruction and creation are two sides of the same coin, a principle that finds expression in Eastern Taoism and underpins the ancient Chinese *I Ching (The Book of Changes)*, often used for divination. Negativity can be transformed into healing energies through positive ritual.

The Goddess is the source of all creation, from whom, in the original virgin birth, her son–consort, the Horned God, came. The Horned God and the Goddess are the creative male and female principles that act and react, not in opposition to each other, but as complementary and necessary parts of a whole. There are variations on this idea within the teachings of Wicca. Some traditions consider the Goddess to be of greater significance than her male counterpart. Others regard them as equal, assuming different aspects according to the season and ritual: she as the Earth or Moon deity, ruler of the summer months, he as the Sun or Corn God, ruler of winter and Lord of the Underworld after his death.

Along with other nature deities, the Horned God became demonised with the advent of Christianity, and the Goddess was either depicted as a wicked witch or downgraded to the status of a faerie. Thus the Celtic warrior goddess Maeve became the faerie Mab, described thus by Mercutio in Shakespeare's *Romeo and Juliet:*

She is the fairy's midwife, and she comes
In shape no bigger than an agate-stone
On the fore-finger of an alderman.

Contrary to popular belief, Wiccans do not 'hex' (cast curses) or seek revenge, although some Dutch and Pennsylvanian witches consider that it is justifiable to 'bind' those who harm children or animals or actively promote evil or corruption. Wiccans prefer to rely on the principles of natural justice that under karmic principles will redress the balance, either in this lifetime or the next.

The chief moral codes are the Wiccan Rede and the Threefold Law. The Wiccan Rede states simply: 'An it harm none, do what you will'. This deceptively straightforward statement refers to the self as well as others. I have already mentioned the Threefold Law whereby magical intent – and, many believe, actions and thoughts – return to the sender with three times the intensity.

Because people are responsible for their own actions, everyone – witch and non-witch alike – can choose to do good or evil. Many witches and Wiccans believe that they are reincarnated in some form and also that the results of past deeds can follow a person from one life to the next. You can compare this to the concept of *karma* found in Hinduism and Buddhism, which says that the thoughts and deeds we accumulate in our lifetime may either progress us towards spiritual perfection – if good – or indicate, if bad, that we need to learn lessons in subsequent lives to right our mistakes or attitudes. Other witches say there is an afterlife, spent on another plane of existence. Known as Summerland, Avalon or Valhalla, and akin to Tir na n'Og, the Celtic otherworld of eternal youth, it is a place where joy and light are experienced. Reincarnation, on the other hand, is a form of bodily transformation. Some may choose to be reborn in another body, perhaps as an animal or bird, sometimes to teach or to complete unfinished work. For example, Merlin, the magician, was believed to have been incarnated in several lifetimes and to have entered willing bodies, including the sixth-century bard Taliesin.

Wiccan rituals are held at esbats and sabbats. An esbat is a monthly coven meeting, traditionally held 13 times a year during each full moon. The eight sabbats are described in the chapter Seasons and Festivals (see page 245), and celebrate the eight major divisions of the Celtic year on the solstices, the equinoxes and the old Fire festivals. These festivals mark the coming of early spring, the start of the Celtic summer, the first corn harvest and the start of the Celtic winter.

There are also many lovely ceremonies to mark the transitions in the life cycle, such as handfastings, or weddings, and rites of passage to welcome recently deceased Wiccans to the familiar circle whenever they wish to draw near.

Solitary witchcraft

There are many reasons for performing witchcraft alone: your personal circumstances or the location of your home may mean that you cannot travel to a group, or you may live in an area where there are few others who share your interests. Many witches like myself choose to practise alone, drawing in my family and close friends to celebrate with me on the festival days. Most solitary witches initiate themselves, though some traditions, such as the Saxon Seat Wicca founded by Raymond Buckland in the USA, do admit solitary witches.

Indeed, solitary practitioners are said by some to have been witches in seven previous lifetimes and to possess within them all they need to know about the Craft. Truth or myth, no one should underestimate the number of private practitioners who do work alone, some coming together occasionally in small, informal groups.

Solitary witches can use ceremonial magick very successfully, but many do follow the less formal folk magick, linked to the land and the seasons, that was practised by our ancestors in their homes. For this reason, some call themselves hedge-witches, from the times when a hedge, often of hawthorn, bounded the witch's home, and it is sometimes said that they are walking on the hedge between two worlds. Such a witch may be in the tradition of the village wise women who knew about herbs and about the cycles of nature and used the implements of their kitchens rather than ceremonial tools. She may also be gifted in divination, in spell-casting and in astral projection. Usually a woman, but occasionally a man, the solitary witch practises eclectic magick drawn from a variety of traditions. In the Further Reading section on page 301, you will find some suggested books in which you can read about some of these different traditions.

Those expert in brews and potions are also called kitchen witches. Indeed, many of our grandmothers and great-grandmothers who possessed a remarkable intuition, read the tea leaves and made herbal concoctions, were jokingly called witches by their own families – and were just that!

All the rituals in this book can be carried out by a lone witch. You have your choice of groves, stone circles, the ocean shore, your garden or balcony, where you can connect with the powers of nature and work unobtrusively. Whether you are working alone, or in a group, or coven, you will share the same aims and will need much the same equipment.

Tools and treasures

You will need to collect some basic tools for your spells and rituals. If you are working in a group, these can be kept either by different members or in a safe place and brought out at meetings. They need not be at all expensive. Magick was traditionally carried out with the equipment of the home: the broom for sweeping the magical circle was the besom used for sweeping dirt (and negativity) out of the door and was stored with its bristles upwards to protect the home. The cauldron was the iron cooking pot on the black kitchen range that served to heat the home as well as for cooking. Items often can be gathered from around your home: for example, a silver bell, a crystal bowl or a large wine glass. Attractive scarves or throws make ideal altar cloths. Car boot sales are an excellent source of magical equipment. Keep your magical tools separate from your everyday household equipment in a large box or chest, so that you can keep them charged with positive energies for magical and healing work.

Some items, such as the pentacle (see page 189), you can make from clay, and herbs can be grown in pots or in gardens and chopped in a mortar and pestle. Fresh herbs have more immediate energies than dried, though the latter are better in sachets and poppets (see pages 107–09).

Always bear in mind that the magick is in you, not in your tools, and a wand cut from a fallen hazel or willow branch in the right hands can be more magical that the most elaborate crystal-tipped one purchased from a New Age store.

Spell casting

Spell casting is part of some, but by no means all, Wiccan activities. Most spells are carried out with the purpose of changing someone's life for the better or sending healing energies to others. For example, love magick could, if you wish to bring love into your life, be focused on increasing the love in the world, thereby attracting love in its many forms, and not just romance. More specifically, you may wish to attract one special person, to deepen an existing relationship or bring back a straying partner. For this, however, you would need to build into the ritual a proviso that this happening should be right for that person as well as for yourself.

Modern witchcraft is all too aware of the need not to infringe on the free will of others. As I have mentioned, binding or banishing spells work by lessening a negative influence or by protecting potential victims (see page 148, Crystals and Protective Magick), rather than by attacking a person, however destructive they may be.

A Book of Shadows

Whether you are working alone or in a coven, you might like to start a Book of Shadows, a record of rituals that have worked well, names of those who need healing and herbal brews and incenses that are especially evocative. In time, this will become a source not only of reference but also of inspiration to you. Books of Shadows are so-called because early witches kept them secret for fear of persecution. They were often burned or buried with witches who died.

You may decide to have two Books of Shadows, one as a permanent record, traditionally copied out by hand, and the other an ongoing working almanac in which you note moon phases for the month. If you are working in a group that includes someone with a mathematical bent, they can calculate and note here the times of the day at which particular planets and angels hold sway (see the tables on pages 235 and 239 for methods of calculation). You can also note the phases of the Moon. I find a diary section of a Filofax serves well, but if this information is kept on computer, then copies can be printed out if required for other members.

Some covens keep a single main Book of Shadows in a safe place. From this, members – especially new ones – can copy rituals and magical lore in their own smaller Books of Shadows, which can then be handed down in future times to any member of their family who shows an interest in such matters as they reach adulthood.

Apart from the suggestions I have made for possible rituals and books you can read, there are countless Books of Shadows on the Internet that can act as inspiration. There are no rules set in stone; rituals carried out in love and even laughter, perhaps when a candle will not light, are far more effective than the most elaborate ceremony in which everyone is so focused on getting it right. If the ritual rather than the intent is all, the power becomes dissipated and anxiety blocks the innate magick we all experienced as children. Magick works best when we can leave behind our innate demands for precision and order. The more formal and lengthy rituals may act as a powerful aid to focus, but they may, equally, ignore the importance of learning through experience and the heart.

Witchcraft within covens

A coven is a group of members of a unit of witchcraft and, in fact, can number anything from two to 13, or even more. The number 13 is traditionally designated by the 13 moon cycles that make up one year, and 13 is the number of the Goddess (hence it became unlucky under Christian influence). Gardenerian covens generally number 13. Some covens are affiliated formally or informally to specific traditions, but they increasingly unite for organisational as well as legal and political strength, particularly in Australia and parts of the USA. On-line covens are also springing up and they are an excellent way for solitary practitioners to gain support and information. Reliable, bona fide covens will offer the same safeguards as any ordinary coven (see page 306), but of course the normal restraints you should show on contacting any Internet site will apply.

The beginning of the path to learning about Wicca within a formal coven is usually marked by a dedication. Initiation, after a year and a day, or a similar recognised magical period, will confer formal entry. Further different levels of knowledge and responsibility may also be involved, for example elevation to a second or third degree, so that eventually initiates can begin their own covens if they wish.

Starting your own coven

You can start a coven without subscribing to any particular form of Wicca or witchcraft. Some of the most spiritual covens are those that do not have anyone in the role of High Priestess or Priest, but instead take it in turns to organise the meetings and rituals and take responsibility for any events. However, if you do want to follow a particular tradition, I have included listings of organisations and books that will help you (see Useful Contacts, pages 306–07 and Further Reading, page 301).

Have a preliminary meeting in which you can plan for about six meetings ahead, deciding on the topics, the different venues and equipment you will need to buy. Using a good almanac and Moon diary, you can arrange to meet on the crescent moon some months to light candles and make wishes as well as on the full moon and on the major festivals. You may arrange a special evening also for healing work, especially if this is an area that you would like to develop collectively.

You can hold separate meetings for planning, but if you wish to make practical decisions at a meeting before an esbat, always carry out a ritual to strengthen harmony after such discussions as Earthly issues can intrude on even the most spiritual gathering. Another good time is afterwards when you are eating and drinking and so are relaxed and full of good feelings. Even then, have a short collective rite before you separate.

You can decide what equipment you need to buy at these planning meetings and one person can act as co-ordinator. Set up a joint fund for candles, crystals, incense, etc., and appoint one person to check and replenish supplies. Large supermarkets have an amazing array of candles, incenses and oils, as do gift shops and herbal pharmacies, while on the Internet there are a vast number of New Age mail-order outlets. I have also listed some in the back of this book.

Appoint one person to organise a specific festival and to act as High Priest or Priestess for that occasion. Hierarchies rarely work in less formal groups of friends. Remember, too, that sometimes the most reticent member may prove the most dynamic at singing chants and raising energies.

You may discover that particular members have special gifts – perhaps for leading the dancing or creating spontaneous rituals – but it is important that the most forward members do not take all the leading parts, leaving others to polish the chalice and sweep up the incense. When you admit new members, you may decide to allow an initial time before the person decides to commit themselves – sometimes even the nicest people can bring personality mismatches that can make harmony difficult, even when dealing with rituals and with goodwill on all sides. You may also find that one personality automatically assumes leadership and if this does not prove beneficial, it needs to be tackled with humour and sensitivity if you are not to have a quasi-deity in your midst.

You may wish to choose a particularly wise member to look after newcomers, explain basic rituals and suggest reading material and meditations and visualisations that can be done at home. Other members may undertake to research aspects of the Craft that interest them, or collect information about deities and then run informal teachings sessions perhaps on a special evening. One person may undertake to update the Book of Shadows regularly.

Joining a coven

Before joining a coven, consider what you are looking for. Some covens emphasise set ritual and ceremony and a learning path that can take years rather than months, along which you progress in an orderly fashion, gradually building up a great store of wisdom and experience and allowing your psychic powers to unfold slowly – is that what you want? It is important also to establish what you may be able to give to the coven. Can you devote the necessary evenings for the coven, or do you have a packed schedule and many commitments, which prevent you from setting aside a regular time?

Perhaps you may want to explore magick more informally with like-minded people where the emphasis is on spontaneity. It is important that you choose a coven that operates in a manner with which you feel comfortable.

Some modern covens do practise sky-clad, or naked, but I would advise you to avoid this, as this can make some people feel very self-conscious and needs very strong parameters to prevent ceremony from spilling into everyday relationships. It can also detract from the spirituality of the ritual. If sexual attraction or spontaneous sexual fantasies are allowed to arise between members of a group, this can make ritualistic contact very difficult, especially where members are in relationships with people outside the coven. The Sacred Marriage, which involves ritual sex between God and Goddess, is an important part of seasonal celebrations. However, modern covens often celebrate the ritual coupling of Earth and Sky by plunging a knife into a chalice of water, or by the use of physical sex carried out in private, by an established couple, out of sight of the coven. In this way, any very human complications may be prevented from creeping into the ritual.

It is also possible to come across well-meaning but totally inexperienced groups who attempt to practise the kind of work that a medium, white witch or healer would take years even to approach. Unfortunately, it is all too common for lovers of occult movies to set themselves up as gurus and wreak unintended havoc on the psychological and psychic well-being of others.

You should be sure, when you choose a coven, that its members are kind and gentle and do not indulge in spirit summoning or spirit possession, even for trance purposes, unless under the supervision of an expert leader who has benefited from a very long training. If these warnings sound a little dire, it is because witchcraft involves very personal and spiritual experiences; it is also, by nature, a very hidden practice, and this means that it may be hard to tell the genuine from the charlatans.

Beware also of strangers or acquaintances who regale you with supposed Wiccan practices or offer to do spells for you, usually for money. True Wiccans are among the most tolerant of people and would never seek to impose their beliefs on others and are usually incredibly reticent with people they do not know.

In the meantime, it is wise to follow an indirect route to find your coven, perhaps through 'green' organisations and reputable New Age stores, or by attending workshops and celebrations arranged by pagan federations and healing organisations, and talking to people there. You can also visit healing festivals and buy established pagan magazines. Take your time until everything feels right and you have answered all the questions you need to ask.

No reputable coven will be in a hurry to sign you up – the reverse is usually the case. You certainly do not want to find yourself signing in blood, being initiated by having sex with the High Priest or Priestess or promising to fall on a sword should you leave the coven or betray their secrets. Nor should you pay huge sums of money in advance for training; for membership of an established pagan organisation, yes, but these tend to ask for remarkably little. Even a full Druidic or Goddess training, for example, costs no more than a few hundred pounds over several years. Most covens and healing groups expect you only to pay for your expenses.

I hope that, one day, joining a coven will be totally open, like joining any other organisation, and then the nasty elements who hide behind the name of magick will be exposed for the frauds they are.

Children and Wicca

Many people are suspicious of witches and all the more so if the practitioner has young children. They seem to fear that witches will exert some kind of evil influence on innocent minds. In my experience, nothing could be further from the truth. Children of Wiccans are almost invariably kind to animals and aware of environmental issues. Some groups have family celebrations and no responsible parent would introduce their children to any experiences before they were ready, least of all Wiccans to whom life is sacred and children the blessing of the Goddess.

Lisa, a Wiccan from Berkshire, describes how her daughter has grown up:

'Becoming a mother has touched me more deeply than I could ever have imagined. I am sure that every mother, pagan or otherwise, has felt and appreciated the magical connection between mother and child: eyes and hearts locked together during a breast feed; waking to silence in the middle of the night, only to hear the baby wake and cry out moments later; being able to recognise one's own child's cry in a room full of noisy babies.

'Being a pagan has brought all of these experiences into a spiritual focus that has brought me closer to the Goddess in a way that I don't think could have happened if I hadn't chosen to become a parent. It has allowed me to experience the Mother aspect first-hand; it gave new meaning to the moon cycles of a woman, it allowed me to become the microcosm of the great Earth Mother as I watched my own body grow and give birth to a new life. It gave me the protective instinct of Sekhmet [the lion-headed Egyptian goddess of fertility], when I realised that I would fight to the death to protect my child. It showed me the true and profound power of the female body; to create and sustain life within the body, to bring forth that life and nurture it with a perfect food made by the body.

'All of these are precious gifts to me as they are all a reflection of my deepest spiritual belief and faith. When my daughter Skye is older, I will share with her what I have learned. For now, we just walk in the forest or along the river and my partner Jim and I give her the opportunity to explore her environment. She already has an image of faeries, elves and other magical beings and we try to encourage her to see the spirit in the tree or in the running water. We collect stones and leaves just to look at and admire their colour or shape. Some we take home, but most we leave where we find them. Skye loves these adventures and I am so happy to be part of her experience.

'On the sabbats, we and our friends celebrate with seasonal games, activities, myths and feasts, and the children in our lives are always eager and excited to join in. Skye is still a bit young for much of it, but even a two-year-old can dance around a maypole, pick berries, plant seeds and help bake bread or biscuits. It's exciting to think that the Wheel of the Year will have deep significance to her; that Samhain and Beltain will hold the same excitement that Christmas held for me as a child.

'I don't know if Skye will ultimately choose Wicca as her spiritual path, but I feel that growing up in a pagan home will give her the best tools for making choices in her life. She will learn to be aware of her environment and will feel a part of it, not above or outside it. Hopefully, this will inspire her to care for it and for others around her, and to encourage others to do the same. Wicca is self-governing, and I hope that Skye will have integrity and confidence in herself.

'Having a goddess as well as a god in her life will certainly give her a better spiritual balance than either Jim or I had as children. I wish for her to be strong and sure of her self, and not to be afraid to challenge or be challenged. Paganism certainly provides a framework for this, and regardless of the spiritual path she chooses, I believe that growing up with these values will help her immeasurably in her life.

'She is a perfect child of the gods: unspoiled and innocent of the limitations humankind have created for themselves. I believe that my greatest gift to her would be to teach her to stand with one foot in each world, the magical and the mundane, so that she will live her life fully and in true happiness, and perhaps inspire others towards the Craft.'

CHAPTER 2

Creating Spells and Rituals

I have said that magick comes from within the individual, as a spontaneous expression of a higher force. This is not to suggest that it is entirely haphazard, however. In this chapter we shall look briefly at some general aspects of its theory and practice. At the end, I have included a simple ritual to illustrate some of these points.

Folk magick and ritual magick

Whether you are casting a simple spell, using items from your kitchen cupboard, or performing a complicated group ceremony, the source of the power behind it is the same. Every spell or ritual involves channelling the life force that runs through all forms of existence and transforming it into higher spiritual energies. These spiritual powers include our own evolved self, which some say is formed through many lifetimes, and the higher divine cosmic energies, such as a supreme god or goddess, or, more abstractly, some sort of divine light, spirit and goodness. Magick for healing, it must be said, is not so far removed from the prayers of conventional religions, whose positive influence is well documented. The same effect can be created whatever the focus or faith, and I know from personal experience that positive results can be achieved when a Wiccan coven sends healing light to a sick member or a friend.

For hundreds of years, angels have been invoked in magick, just as in religion, both for protection and to act as vehicles for healing or positive energies. Practitioners of white magick may focus on particular aspects of a god or goddess figure, or benign power, personified through different deities from many age and cultures. When I began practising magick ten years ago, I found it very artificial to invoke a goddess who belonged to another time and culture. However, I have since found that such symbols do hold a great deal of power and therefore can concentrate specific energies. I have listed in Chapter 4 a number of deities that seem to be especially potent in ritual or as a focus for meditation. But if you do not find them helpful, there is no need to use them.

Most rituals are related to the basic human needs for health, love, fertility and prosperity. In Chapter 13, Seasons and Festivals, I describe the major solar, lunar and agricultural festivals that formed a focus for attracting abundance and increase to the land, animals, crops and people, tapping into the life force that connected them all. In past time, the well-being of the planet was considered to be the responsibility of peasant as well as king through paying tributes and enacting age-old ceremonies to invoke the necessary energies for the Wheel of the Year to turn. So individual prosperity or fertility was attained both through private spells and charms and by sending positive energies to the Earth and the cosmos and, in a sense, receiving bounty as those beams were amplified and returned to the sender.

Folk or domestic magick was an important part of people's everyday lives right up until the nineteenth century. In rural areas, the implements used in and around the home and garden could be easily adapted for use in magick; and for town-dwellers, flowers and herbs could be gathered on a day in the country or grown on allotments or in urban back gardens.

In the days before central heating systems, the focus of the home was the family hearth. *Focus* is Latin for 'hearth' and from Ancient Rome to China, the household deities have always had their place, being offered morsels of food, nectar and flowers and consulted on family happenings.

It was believed that the ancestors as well as the living gathered around the family hearth, and so it became a natural focus for magick. The witches' cauldron started off as the iron cooking pot that hung over the fire (such pots are still used in country regions of Europe – I saw one for sale quite recently in the market in Rouen in France).

Herbal brews were not only created to cure coughs and colds but also, with magical words spoken over them, transformed into potions to bring a desired lover, employment or an unexpected helping hand in times of sorrow. A grandmother would put any small coins she could spare into a money pot and warm it near the fire to 'incubate' the money into sufficient to mend the roof or buy new coats for the winter. A young wife eager to be pregnant would secretly prick a fertilised hen's egg with a needle on the night of the full moon immediately before making love. Such actions were quite a normal part of life, a way of tapping into the same energies that made the cattle fertile and the corn set seed.

Farmers would leave milk for the faeries that they might bring good fortune, young girls recited love charms while planting herbs in soil embedded with a would-be lover's footprint. On Hallowe'en, housewives opened their windows and placed garlic on the window ledge so that only the good family dead might enter and take shelter from the cold.

This simple folk magick, rather than ceremonial magick, forms the basis for the majority of spells. 'As above, so below', the words of the semi-divine father of magick, Hermes Trismegistos, may originally have evolved from popular magick that is practised in many different cultures around the world to this day. They are certainly as applicable today as they ever were.

Whatever the aim of your magick may be, if you look around your home, garden, workshop or even office, you have the necessary tools for the spells you require. What is more, rooted as they are in domesticity and the daily world, these implements could not be safer: fruit, vegetables, salt, sand, seeds, flowers, coins, pots and jars, together with your crystals, candles, incense and oils, and perhaps a few coloured scarves or ribbons to tie knots. Whether your spell is small and personal, or vast and universal, whether you are working to attract love, harmony in the home, prosperity or fertility for yourself or loved ones, for people in the wider environment or the planet, these are all you need.

Thoroughly modern magick

Not everything you use for magick must be of ancient origin, however. Even your computer can be a magical tool, used to draw magick circles. You can draw figures to represent lovers, estranged family members or yourself and a baby you hope to conceive and draw them closer with your mouse until they join. You can draw a square on the screen and enclose in it anything you wish to bind from harming you, perhaps the name of a destructive habit or a malicious person, and send it to the recycle bin where the energies will be transformed. Alternatively, you can reduce the size of a word or image symbolising something you wish to rid yourself of, and as you make it disappear from your computer screen, create sympathetic banishing magick to remove it from your life. You can attract objects or people by filling your screen with them, then print out the images on the screen and burn the paper in a candle flame to get the energies moving. You can even e-mail empowerments to yourself!

Different kinds of magick

What is certain is that whether folk customs or more formal ceremonies are used, the underlying principles of all types of white magick are the same throughout the world, and can be categorised under the following headings.

Sympathetic magick

This involves performing a ritual that imitates what you would desire in the outer world, so bringing on to the material plane a desire or need or wish from the inner or thought plane. This is done using appropriate tools and symbols. So in a spell for the gradual increase of money, for example, you might grow a pot of basil seedlings (a herb of prosperity) and light a green candle (see page 96).

Contagious magick

This involves transferring and absorbing power directly from a creature or an object, such as an animal, a bird, a crystal, a metal, the wax of an empowered candle or even the Earth itself. This principle is central to the potency of talismans and amulets; for example, traditionally, hunters might wear the pelt of a lion to bring them the beast's courage and ferocity. So, by the same token, if you wished to become pregnant, you might make love in a newly ripening cornfield (near the edge so as not to damage the crops); alternatively, you might try one of the ancient power sites of Earth, close to the phallus of the chalk Cerne Abbas fertility giant that is carved in the hillside at Cerne in Dorset.

Attracting magick

This type of magick embraces both sympathetic and contagious magick to bring you something you desire. For example, you could scatter pins across a map between the places you and a lover live and with a magnet collect them, while reciting:

Come love, come to me, love to me come, if it is right to be.

You would then place your pins in a silk, heart-shaped pincushion or a piece of pink silk, also in the shape of a heart, and leave it on the window ledge on the night of the full moon, surrounded by a circle of rose petals.

Banishing and protective magick

This involves driving away negative feelings, fears and influences by casting away or burying a focus of the negativity. For example, you might scratch on a stone a word or symbol representing some bad memories you wished to shed, and cast the stone into fast-flowing water. Alternatively, you could bury it, together with quick-growing seeds or seedlings to transform the redundant into new life.

Binding magick

Binding magick has two functions, one to bind a person in love or fidelity and the other to bind another from doing harm. This may be done in various ways, using knots in a symbolic thread, or by creating an image of the object or person and wrapping it tightly. But all binding can be problematic in terms of white magick, for whatever method you use, you are very definitely interfering with the person's karma, or path of fate.

However, it is tempting to think that if someone is hurting animals, children, the sick or elderly, you may be justified in binding them. And what if your partner has deserted you on the whim of passion, taking all the money and leaving you and your children penniless? These are very real dilemmas; in dealing with them, I have always performed such rituals adding the proviso '… if it is right to do so.'

I believe that it is essential to include that phrase in all binding magic rituals.

My friend Lilian, a white witch and healer, used to wrap the perpetrators of crimes in a mantle of pink and visualise them in a sea of tranquillity so that they might be diverted from a destructive course of action. However, I usually cast a protective barrier around the victims (see page 148 for various protective devices) and I think this is the best answer to a very difficult problem. We must harm none, not even the evil, hard though it is, and we should leave the punishment to natural justice. In my own experience, few who find happiness at the expense of others achieve more than temporary, superficial pleasure, and in time they do seem to end badly. We should never use magick in order to act as judge and jury. After all, some who do act badly do so only out of unhappiness or ignorance.

What are spells?

There is a clear difference between spells and rituals. 'Spell' tends to be the term used for the less formal folk magick that, unlike ceremonial magick, is not so rigid about such things as circle casting (see page 49) and the use of specific tools, though it may be based in forms and use words that date back hundreds of years. Our kitchen witch ancestors swept clean their magical areas and danced in circles under the Moon or round sacred fires on one of the old festivals to bring fertility to land and people, but most of their magick was done by firelight or the light of smoking tallow candles in a cramped living room or in muddy fields.

It is a serious mistake to regard informal spells as inferior to the kind of magick in which the appropriate planetary hour is carefully chosen, incense is burned, the tools laid out in the correct position and the names of all the archangels recited without a mistake. Both have a place and even if there were an actual deity watching the minutiae of the ritual, he or she would be less interested in whether a correct elemental pentagram was drawn than if the intent and the heart were pure and the need was genuine.

The purposes of white magick

There are three distinct and yet related types of magick, all of which can be used informally, in spells, or formally, in ceremonial rituals.

Personal magick

As I have already said, it is quite permissible to use magick to empower your personal needs, though this does not bring lottery wins or the object of your romantic fantasies delivered gift-wrapped to your door. Magick has traditionally encompassed material needs, and spirituality is very difficult to achieve at a time when there is a crisis of physical need or emotional shortfall in your life. For example, in days when having sufficient food and heating was an ongoing concern, abundance for the coming winter months was a prime focus of Mabon, the harvest festival at the autumn equinox. Many kitchen witches would carry out private spells using the equinox energies, to empower talismans and cast spells to ensure their own family would survive the inhospitable months of winter.

In the modern world, concerns are different, but no less urgent, and for many of us still centre on the home, family and employment. We need money to fulfil obligations, help for a child who is studying for exams or perhaps suffering bullying, a partner to share joys and sorrows, better health for ourselves and our loved ones. There are subjects for spells for yourself, your partner or lover, your children, close relatives and friends. They are usually the strongest in terms of emotion and so can be very simply carried out at home, in the garden or on the balcony, often with everyday items.

Magick for others

You may, however, wish to carry out rituals for people or groups with whom you are less intimately involved, who are vulnerable or to whom you relate in a caring, social or a professional capacity. These might include the people in your workplace, a sick neighbour, or a colleague you know is unhappy or worried; or perhaps it could be an animal park or environmental project that is under threat or needs help financially, legally or practically or even a local disaster.

As you send out loving or healing energies, so you will receive them in return, often in unexpected ways or perhaps at some future time when you yourself are vulnerable. This is part of the cosmic banking system and in practice there is considerable overlap between this and personal spells.

Magick to increase positivity

These are the least focused kind of spells. They are used to send out energies to whoever needs them, for example of love, happiness, health or abundance. They may be for an endangered species, a war-torn land, a country in need of water or the planet itself. If a large number of people do send positive energies either to a large-scale project or into the cosmos, followed where possible by practical help or support, then this can really make a difference. Again, by sending out healing you will receive in return threefold healing in indirect but powerful ways.

The four stages of magick

Although there are many different kinds of magick, in practice all spells and more formal magical rituals tend to follow four stages, though informal spells may combine one or more steps.

The focus

This defines the purpose of the ritual or spell and is generally represented either by a symbol or a declaration of intent. These could take the form of a candle etched with the name or zodiacal glyph of a desired lover, a little silver key charm or an actual key in a spell to find a new home, a picture of an ideal holiday location, and so on.

In a sense, this part of the spell begins before the actual rite and involves verbalising the purpose. As you define it in a few words or a symbol, you may realise that what you are really seeking lies beyond the immediate external purpose. Spending time at this stage is quite vital as it is said we tend to get what we ask for, so we should take care to ask for what would truly fulfil our potential, rather than what we think we need immediately.

If you are working alone, hold the symbol while speaking words that summarise the purpose of the magick. You may be surprised to discover that it is your wise psyche speaking, guiding the intention towards what you truly need or desire – and afterwards you realise it could have been no other way.

If you are working in a group, a declaration of intent, created by the group collectively before the ritual, is a good way of focusing the energies. After the initial circle is cast, the symbol can be handed round while the person leading the ritual speaks the intention. Alternatively, each person can add his or her special interpretation while holding the symbol and so the declaration is worked as part of the ritual. As others are holding the symbol, visualise it within your own hands; this provides the transition to the next stage of the ritual.

Concentration is the key to this first stage.

The action

This is the stage where you use actions to endow the symbol with magical energies. This is part of the continuous process of translating your magical thoughts and words from the first stage, the inner plan, to manifestation as the impetus for success or fulfilment in the everyday world. These energies amplify your own. For example, passing incense, representing the Air element, over the symbol activates the innate power of rushing winds that cut through inertia and bring welcome change, harnessing the energies of wide skies in which there are no limits, soaring like eagles, carrying your wishes to the Sun. You can unite other elemental forces by using the appropriate tools and substances (see Chapter 10).

Similarly, you might begin a chant, a medley of goddess names or a mantra of power linked with the theme, or a slow spiral dance around the circle. You could try drumming or tying knots either on individual cords or in a group, creating a pattern with the longer cords of fellow witches, perhaps looped around a tree.

The action of the magick is limited only by the environment and your imagination. You may find that improvisation enters quite spontaneously as the energies unfold and spiral.

Movement is the key to this stage.

Raising the power

This is the most powerful part of the magick, as the magical energies are amplified and the power of the ritual carries you along joyously. Ecstasy forms a major part of shamanic ceremony and the old mystery religions; it is akin to the exhilaration you experience riding on a carousel or running barefoot along a sandy shore with the wind lifting your hair.

You might repeat a chant of power, dance faster, drum with greater intensity, bind your cords in ever more intricate patterns or add more knots if working alone, visualising a cone of spiralling, coloured light, rising and increasing in size and intensity as this stage progresses.

Stretch your arms and hands vertically as high as possible to absorb power from the cosmos. If you are in a group and have been linking hands, as the power increases to a great intensity, this is the time to loose them.

As the power builds, you will create what is known as a cone of power. The cone-shaped hats traditionally associated with witches and bishops' mitres reflect the concentration of spiritual potency. The purpose of the cone, like the sacred pyramid, is to concentrate energy in a narrowing shape so that it reaches a pinnacle of power, which can then be released at the end of the ritual to carry your wishes or desires into the cosmos. In order to create a cone of power in magick, you can visualise these energies as coloured light (for the meanings of colours, see page 94) or as gold. Alternatively, you can visualise different rainbow colours to create a cone of every colour that merges to brilliant white at the apex. In healing work, some people see this as silver blue light that becomes brilliant.

Whether working alone or in a group, as you build up the power, breathe in pure white light and exhale and project your chosen colour, seeing it become ever more vibrant and faster-moving as the intensity increases. After you have been practising magick for a while, you will notice that the cone of colour builds up quite spontaneously, with no apparent effort. It has also been described as a cloud of energy. At the point when the climax is reached, comes the release of power.

Note that for some people the cone concept interferes with their own natural magical abilities – some of the most skilled witches and healers see circles of light, shimmering golden beams or rainbows with their psychic eye. Some see nothing at all, but instead feel power pushing their feet almost off the ground.

Growth is the key to this stage.

Release of power

When you release the power in the final stage, you may see the cone exploding and cascading as coloured stars or light beams, which surge away into the cosmos and break into brilliant rainbow colours.

If you wish, you can direct the energy after the final release of power by pointing with your hands, or a wand or knife, so that the energies cascade horizontally and downwards, for example into herbs on the altar that you are empowering to make into herb sachets. Or you can direct the cascading energies in a specific direction, perhaps towards a person who is ill or in need of magical strength.

Release is the key at this stage.

This release may take the form of a final shout, a leap, or words. As you extinguish your candle of need, you may shout:

It is free, the power is mine!

Or, at the point of release, you may throw your extended hands wide in an arc above your head. If the ceremony is formal and you are using an athame (see page 50), you can at this moment bring it in front of you to mark the invisible cutting of the knot holding the power. Pull your visualised or actual knots tight, cut them, leap into the air, shouting:

The Power is free! or *It is done!*

Sometimes there is just a sudden stillness, as the power leaves.

Afterwards, you need to ground the energies by sitting or lying on the ground and letting excess energies fade away into the Earth as you press down with your hands and feet.

The four elements

I have mentioned the use of the elements in rituals. In magick, there are four elements – Earth, Air, Fire and Water. They all contain symbolic qualities and powers that together form the energies used in rituals. Each element controls a quadrant in the magical circle.

Earth, in the North, represents the stability, security and strength of old stone circles, mighty castle walls, tall craggy rocks and mountain peaks. It is also associated with the time of midnight and winter. Salt is often used to represent Earth in spells and rituals.

Air, in the East, is action, freshness and power for change, the winds blowing across plains, vast, cloudless skies stretching endlessly, storms and whirlwinds stirring stagnation but also bringing destruction of the old. Air is also associated with the dawn and spring. Incense is often used to represent Air in spells and rituals.

Fire, in the South, is the quicksilver, inspirational energy and clear light of the Sun, the lightning flash. It is the hearth fire that warms, the ritual fire that cleanses, the forest fire that sweeps all away. It represents the full power of the Sun and light at noon and in summer. Candles are used to represent Fire.

Finally, in the West is Water, that falls as refreshing rain, tides that ebb and flow, watercourses always finding a way, moving ever onwards, never backwards. Water is associated with autumn and sunset. It represents the changing responsive, human emotions of life cycles, and personal ebbs and flows of energies. Water is used to represent its own element.

Magick in the southern hemisphere

In magick, time and direction have an important place and it is necessary to understand that there may be differences according to which hemisphere of the globe you are working in. In the northern hemisphere, magical circles are cast clockwise, or 'deosil', which means 'in the direction of the Sun'. In the southern hemisphere, however, practitioners casting their circles deosil should normally cast them anti-clockwise, because that is the direction of the Sun in that hemisphere. For this reason, I have used the term 'deosil' (and its opposite, 'widdershins') throughout this book when referring to the direction of circles. These terms are clearer than clockwise and anti-clockwise, because as long as you think in terms of the direction of the Sun, the terms can be applied wherever you are standing on the globe.

Practitioners in the southern hemisphere will also need to alter the dates I have given. For them, for example, the mid-winter solstice is celebrated on or around 21 June (see page 245 on seasonal magick) and the summer solstice, when the Sun is at it most powerful, is around 21 December. In the same way, the two annual equinoxes, when there is equal day and equal night, move round so that the spring equinox falls around 21 September and the autumn equinox around 21 March. It is perhaps better to think in terms of the Wheel of the Year, rather than our modern-day calendar, for what matters is not the date but what is happening with the cycle of growth and fruition. So the autumn equinox is the time of harvest, whenever that may be in your part of the globe.

Things are a little more complicated, however, when it comes to the use of the quadrants of your magical circle and the directions, North, South, etc. I explained on page 41 that North is the direction of Earth and winter. However, in the southern hemisphere since the equator, the area of maximum heat, is to the North, this direction will more naturally be regarded as Fire. To face the colder direction of winter, you must turn away from the equator, towards the Antarctic – the South. This means that when following the instructions in this book practitioners in the southern hemisphere should substitute the opposite for each direction. So, for example, where I have said you should set up your altar in the North, and enter your circles from the East, you would set up your altar in the South, and enter from the West.

If you find this too complicated, don't worry. Some practitioners in the southern hemisphere follow the northern traditions, especially if they have ancestors from colder climes. It really is a matter of preference and all this diversity actually has a very positive effect, because it means that you can weave the natural forces into your personal creation of magick. The only important thing is that you are consistent in your attitude.

A ritual using light and cosmic power

The following ritual can be carried out anywhere at all, as direction is not important. It is most powerful when performed standing beneath a tree that perhaps has stood for hundreds of years. If sunlight is filtering through the leaves, so much the better. You can work alone, with a group of friends, or in a more formal coven. You may want to decide in advance on a focus for the power, for example healing a particular place or a person you know. Alternatively, you can let the energies find their own target as they cascade though the cosmos, increasing the positivity of the universe.

✿ Stand with your feet apart and your arms outstretched above your head like the branches of a tree. Through your feet, draw up rich, golden light from the Earth and let it flow upwards, becoming lighter and more golden as it rises to your fingertips. Feel the light from above flowing downwards to merge with it.

✿ If you are working alone, then, holding a long, silk scarf in either hand, move around the tree with your hands rising and falling in a spiral path to create swirls of energies, the most ancient of the Mother Goddess sacred geometric forms, while chanting and dancing. If you are with friends, join hands around the tree and pass the light and energy between you from hand to hand, deosil, until you can feel the circle of light (you may even see luminous energy transferring from hand to hand).

✤ Begin to circle the tree deosil, reciting faster and faster:

> *Tree power, Earth power, Sun shower and light,*
> *Encircle me, enfold me, Goddess radiance bright.*

If you do not want to use the Goddess as a focus for your magick, you can substitute the word 'god' or say 'golden radiance bright'. You can also create your own chant, if you prefer, that may change from line to line, or use a simple mantra, such as:

> *Touch me, enfold me, enclose me.*

✤ When you feel the power reaching a climax, cast the scarves high into the air and hug the tree, pressing your feet down hard to ground your energy and receive healing light from the trunk. If you are working alone, you may feel that in a sense you are not alone but are joining with the tree spirits and Devas, the higher forces of nature who will dance with you as you spiral. You may even see their luminous outlines.

✤ If you are working in a group, when you feel the power has reached a climax, unclasp your hands and with a final call,

> *Above!*

raise them straight above your head and allow the energies to spiral through the cosmos.

✤ Then sink down so that your hands and feet are pressing the ground and let any excess golden radiance and power return to the Earth. (If you do not do this, you will be buzzing all day and night as though you had been drinking too much coffee.)

CHAPTER 3
Beginning Magick

You can create magick in all kinds of ways and you can use it for an almost infinite variety of purposes. Your magick can be solitary or group-based, self-centred or entirely altruistic. It can be personal and informal, or it may be framed in rigid ceremony. But whatever kind of magick you wish to practise, you will need to create a special place to work in, a personal area at home for your private healing and personal development work.

A magical place

When you were a child, you probably had a special place, perhaps a tree house, a den under a table with a curtain draped over, or a corner of the garden hidden by bushes that only you and chosen friends visited; in this place you wove your dreams and played with your treasures. The magical place I am describing in this section is just such a special place, an extension of and, in a sense, a return to that time of enchantment, for you are once again making an area separate from the everyday world, where you can set up your special artefacts. But it will also be very different from your childhood place, because as an adult you can learn to control and direct the energies that then ran free and unstructured. Your imaginings can be refined as visualisations, your daydreams as altered states of consciousness; you can make wishes and dreams come true, not just in faerieland but in the here and now.

If you have sufficient space, you may set aside a room, perhaps a conservatory, attic or basement, or a sheltered spot in the garden for your special magical place. Alternatively, you may need to use a corner of your bedroom or draw a velvet curtain across an area of a room where you can be quiet and private. In the summer, I like to work out of doors at my caravan and go down the winding track to the beach for my sea rituals (and puff and pant up again). In winter, I work either round the hearth that is the focus of the small, dark family room where I write, or high in the attic bedroom of my narrow house overlooking the hills.

Altars

Your special place will need to contain an altar. To many people, the word 'altar' summons up images of vast churches with golden crosses or B-movies with dark-robed figures sacrificing damsels on a stone slab in the middle of a deserted moorland. But in magical terms an altar is simply the term for a sacred work space on which you place your tools, candles, incense and symbols for rituals.

In practice, many people use their altar every day, as a focus for quiet meditative moments, perhaps at the end of a busy day or early in the morning. Such use does not make it any less special. Indeed, by becoming a part of your daily world, it becomes charged with your own essential magical qualities, and provides a repository of magical and healing energies, even if you only spend a few moments each evening in personal, informal work.

It is your place and the rituals you hold there are limited only by your own desires and ingenuity.

Setting up your altar

You will need a large, flat surface for your altar; a table or a cupboard will do – you can use the drawers for storage and cover it with a cloth. It does not really matter what shape the surface is – circles and squares are both sacred shapes and easy to divide into quadrants for the four elements, Earth, Air, Fire and Water, that are central to traditional magic and play a part even in informal rituals. A round altar, the shape of the sacred circle, works especially well.

If you do not have a suitable piece of furniture, a piece of uncut stone or unpolished wood, such as hazel, ash, rowan or oak supported on stones or bricks will do. Ensure that it is high enough, so that you are not constantly stooping.

In good weather, if you have a sheltered private place in your garden or back yard, you can adapt a tree stump or tall, flat rock as your work space. But perhaps the best altars of all are those impromptu ones you make – such as the top of a standing stone with a circle of your favourite crystals, or a rock on the beach with a circle of seaweed and shells to mark the directions.

The altar need not be large but you will need to have room to move all the way round it. Many rituals demand that you move in a circle with the altar in the centre, although some place the altar in the North of the circle and you stand to the South, facing North.

The central position of the altar/circle represents the realm of Spirit, or *Akasha*. Akasha is the name given to the fifth element formed by the combination of the four ancient elements of Earth, Fire, Air and Water that were considered in classical times to be the components of all life and matter. It is greater than the other four.

In formal magic, artefacts and lighted candles are kept on an altar but this is not vital. It is quite possible, even if you are using a communal room in an apartment or house, to leave your altar partly prepared, although items such as salt and water are best added immediately before a ritual so they will be fresh. A garden altar can be set with an outdoor candle or torch and stone figurines, perhaps shaded by bushes.

Keep pot pourri or living plants on your indoor altar when it is not in use to keep the energies fresh and moving. If it feels stagnant, sprinkle an infusion of lemon or peppermint widdershins, to remove negativity that has come in from the activities of the day, and then deosil, to charge it with power. You can also cleanse it with incense, creating a protective circle of pine or myrrh, again widdershins and then deosil.

Each night, or whenever you have time, you can explore your inner psychic powers at your altar. For example, you can gaze into a candle or scry into a bowl of water on the surface of which you have dripped coloured inks. Try holding the different crystals that you place on your altar and allow impressions to pass through your fingertips, manifest as images, sounds or feelings. This psychic art is called psychometry and is one that will emerge spontaneously.

You may, however, have a more specific aim in mind. For example, to improve your finances, place a pot of basil herbs, surrounded by golden coloured coins and light a green or golden prosperity candle while visualising golden coins showering upon you. If you have a friend who is sick, and wish to send healing thoughts to them, place a photograph of them on the altar, and surround it with pink flowers, pink rose quartz crystals and a circle of tiny pink candles. Send your message of healing or visualised golden light, then blow out the candles deosil, sending the energies to where they are needed.

When you are not carrying out formal magick, keep on the altar any crystals that are of personal significance to you (see page 153). You might wish to have a clear crystal quartz for pure energy, a blue lapis lazuli flecked with gold for wisdom, a purple amethyst and rose quartz for healing and harmony, or a gleaming, golden-brown tiger's eye for grounding. You can also keep different herbs there according to your current focus (see page 110).

Empowering your altar

You can further empower your special place as a reflection of the positive aspects of your changing life by placing on it other small items that carry happy memories for you. These might include stones or shells found on an enjoyable outing, presents from friends or family, a letter or even a printed e-mail written in love, pictures or photographs of places and people that are endowed with emotional significance. Holding these can restore the pleasure of the moment and fill you with confidence, so they are magical objects because they are endowed with the power of good feeling.

Some practitioners keep a book, for example a book of poetry, a copy of the psalms, the works of Shakespeare or the *I Ching*. Whenever you lack inspiration, close your eyes and open your book – the page will be chosen apparently at random but in fact your deep unconscious mind has chosen the most appropriate answer by a process akin to psychokinesis.

Occasionally, gently energise these personal artefacts by burning a candle scented with chamomile or lavender. The domestic altars of many lands were originally the family hearth and an unused hearth will serve well as an altar. They depended for their power on herbs and flowers gathered from the wayside in the days before petrol fumes. Many witches who have a hearth do still keep it well swept and fresh with flowers or seasonal greenery.

Between your altar candles you may like to place statues, a god and goddess figure from either your own spiritual background or from a culture that seems significant to you; this will balance the *yang*, or male, energies with the *yin*, or female. The god figure may be represented by a horn, and the goddess by a large conch shell.

There are a great variety of deity figures in museum shops as well as New Age shops and those selling goods from particular areas of the world. You may, however, feel more comfortable with a ceramic animal, bird or reptile for which you feel an affinity: a tiger for courage, an eagle for vision, a cat for mystery and independence, a snake for regeneration. This is what Native Americans call our personal totem or power creature. You may find some of these are, in some cultures, the symbols of divinities. There is, for example, Bast, the cat-headed Egyptian goddess who protected women – especially in pregnancy and childbirth – the home, pleasure and joy. Bast was originally a lion goddess who symbolised the fertilising rays of the Sun.

Casting a circle

All spells and rituals, however formal or informal, are based on a magical circle. This may be large enough for an entire group of practitioners to stand in, or it may be small enough to fit on your personal altar. I have known practitioners who have only a small area create a circle on a table-top and sit facing North, physically outside it but spiritually within, manipulating the symbols within it. I have also known modern witches who will create an instant circle on paper or even on a computer screen.

If you have the space, you can keep a magick circle marked out with stones in a corner of your garden or painted on the floor of a room covered with a large rug. Attics are especially good since you are nearer the sky. If you are able to keep a special area for your circle, scatter dried lavender or pot pourri on it before each use, and sweep it in circles widdershins to remove any negativity.

Whatever the form or size of your circle, mark the four main compass directions within it. In the marker positions, you can use stones, lines on the floor, four crystals hanging on cords on the four walls or candles in the appropriate elemental colours (see page 91).

Once you know your directions, you can mark out your circle, beginning in the North (although some practitioners begin in the East), and working deosil. Draw your circle in one sweeping movement. You may wish to chant as you go.

If you are working in a group, or if this is a circle for a more formal ritual, you may wish to add god/goddess–power forms as an interspersed chant, with the voices of the group ebbing and rising in waves. You may wish to welcome the Archangels, or Guardians of the Four Watchtowers at the four compass points as you cast your circle. (The Archangels represent the celestial beings that feature in the cosmologies of the three main religions of the Western world – Christianity, Judaism and Islam. For more information, see pages 200 and 236). Alternatively, you may wish to call upon powerful goddess forms:

Isis, Ishtar, Cerridwen, Innana, Shakti, Yoruba, Danu, Kali and Aine,
protect, empower and inspire this magical endeavour.

You can embellish the casting ceremony as much as you like, perhaps drawing pentagrams (see page 203) in the air at the four main compass points, and combining this with lighting the four elemental candles.

Some practitioners like to cast a circle and then welcome other members of the group to enter, sealing the circle with a diagonal up-and-down slashing movement of their power hand (the one they write with), or a wand or an athame. (An athame is a double-edged knife used in formal rituals. It represents Air and is placed in the East of the circle. As well as drawing circles, it may be used to conduct magical energies into a symbol.) But I think it is more powerful if one person actually walks around the outside of a circle of people, enclosing them in light. In this way, the circle is created in human dimensions and is as large or small as is required by the actual formation. The circle made to fit the group is far better magically than the group made to fit the circle, for the group is the circle.

If you want to visualise a circle, use a clear, pointed quartz crystal, or wand, or the forefinger of your power hand, and draw an outline, in the air at chest level or on the ground. The circle extends wherever you draw it from the ground upwards to above your head like a wall of gold. Again, begin in the North, and continue in an unbroken, circular movement.

Remember, the circle is created with your own power, amplified if you wish by the sacred Guardians or powers you may invoke. For this reason, creating a light body and thus drawing energy from the ground (see page 124), before casting the circle, is a powerful preliminary. Some practitioners, having drawn the light, extend their hands upwards so that light from the cosmos can also enter. Do this before joining hands if you are creating the circle as a group.

In a conventional coven, the High Priestess casts and uncasts the circle, but you may prefer to allow the person leading the ritual to cast the magical boundaries.

Casting a dual circle

You can create a dual circle if you wish.

☙ First consecrate the salt symbolising the Earth element in the North of the altar by stirring it three times with an athame, wand or crystal, and visualise radiance pouring into it.

☙ Stir the water, also three times deosil with the athame, wand or pointed crystal, asking the light and the Goddess to enter it.

✿ Add a few grains of salt to the water and stir it, saying:

May power thus be doubled, thus increased, as life joins life to create a greater force even than these.

✿ Stand either just within or beyond the first circle perimeter.

✿ Walk deosil round the circle, sprinkling the circle line, physical or envisaged, with your salt water.

In formal rituals, the High Priestess consecrates the salt and the High Priest the water and they mingle them. The High Priestess then creates the first circle and the High Priest the second.

Casting a triple circle

Three is a sacred number in magick and for special ceremonies you can create a triple circle of both power and protection. The number three represents the three aspects of the god figure in many religions: the Holy Trinity, the Triple Goddess, the three aspects of the Moon – maiden, mother and wise woman or crone – the trefoil or triple god of the Celts, and the even older Egyptian trinity of Isis, Osiris and Horus, the young Sky God. This triplicity is still celebrated when we turn our money over and bow three times to the Moon for good luck.

✿ Create your first two circles of light and salt water.

✿ Return to the place where you began.

✿ Place the bowl on the altar and light your incense; you can either light a stick in a secure holder or sprinkle incense on a charcoal block burning within the censer (see pages 138–39).

✿ Make your final circle with incense, just beyond the lines of salt and water.

There are other variations of this, including creating your outer circle of light by walking with your candle in a broad-based holder, followed by the salt water and the incense.

Uncasting the circle

When you have completed your spells or rituals, you should close the circle. This is done by simply reversing the casting process.

- Thank the Guardians and send the light of the elemental candles to whoever needs it.
- Extinguish the elemental candles in reverse order of lighting. Visualise the light fading and say, together with any present:

Let the circle be uncast but remain unbroken. Merry meet and merry part and merry meet again.

- Leave the altar candles to burn down.

Preparing your mind for magick

As well as preparing the physical area for magick, you also need to prepare your mental state.

It is universally agreed that we have two hemispheres of the brain – the left, logical, and the right, intuitive, side – and that generally in the everyday world the left brain predominates. This may be no bad thing; after all, buying golden sunflowers and oils pressed from fragrant herbs may lift the spirits, but they will do little for us if we are so disorganised that we fail to remember the cereal and cat food – and the yowls of hungry children and cats ringing through the early morning air are not conducive to relaxation.

These demarcations within the mind have not always been so clear. Julian Jaynes, in his book *The Origin of the Consciousness in the Breakdown of the Bicarmel Mind,* suggests that self-awareness in humans has existed for only about 3,000 years. In stating this, he was defining self-awareness as the awareness of our own separateness and our private thoughts. This state of mind, normal in adults, is very different from the more primitive state of mind of small children, who keep up a running commentary on their actions. But young children are also incredibly skilled at mind-hopping and reading the thoughts of others. This is precisely because they do not have the adult's strong sense of the individual and private self. In so-called primitive societies, the individual does not have the same importance: it is the collective responsibility that matters. So the rituals that are carried out to ensure the fertility of the crops and animals and the community are performed in a group.

In a sense, magick is about using the bicarmel mind, placing the brain's right hemisphere in the driving seat, taking concentration, focus and determination from the more logical side as fuel and a map, and reconnecting our unified self with the undifferentiated universe.

You can carry out magick absolutely anywhere as long as you are in a positive frame of mind. But many practitioners believe that by entering an altered state of consciousness, you remove all the conscious blocks and allow the intuitive brain free access to the unconscious mind and with it the repository of human and cosmic wisdom. This brings about a state of mind in which energies can flow between the dimensions.

You are in your most relaxed state when your brain is generating alpha waves. They oscillate about ten times per second (the range is eight to 13 cycles per second) and are less common in our modern stressful lives. But they are naturally generated, for example, when you daydream, or sit by a fountain and let the rushing water fill your mind, or gaze into a candle flame, or have a lavender- or rose-scented bath. Compare these with the traditional routine preparations of fasting and ritual bathing of practitioners of the craft and you begin to see why these are important.

Invoking your protective angels to stand at the four corners of your magical circle, performing the rituals of preparing your magical tools and, in more formal magick, casting a circle – these are all ways of marking the limits of the everyday world and the entry into this magical space in which all the normal laws are suspended. There are many ways of reaching this state, techniques to still inner turmoil and outer demands that block the easy access to the deeper psychic states.

At times when you feel unhappy, tense or anxious, you may need tranquillity; alternatively, there may be times when you need an infusion of power to meet a challenge, restore confidence or gain energy when all you feel like doing is sleeping.

Breathing in light and colours is a method of creating a cone or vortex of power, that can be released as magical energy or healing power in the cosmos. In addition, by absorbing the light of the Moon or Sun you may take in either tranquillity or energies for those moments when you are particularly in need. Perhaps you will find yourself in an artificially lit building, crammed on a commuter train or rushing to get the children to school and go to work. At such times you may feel like one of the hags from _Macbeth,_ ready to turn the entire carriage of commuters into toads – that's when good magick is what you need.

A Moon magick ritual for calm

❄ Wait until the Moon is moving towards full, and is quite bright in the sky.

❄ Find somewhere as dark as possible so the light is undiluted and slowly 'inhale' the light through your nose, looking at the Moon and drawing its light towards you.

❄ Hold your Moon breath for a count of 'One and two and three'. Remember to say the 'ands' to stop yourself rushing – this is relaxing, not a race.

❄ Close your eyes and exhale the darkness of your panic, frustration or unhappiness.

❄ Continue alternately inhaling with your eyes open and exhaling with your eyes closed until you feel that you are filled with silver light.

❄ Now gently exhale a little of that light in a single breath, this time with your eyes open, directing it in your vision towards someone you know who is also feeling stressed or anxious.

❄ Inhale more moonlight and continue to exhale, still with your eyes open, continuing to direct the healing light.

❄ Let the Moon shine into a silver or crystal bowl of water. Before bedtime, tip the water into your bath so you can absorb the Moon energies through your pores.

Whenever you feel stressed, visualise the Moon, close your eyes and gently inhale; peace will come to you because you gave it out to others.

You will find more detail on Moon magick in the chapter on Moon energies, starting on page 211.

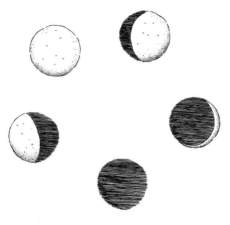

A Sun magick ritual for energy

Because it can be dangerous to look directly at the Sun, catch your sunlight close to noon in a large crystal or in water in a brass dish.

❀ As before, 'inhale' the sunlight via the crystal or water with your eyes open. Hold the Sun breath, counting 'One and two and three', then close your eyes and exhale the darkness of your doubt, anger or lack of confidence. With practice, this will become a single movement.

❀ Continue until you are filled with light and energy, then exhale a Sun breath, directing it to someone who is exhausted, frightened or ill.

❀ Inhale the Sun and again exhale it towards a person or people in need.

❀ Rinse your face in the Sun water, then tip the rest into the ground to energise a plant.

Whenever you feel tired, recall the Sun and inhale its light in your mind's vision.

Repeat both these intakes of power once every month. If you have a particularly stressful or challenging time, hold a moonstone for your Moon energies in your power hand. Hold a sparkling crystal quartz for the Sun in the other (receptive) hand to boost the flow as you visualise the natural sources. In this way, you can balance the energies in both spheres of the brain for integrated mind and soul flow.

CHAPTER 4
Gods and Goddesses

The mechanics of witchcraft

Magick takes place at what TS Eliot in *The Four Quartets* called the 'still point of the turning world', that moment of timelessness that enables thought to be turned into reality on the material plane.

It operates on the principle 'As above, so below'. This phrase comes from the beginning of *The Emerald Tablet*, attributed to Hermes Trismesgistos (thrice-blessed Hermes), thought to be a powerful first-century Egyptian sorcerer who became worshipped as a god after his death. This tablet is said to contain all magical knowledge as well as the principles of alchemy, and states that human action and events reflect what occurs in the heavens. And so by releasing magical intentions into the cosmos, as I said earlier, they will be reflected back as actuality.

Since time immemorial, humans have called upon the power of higher beings to help them, whether it be to deliver them from enemies, to bring rain for their crops or to cure their children's illnesses. Every religion and every culture believes in a divinity of some sort, whether it be god, goddess or spirit, good or evil. Evocations were performed by medieval practitioners of magick to summon up angels (and sometimes demons) and bind them to perform tasks, rather like the Middle Eastern *djinn*, or genie, who, in faerie tales, would appear from a magick lamp or corked bottle and grant wishes. Incense would be used to give substance to the etheric form of the angel or demon concerned. (Modern magick tends to be a little wary of calling up spirits, however, whose malevolent energies may cause harm.)

In contrast, invocations were used to endow the practitioner with the power to carry out magical purposes through a form of possession, with the angel or god acting directly from within the practitioner's body.

Elementals have also been associated for hundreds of years with more formal magical traditions. Elementals, rather than having a permanent form themselves, are the forces or energies that give shape to living things. They also bring thoughts and desires into actuality, invoked by symbols. Thus medieval occultists sought mastery over the elemental beings that they fashioned by their incantations. Sometimes, if practitioners used the elemental forces for negative purposes, they would create a _tulpa,_ or thought form, that became an elemental demon. This was hard to banish, even though the magicians worked within a square enclosed by two magick circles – hence the origins of warnings about magical effects coming back threefold.

The Goddess and the Horned God in Wicca

Neither evocation nor invocation is part of modern witchcraft, however, and white witches do not recognise any demonic figures in their religion. When we refer to the Goddess and her son–consort, the Horned God of Wicca, we are referring to the archetype or source energies of the feminine and masculine aspects of ultimate power. They are the creative female and male principles, acting not in opposition to each other but as complementary and necessary parts of a whole. All the named goddesses and gods in witchcraft represent the different qualities of these supreme forms, for example the goddesses of the hunt, or specific forms in different cultures.

There are, of course, variations within Wicca; some traditions emphasise the importance of the Goddess, while others regard the Horned God as her equal, with each assuming different aspects according to the season and ritual. For example, the Goddess may appear as the Earth or Moon deity, and her male counterpart as the Corn God or the Sun.

Reaching gods and goddesses in trance

Modern Wiccans call into themselves the energies of the Goddess to amplify their own innate divine spark and at times may work in a deep trance, uttering words of prophecy or profound teaching. This is said to increase the power entering the body, like turning up the current from a power source. But until you have practised magick for many years, I would advocate working only in light trance and then only in the controlled situation of a very spiritual group. You can think of this as opening a channel between your own higher energies and the Goddess or powers of light.

I said just now that the power of a trance can be compared to an electric current. The analogy can be taken further: just as sending a sudden surge of electricity can cause a power failure, deliberately inducing a deep trance can be dangerous. Those who use drugs to induce such experiences are, in my opinion, playing with fire and may in fact be blocking their innate wisdom in return for an artificial mind-bending experience.

Most people quite rightly shy away from the idea of possession by a force, however benign, preferring to work with the energies indirectly – and this is what I believe is safest and most effective. For even if you are working with an experienced group in healing magick and do want to allow power of light or the Goddess to manifest in you directly, it is pretty heady stuff. So go cautiously, work only in the most positive of minds for the good of all, and for trance work have other experienced witches or mediums to guide you and help you to centre.

The gods themselves can offer protection when you are performing rituals. In formal magick, the Guardians, or Devic Lords of the Watchtower, are invited to guard the four directions of a magical circle. The term *deva* in Sanskrit means 'shining one', and the Devas represent the higher forms, akin to angels, who watch and direct the natural world. They communicate with people by psychic 'chanelling' and rule over the beings associated with the four elements, Fire, Air, Water and Earth. In less formal practices, either archangels or pillars of light may be visualised in the corners of the room to offer protection at a time when a person is opening their psyche to the cosmos, to keep out all negativity, earthly or otherwise. But the greatest protection is a pure heart and pure intent, much harder to attain than learning any complex ritual.

The Goddess as focus

Many beliefs emphasise the polarity of the female/male, Goddess/god and anima/animus energies. The bringing together of these two powers, the Sacred Marriage that is celebrated symbolically in the Great Rite of the union of Earth and Sky, is a ritual that permeates all cultures.

In Egyptian mythology, Isis, the sister–wife of Osiris, sought and reassembled his body after his murder and dismemberment by his brother Seth. In this connection, she took on the role of the goddess of rebirth, the Bone Goddess, and restored him in a more evolved form. The annual celebrations of this event coincided with the rising of the dog star, Sirius, which heralded the flooding of the Nile and the restoration of fertility to the land and symbolically to the people.

As the Sky Gods gained supremacy, they married the Earth Goddesses who slowly evolved into patronesses of women, marriage and childbirth. So, for example, Odin the Norse All-Father married Frigg, goddess of women, marriage and motherhood.

But in witchcraft, though the Sky Fathers and their wives are used for the focus of specific rites, the Goddess retains the earlier form as the creative principle. As the Triple Goddess – maiden, mother and wise woman or crone – she is frequently central to coven work.

Generally in magick the Goddess is recognised as the prime mover of existence, bringing forth from herself in the first virgin birth the animus, or male, principle. For this reason, it is often the High Priestess who casts the circle, though in some covens the Goddess rules over the spring and summer and the Horned God over the autumn and winter.

Other gods and goddesses

There is a vast selection of gods and goddesses from many different cultures that you may choose to form a focus for particular energies in rituals. I have given a list of these later in this chapter, but I have not given much detailed description, as it is important we create our own deity images. There are many excellent sites on the Internet, illustrated with paintings and statues of the deities, where you can read their mythical stories.

Because the deities come from so many cultures and times, it is important to invoke only the positive qualities you need and to remember that some did reflect dark as well as benign aspects of divinity. For example, Diana, the goddess of the Moon and the hunt, is thought by most to be a sympathetic soul; but you might be surprised to learn that she would, according to myth, have her rejected lovers torn apart by her hounds. So, when setting up your icons, read about them first, and decide which are the attributes that will assist your magical workings. Some deities fit into more than one category, so I have listed them under their most significant one. For more information, see Further Reading on page 297.

Deities of love and passion

Aphrodite

Aphrodite is the Cretan and Greek goddess of love and beauty. Her name means 'born from the foam'. She can be invoked for the gentle attraction of new love as well as for sexuality and passion (hence the term 'aphrodisiac'). Aphrodite is especially potent in candle and mirror spells, romance and for love rituals involving the sea.

Artemis

Artemis is the twin sister of Apollo, the young Greek Sun God, and is goddess of chastity, virginity, the hunt, the Moon and nature. Although a virgin goddess, she also presides over childbirth. Because of her connection with the hunt, she is altogether a more active goddess than Aphrodite if you are seeking love or, perhaps, trying to encourage a reluctant lover of either sex or win love under difficult circumstances. She is perfect for outdoor love spells and for casting your love net wide to attract an as yet unknown lover.

Freyja

Freyja is the Viking goddess of love and sexuality and can be invoked for rituals to increase confidence in inner beauty and worth, for the increase of passion and for fertility in every aspect. A witch goddess, she is potent for all magick, especially astral projection and crystal and gem magick.

Venus

Venus, the goddess of love, is the Roman form of Aphrodite and by her liaison with Mercury gave birth to Cupid. Although she had many lovers, she was the goddess of chastity in women and is a joy-bringer, and so represents not only sexual pleasure, but also innocent love and especially love in the springtime. Her planetary associations mean she is the focus in all kinds of love rituals. As the evening star, Venus takes on a warrior aspect and so can be invoked in fighting for one's lover or tough love in relationships.

Deities for power

These deities may be invoked for strength, success, energy, inspiration and increase.

Apollo

Apollo, the Greek Sun God, was twin brother of Artemis, the Moon Goddess. As god of the solar light, Apollo made the fruits of the Earth ripen, and at Delos and Delphi where he slew Python, the first crops were dedicated to him.

(Python, the great lightning serpent, was the son–consort of the Mother Goddess in her form of Delphyne, the Womb of Creation, fertilised by Python. Python in this sense predated all other gods and was later called the Dark Sun, Apollo's alter ego. The Ancient Greeks rededicated his shrine to Apollo.)

Apollo was god of prophecy as well as music, poetry, archery, healing and divination. He is very strongly animus and is good for all rituals of power, ambition and inspiration, as well as those areas under his patronage. Men tend to work better with him than women.

Aine

Aine is daughter of Manananann, Celtic Sea God and ruler of the Isle of Man and goddess of the cycles of the solar and lunar year. Even during the twentieth century, she was remembered on the Hill of Aine in Ireland, by torchlight processions and burning straw at midsummer and also at the old corn harvest, Lughnassadh, at the beginning of August. She is also linked with love, fertility and healing.

Ama-terasu Omikami

Ama-terasu Omikami is the Ancient Japanese Sun Goddess. Her name means 'Great August Spirit Shining in Heaven' but she is also called Shinmet, 'Divine Radiance' and O-hiru-me-no-muchi, 'Great Female Possessor of Noon'.

She is good for female-focused Sun rituals and for ceremonial magick.

Helios

The Greek god Helios, known to the Romans as Sol, was regarded as the Sun itself. He ascended the heavens in a chariot drawn by winged snow-white horses to give light and in the evening descended into the ocean. Homer wrote:

'Drawn in his swift chariot, he sheds light on gods and men alike; the formidable flash of his eyes pierces his golden helmet, sparkling rays glint from his breast and his brilliant helmet gives forth a dazzling splendour. His body is draped in shining gauze, whipped by the wind.'

He is especially associated with the life force and renewing health and energy.

Horus

Horus was the Ancient Egyptian Sky God, represented as a falcon or a falcon-headed man. His eyes were the Sun and Moon and his wings could extend across the entire heavens. He was frequently associated with the morning aspect of Ra, the Sun God, and worshipped as Re-Harakhte. The son of Isis and Osiris, he is often depicted as an infant on his mother's lap and together the parents and child form a trinity.

Horus brings clarity of mind and purpose and the ability to seize upon an opportunity, and is effective for uncovering secrets, deception and illusion.

Lugh

Lugh, the Celtic 'shining one', who gives his name to Lughnassadh, Celtic festival of the first harvest, was the young solar deity who replaced the Dagda, father of the gods, as supreme king. He was associated with sacrifice, as the Sun King who was reborn each year at either the mid-winter solstice or the spring equinox.

Legend has it that when Lugh arrived to join the Tuatha de Danaan, he went to the palace of Tara and asked for a position in the court. (The Tuatha de Danaan were the ancient Irish gods and goddesses, literally 'the tribe of Danu', who was the creatrix goddess.) He said he was a carpenter, but was told that the company of gods already had one. Lugh then declared he was a smith but again was told that the deities possessed such a craftsman. He then announced that he was a poet, then in turn a warrior, historian, hero and sorcerer. Each position was filled. Lugh then demanded whether any one person could perform all these tasks as he could. As a result, he was admitted to the Tuatha de Danaan and eventually became their leader.

You can invoke Lugh especially at the time of Lughnassadh, for the reaping of benefits sown earlier in the year, but also at any time for adaptability, versatility, innovation and originality.

Deities of the Moon

Invoke these for gentle increase, power and banishing energies, fertility, intuition, magick and dreams.

Arianrhod

Arianrhod is a Welsh goddess of the full moon and also of time, karma and destiny. She ruled over the realm of the Celtic Otherworld, called Caer Feddwidd, the Fort of Carousa. Here a mystical fountain of wine offered eternal health and youth for those who chose to spend their immortality in the Otherworld. She brings inspiration, renewal, health and rejuvenation, and is a focus for all magick, as she is a witch goddess.

Diana

Diana is the Roman counterpart of Artemis, and because of her strong association with the Moon in all its phases, is a goddess of fertility as well as love. Like Artemis, she is goddess of the hunt and a virgin goddess, but can be invoked in her role as an Earth goddess and as protector of women in childbirth. Her beauty and hunting skills make her a perfect focus for the pursuit of love, especially from afar.

Myesyats

Like the lunar goddesses, Myesyats, the Slavic Moon God, represented the three stages of the life cycle. He was first worshipped as a young man until he reached maturity at the full moon. With the waning phase, Myesyats passed through old age and died with the old moon, being reborn three days later. As he was the restorer of life and health, parents would pray to him to take away their children's illnesses and family sorrows. Other sources have a female version, Myesytsa, a lovely Moon maiden who was the consort of Dazhbog the Sun God, and became mother of the stars.

Myesyats brings healing and family harmony.

Selene

Selene is the Greek goddess specially associated with the full moon, sometimes forming a triplicity with Diana and Hecate, the twin sister of Helios the Sun God. Selene rises from the sea in her chariot drawn by white horses at night and rides high in the sky in her full moon.

At the time of the full moon, she is invoked by women for fertility and by all who seek the power of intuition and inspiration.

Mother Goddesses

Mother Goddesses are for fertility, abundance of all kinds, female power and all rituals for women.

Astarte

Astarte is the supreme female divinity of the Phoenicians, goddess of love and fertility, associated with the Moon and all nature (see also Ishtar, page 66).

Invoke her for power and wisdom, seduction and passion as well as fertility.

Cerridwen

Cerridwen is the Welsh Mother Goddess, the keeper of the cauldron and goddess of inspiration, knowledge and wisdom. She is a natural focus for rituals involving all creative ventures and for increased spiritual and psychic awareness. Invoke her for divination and especially scrying and for all rituals of increase.

Ceres

Ceres is the Roman goddess of the grain and all food plants. Her daughter Proserpina was taken into the Underworld for three months of the year by Pluto, causing Ceres to mourn and the crops to die. This was the origin of winter.

Through this, she is seen as goddess of fertility and abundance, as well as a deity of the natural cycles of the year. She represents loss and is a focus for rites concerning grief and mourning, with the hope of new joy ahead for women and especially for mothers. Her Greek counterpart is Demeter.

Demeter

Demeter, the Greek Corn Goddess or Barley Mother, was the archetypal symbol of the fertility of the land. Demeter is often pictured as rosy-cheeked, carrying a hoe or sickle and surrounded by baskets of apples, sheaves of corn, garlands of flowers and grapes.

Like Ceres, she mourns for her lost daughter Persephone for three months of the year and so is another icon for those who are feeling sorrow or loss and for maternal sacrifice. But she can be invoked for all matters of abundance, for reaping the benefits of earlier work or effort, for all mothering rituals and as a protectress of animals.

Innana

Innana was a Sumerian goddess, known as the Queen of Heaven, who evolved into the Babylonian goddess Ishtar. Innana was goddess of beauty, abundance, fertility and passion, famed for her loveliness and her lapis lazuli necklaces. She was the first goddess of the morning and evening stars, a legacy that has passed to Aphrodite and Venus.

Like many of the Mother Goddess icons, she descended into the Underworld annually to face and overcome many trials, to bring back to life her shepherd god consort Dumuzi.

Ishtar

Ishtar, the Babylonian version of Innana, also descended into the Underworld each year to restore her consort Tammuz to life. She was a fierce goddess of weapons and war. In Ancient Babylon, a sacred marriage took place each year between Tammuz and Ishtar. This was celebrated at the festival of Akitu, or Zag-Mug, which marked the rising of the waters of the Tigris and the Euphrates and the coming of the spring rains, to bring fertility, at the spring equinox.

Like Innana, she is a goddess of fertility, restoration, renewal, birth and the life cycles; she also represents power with responsibility and necessary sacrifice for future gain, but above all transformation.

Isis

The Egyptian goddess Isis is the most powerful and frequently invoked goddess in formal magick. She is mother, healer and the faithful wife who annually restored her consort Osiris to life, thus magically causing the Nile to flood and fertility to return to the land. She is the patroness of magick and spell-casting, having tricked Ra the Sun God into giving her his secrets. Some accounts say she was taught by Thoth, god of wisdom and learning. Her cult spread throughout the Roman Empire and she remained in Mediterranean lands in her guise as the Black Madonna, holding her infant son Horus, until the Middle Ages. She is sometimes represented as a vulture, in which form she appears on amulets (protective charms) with an *ankh*, the symbol for life, engraved on each talon. Isis demonstrated the power of maternal protection when she hid Horus in the marshes from his evil uncle who would have destroyed him.

Deities of marriage

These deities can be invoked in rituals concerning the family and the home.

Frigg

Frigg was the Viking Mother Goddess whose jewelled spinning wheel formed Orion's belt; as patroness of marriage, women, mothers and families, she can be invoked for all rituals concerned with families and domestic happiness. She invited devoted husbands and wives to her hall after death so that they might never be parted again and so is goddess of fidelity.

As Ostara, goddess of spring, she was known among the Anglo-Saxons and is remembered in the festival of Easter as a fertility goddess and bringer of new beginnings.

In her role as Valfreya, the Lady of the Battlefield, Frigg recalls the Northern tradition of warrior goddesses and offers courage to women.

Hera

Hera, the wife–sister of Zeus, is a the supreme Greek goddess of protection, marriage and childbirth whose sacred bird is the peacock. She is a powerful deity of fidelity and is called upon by women seeking revenge upon unfaithful partners.

Hestia

Hestia is the Greek goddess of the hearth and home, all family matters and peace within the home. She is a benign, gentle goddess and so can be invoked for matters involving children and pets.

Juno

Juno, the wife–sister of Jupiter, is the Roman queen of the gods, the protectress of women, marriage and childbirth and also wise counsellor.

Together with Jupiter and Minerva, the goddess of wisdom, she made up the triumvirate of deities who made decisions about humankind and especially Roman affairs. Her month, June, is most fortunate for marriage and, like Hera, her Greek equivalent, her sacred creature is the peacock. She is invoked in sex magick as well as for all matters concerning marriage, children, fidelity and wise counsel.

Parvati

Parvati is the benign and gentle Hindu Mother Goddess, consort of the god Shiva and the goddess daughter of the Himalayas. Her name means 'mountain' and she is associated with all mountains. She and Shiva are often pictured as a family in the Himalayas with their sons Ganesh, god of wisdom and learning, and six-headed Skanda, the warrior god. She is invoked for all family matters and those concerning children and by women in distress.

Vesta

Vesta is the Roman goddess of domesticity and of the sacred hearth at which dead and living were welcomed. The Vestal Virgins of Rome kept alight the sacred flame in Vesta's temple and this was rekindled at the New Year, as were household flames. Vesta can be invoked in rituals centred around the element Fire.

Father Gods

The Father Gods represent authority, channelled power, benevolence and altruism, nobility of purpose, expansion and limitless potential.

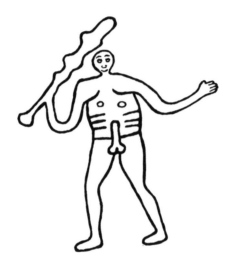

Dagda

Dagda, the Father God in the Celtic tradition, was also called Eochaid Ollathair (Father of All) and Ruadh Rofessa (the Red One of Knowledge). He was the first King of the Tuatha de Danaan, the Irish gods, and it was believed that he performed miracles and saw to the weather and the harvest.

Dagda was lord of life and death and the primary god of fertility. With his huge club, he made the bones of his people's enemies *'fall like hail beneath the horses'*. With one end of the club, it was said, he could kill nine men with a single blow and with the other could instantly restore them to life.

His great cauldron was handed on to his daughter Brighid (Cerridwen in the Welsh tradition). In some legends, Dagda is associated with Balor, the Sun deity of the Formoiri, enemies of the gods, who was slain by Lugh, the young solar god, at the Battle of Moytura, thus representing the ascent of the new Sun.

The death of the old order, as a necessary requirement for the new, is a central motif in spirituality and so Dagda can offer a focus for rites of passage where change is necessary, but not necessarily welcomed.

Odin

Odin is the Viking Father God, known as the All-Father, god of inspiration, wisdom and poetry as well as war. Odin was desperate to acquire the wisdom and knowledge of the older order of giants. He traded one of his eyes for wisdom and obtained the knowledge of the runes, the ancient symbols of spiritual knowledge, by sacrificing himself on the World Tree.

Odin can be invoked for magic and divination, especially for casting runes, for inspiration with words and oratory, for expansion of horizons and for male power magic. If Frigg is also invoked, the energies are more balanced.

Deities of change

These deities may be invoked in rituals involving not only change but also good fortune.

Oya

Oya is the African goddess, also known as Yoruba, who rules the winds and so controls the winds of change. She oversees trading and the marketplace, and brings good fortune to all honest traders and those who work with finance. She is very powerful, described as an Amazonian warrior and life-giver with dominion over the storms. She can be invoked at times of change and for all matters of employment, commerce good fortune and taking control of one's destiny.

Lakshmi

Lakshmi is the Hindu goddess of wealth, beauty, joy, pleasure and good fortune.

At Divali, the Hindu autumn festival of light, lamps and candles are placed in windows so that Lakshmi will look in and endow prosperity upon the family. *Rangolis,* or coloured patterns, are painted on floors and walls to attract her. Rituals to invoke her usually involve candles and use gold or jewellery as a focus for her benevolence.

Deities of power

These gods and goddesses bring psychic self-defence, protection, righteous anger against injustice, also change, regeneration and survival.

These deities are very powerful and should only be invoked in their most positive aspects for the purpose of defending the weak and never for revenge or personal anger. Experienced witches call on them only rarely and with the purest intent under the law of threefold return. The exception is Bellona, who is a benevolent and effective focus for female power and courage.

Bellona

Bellona is the Roman goddess of war, the female counterpart of Mars whose chariot she drove into battle. She is especially good for women's assertiveness and self-confidence rituals. She carries a sword and wears a helmet.

Kali

Kali, the dark side of the Hindu Mother Goddess, came into being when Shiva, the husband of the Mother Goddess Shakti, taunted her for her dark skin. In fury she carried out rituals until her skin became golden inside. Shakti then shed her black outer skin like a snake and it formed the avenging destroying persona of Kali. Kali is depicted with her four arms holding weapons and the heads of her victims, her tongue lolling out, and covered in blood, signifying her power over life and death. She is often pictured dancing on Shiva whose body she trampled on, destroyed and then danced on once more to restore him to life.

Kali is invoked to remove fear and, it is said, to bring bliss to her devotees, and so she brings protection and regeneration after sorrow.

Persephone

Persephone is the Greek maiden goddess of transformation, daughter of Demeter and goddess of spring and flowers. She was abducted by Hades, God of the Underworld, and became Queen of the Underworld for the winter months (see also Demeter, page 65), returning to the Earth as the light-bringer in spring and so representing the cycle of death and rebirth. She is especially powerful in rituals by or for young women, especially those who have suffered loss or abuse, and also for mother–daughter relationships. She is sometimes regarded as a symbol of grain.

Proserpina, daughter of Ceres, is the Roman form of Persephone.

Sekhmet

Sekhmet is the Ancient Egyptian solar and lion goddess created from the eye of Ra. She is sometimes pictured as a woman with a lion's head and so is a good to evoke for courage, righteous anger, protection of the vulnerable, psychic protection and the correction of injustice. As an avenging goddess, she should be used only as a focus for positive rituals, for, like fire, her innate power can blaze out of control.

Shiva

Shiva, or Siva, is the Hindu god of both creation and destruction, good and evil, fertility and abstinence. With Vishnu and Brahma, he forms the trinity of the modern Hindu gods. He is the Lord of the Dance who, it is said, will one day bring about the destruction of the world.

His symbol is the phallus, representing creative power, and many Hindus regard his benevolent, creative aspect as predominant. Shiva has three eyes, represented by the Sun, the Moon and Fire. His third eye allows him to see inwards and also to destroy whatever it looks on. He was not one of the original Vedic deities but became one of the supreme gods, according to legend, at the time when the universe consisted only of water. Vishnu and Brahma were arguing about who was the greatest god when a great pillar of flame appeared between them. Shiva appeared from within the flaming pillar, which was symbol of his masculine power, and the other gods bowed before him.

Invoke Shiva for animus power, potency, survival and male rituals.

Shakti

Shakti, or Matahdevi, is the female energy or power of Shiva. Her name is also used for the wife of any Hindu god. She is the Mother Goddess and, like Shiva, creator and destroyer in her different aspects.

Shakti provides the energy that activates Shiva's male divine power, and her life-giving force animates other gods in difficult tasks. Although there are several other Hindu female goddesses, they all form aspects of Shakti and often their identities merge. One of Shakti's forms is as Parvati, the gentle mother (see page 67). Shakti is potent for all rituals of women's power, especially when they must take the initiative, and she is easier to work with than Kali (see page 70).

Triple Goddesses

The Triple Goddesses are for lunar magic and moving from one stage to another in the life cycle.

Brighid

Brighid, the Celtic Triple Goddess, is patroness of smiths, poets and healers and has the longest enduring cult in Ireland, which merged into that of the Christian St Bridget of Kildare. Her name means 'high one' and she is sometimes seen as three sisters, daughters of the god Dagda, the Divine Father, or as the triple-aspected maiden, mother and crone. She is invoked in fertility and healing magick and also for creativity, especially involving the written word. There are a number of sacred wells throughout England, Wales and Ireland dedicated to her or her Christian counterpart.

Deities of the environment

Invoke these deities for rituals involving all aspects of the environment and for healing the planet.

Gaia

Gaia is the all-embracing and all-nourishing goddess of the Earth. It is said that she supplies in her bounty all the necessary plants to cure any disease and, in spite of human pollution, she constantly heals and renews the planet. She is also a goddess of marriage.

She is the natural focus for all green rituals.

Tellus Mater

Tellus Mater was the Earth Mother of the Romans, the alter ego of Ceres, the grain mother, and guardian of the fertility of people, animals and crops. However, Tellus Mater is also the mother who receives the dead in her womb to comfort and restore and so, like Gaia, she is a excellent goddess for all green magick and rituals for healing pollution or deforestation.

Wophe

Wophe, or White Buffalo Calf Woman, is the sacred creator woman of the Lakotas and other peoples of the American Plains. Legend says she fell from a meteor and as she began her Earth walk, she was discovered by two young Lakota scouts who were hunting for buffalo.

She wore a pure white buckskin dress, her long hair flowing behind her like a sea of corn. She sang into the souls of the men that each should act on his thoughts. Eagerly the first, not recognising her sacred nature, hurried towards her and a white mist covered them. The sound of rattlesnakes was heard and when the cloud lifted, there were only the bones of the young man. She told the other to inform the elders of the tribe that she would come to them next morning with a great gift for the people.

A huge ornate ceremonial tepee was erected and in the morning she entered, carrying a special bundle on her back and singing a holy song. The men kept their eyes lowered when she entered, as she had instructed. She unfastened the bundle and took from it the buffalo calf pipe, which is still the most sacred religious object of the Lakota today.

The woman instructed the men in how to smoke the pipe, which in its smoke symbolised the visible Spirit, in the bowl Mother Earth and in the stem Father Sky, so that it might be used for prayer offerings to her and for bringing peace to divided nations. On her visits she also taught sacred ceremonies for restoring balance and healing to both Earth and people. She then set off to leave the camp, walking towards the West. When she reached the outskirts, she rolled over on the ground and was transformed into a buffalo, changing colours several times. Finally, she changed into a white buffalo calf, rarest of the species, promising that when she was seen again she would restore harmony to a troubled world. The people followed her teachings, the corn grew, the seasons continued to flow in succession and they were hungry no more, as buffalo became plentiful.

By the end of the nineteenth century, however, there were in reality fewer than 200 buffalo left, where only years earlier it was estimated there had been several million. In the summer of 1994, a white buffalo calf was born in Jamesville, Wisconsin. As the prophecy had told, the white buffalo has changed its colours since birth, going from white to black to red to yellow and back to white. Since each colour represents one of the four directions, the buffalo is seen by many Native Americans as a symbol of the rebirth of hope. One visionary interpreted the birth of the white buffalo calf as signifying that the human race will be united, in spite of differences in creed and colour, and join together in peace.

Wophe is therefore an important symbol not only of the revival of the Native American wisdom, but also of healing and reconciliation of all people and of the land and all its creatures.

Deities of the male principle

These deities are for the hunt, instincts, willing sacrifice and ecstasy.

Cernunnos

Cernunnos, meaning 'horned one', was a generic term for the various Horned Gods of the Celtic tradition. The god dates back to the shamanic figures portrayed on cave walls. Cernunnos was lord of winter, the hunt, animals, death, male fertility and the Underworld, and was sometime portrayed as a triple or trefoil god, an image later assimilated by St Patrick with his emblematic shamrock.

Other forms of the Horned God include Herne the Hunter, the Greek Pan, god of the woodlands, and Dionysus, Greek god of vegetation and the vine, whose ecstatic mystery cult involved ritual dismemberment and resurrection.

Cerunnos' importance has been in his continuing presence as the Horned God, the male principle in witchcraft through the ages, in modern Wicca and other neo-pagan faiths. He is also invoked for prosperity, fertility, instinctive power and knowledge of when it is necessary to hunt, whether to find employment or a home, and as protection against predators of all kinds.

Dionysus

Dionysus, sometimes depicted as a Horned God, was a god of the grain, who died and was reborn every year as a child in a basket, representing the seed corn. He was the Greek god of fertility, ecstasy and wildness, who bestowed great abundance on his followers; his cult performed savage rites at Eleusius where human flesh was eaten as the bread of life. Not an easy deity to use, without great experience and restraint, as the excesses carried out under his name need to be kept in check while invoking the free spirit and the renewal of life. He is potent for breaking away from destructive situations or, ironically, bad habits such as alcohol.

Osiris

Osiris became one of the most important and popular gods in Ancient Egypt, mainly because he promised non-royal believers that resurrection and salvation from death were for everyone, poor as well as rich. Originally he was identified with each dead pharaoh, and his son Horus was identified with the reigning successor.

Osiris married his sister Isis, and his brother Seth married Isis's sister Nephthys. According to legend, Osiris was at first made an earthly king by his father Geb, the Earth God. Osiris ruled wisely, teaching his people about agriculture and the arts. But Osiris's brother Seth was jealous and vowed to kill him. Seth invited Osiris to a feast and showed the guests a fine coffer, promising that whoever fitted inside would be the owner. Osiris stepped inside the coffer and it fitted perfectly. Seth slammed the lid tight and he and his followers threw the chest into the Nile.

Isis searched for her husband and at last discovered the chest at Byblos on the Phoenician coast. She brought Osiris' body back to Egypt and conceived a son by her dead husband, hiding herself in the rushes of the marshes of the delta while awaiting the birth.

Seth discovered the body of Osiris, hacked it into pieces and scattered them throughout Egypt so that he could never be restored to life. But Isis searched once more and, assisted by Nephthys, remodelled the bones into Osiris' form and restored her husband to life once more.

When their son Horus, the Sky God, became a youth, he fought to avenge his father against Seth. The divine judges, including Thoth, god of wisdom, met in the Great Hall of Judgment and decided that Osiris should become not a living king once more, but eternal King and Judge of the Underworld.

Osiris was also god of vegetation, the fertile, flooding Nile and the corn, and so represented the annual dying of the land and rebirth with the flood. He is normally pictured as a man, bound in mummy wrappings.

Osiris is an important icon of the annual cycle of sacrifice and resurrection but, as with all the sacrifice gods, it is the female power that causes the resurrection. Like other sacrificed and restored gods, Osiris thereby represents the integration of animus and anima and sacred sex magick. He can be used in rituals for the balance of male/female energies or where the female in the High Priestess role takes the lead. He is also good for any magick that relies on a cycle of regeneration following a natural ending.

Deities of fire

Agni

Agni, the Hindu god of fire, is said to be manifest as the vital spark in mankind, birds, animals, plants and life itself. He appeared in lightning, in celestial sun flares, in the sacred blaze rising from the altar and in household fires.

Agni was the divine priest and acted as messenger to the gods, interceding with them on behalf of mankind. The priest would chant:

> 'Agni, the divine ministrant of the sacrifice, the great bestower of treasure. May one obtain through Agni, wealth and welfare.'

Agni is still important as the god of domestic and ritual fire and for spells for the increase of wealth, material goods, creativity and domestic protection.

Hephaestus

Hephaestus, Greek god of fire and metalwork, was thrown from Mount Olympus by his father Zeus because he took the part of his mother Hera in a quarrel; as a result of the fall, he became lame. He created armour, weapons and jewels for the gods in his workshop beneath the volcanic Mount Etna, in Sicily, and as a reward was given Aphrodite as his unwilling bride. He was among the least charismatic of the gods, but his Roman counterpart, Vulcan, fashioned Jupiter's thunderbolts.

Hephaestus is patron of metal-workers in much of the Western world and in the Middle East from where his cult originated. He is effective in all rituals for craftsmanship, for the acquisition of wealth and treasures, for the development of skills and precision and for controlled power for a particular purpose.

Deities of healing

Aesculapius

Aesculapius was a healer, son of Apollo and the mortal Corona, who lived during the eleventh century BC, and became a god after Zeus killed him with a thunderbolt for raising the dead.

The first shrine dedicated to Aesculapius was built in Athens in the fifth century BC by Sophocles. Other shrines followed in rapid succession, the most famous at Epidaurus, which became a major healing centre. Many were sited at sacred wells and springs. These shrines were dedicated to healing and dreams, and were the principle vehicle for obtaining relief or cure of illness of all kinds.

When Aesculapius appeared to the dreamers, he would tell them the medicine they should use and any treatment that should be followed. He can be invoked for healing and meaningful dreams, for good health and for divination.

Ganga

Ganga is the Hindu water goddess who is manifest as the sacred river Ganges, daughter of the mountain Himalaya. She is a natural focus for healing rituals, as well as for happiness, fertility and prosperity, and for Water magick.

Iduna

Iduna is the Viking goddess of eternal youthfulness, health and long life. As goddess of spring, she possessed a store of golden apples that endowed immortality, fertility and healing and so she can form a focus for healing rituals, and for spells for beauty, health and the granting of wishes, especially those using apples as a symbol.

Panacea

Panacea is the Roman goddess of healing, who takes away pain. Daughter of Aesculapius, she and her sister Hygeia assisted in healing the sick in their dreams at the dream temples.

She is good for healing rituals for women, children and especially teenage girls.

Sulis

Sulis, or Sulevia, is the Celtic goddess of healing and especially of healing waters. Her name is derived from the Celtic word for the Sun and her most famous site is the hot mineral springs that have for at least 10,000 years poured from the ground in Bath, in south-west England. From Celtic times, perhaps even earlier, the springs became a formal centre of healing.

Sulis became Sulis Minerva under the Roman occupation and she maintained her role as a healing deity. The significance of the sacred springs continued and Edgar, the first king of England, was crowned there in AD 973. In medieval times, the springs were still a focus for healing pilgrimages and in the seventeenth and eighteenth centuries Bath became a fashionable resort where the wealthy would come to socialise and take the waters.

Sulis is potent for all healing water rituals. Because curse tablets as well as offerings have been retrieved from the waters, she is also associated with justice through karma and the banishing of sorrows.

Deities of wisdom

As well as wisdom, these gods and goddesses are for knowledge, truth and justice.

Athena

Athena, or Athene, daughter of Zeus, is goddess of wise counsel, both in peace and war, of intelligence, reason, negotiation and all forms of the arts and literature. The owl is her sacred bird and the olive her symbol representing peace, healing and nourishment.

Hathor

Hathor is the Ancient Egyptian goddess of truth, wisdom, joy, love, music, art and dance and protectress of women. She is said to bring husbands or wives to those who call on her and she is also a powerful fertility goddess. Also worshipped as a Sky Goddess, Hathor is frequently shown wearing a Sun disc held between the horns of a cow as a crown.

She was once entrusted with the sacred eye of Ra, the Sun God and her consort, through which she could see all things. She carried a shield that could reflect back all things in their true light. From her shield she fashioned the first magical mirror. One side was endowed with the power of Ra's eye to see everything, no matter how distant in miles or how far into the future. The other side showed the gazer in his or her true light and only a brave person could look at it without flinching.

Hathor can be invoked for all forms of mirror magic and is also associated with gold and turquoise and so jewellery made of these can be a focus for her powers. In the modern world she is guardian of businesswomen. Fiercely protective in defence of her own, she is especially potent against physical and psychic attack.

Ma'at

Ma'at, the Ancient Egyptian goddess of truth and justice, was responsible for maintaining the correct balance and order in the universe. She was daughter of Ra who created her to establish unity and order in the world. Ma'at is pictured as a woman wearing a single ostrich feather as a headdress.

She was all-powerful, even over the king, who had to rule with truth and justice to attain eternal life. After death, a person's heart was weighed on the scales of justice against the feather from her headdress to see if it was free from sin. She can be invoked for all rituals of justice, uncovering secrets, truth and trustworthiness.

Hermes

Hermes is the Greek messenger god who travelled between dimensions. He is associated with the wise Ancient Egyptian god Thoth and the later Roman Mercury. He is credited with great knowledge, healing powers and medical knowledge.

The double entwined snake of Hermes' and Mercury's caduceus, or wand, which is often a living growing staff, is a symbol both of healing and of powerful communication. The snake forms two circles, the interlinked cycles of good and evil, life and death, light and darkness. The wings on the caduceus are for wisdom, guarding against gossip and malicious words as well as illness.

Among Hermes' many patronages were moneylenders and thieves and so he can protect against poverty and trickery, as well as helping you to speak the truth that is in your heart.

Hermes can also be invoked for all medical and commercial matters, for good fortune of all kinds and for peaceful sleep.

Minerva

Minerva is the Roman goddess of wisdom, who ruled with Jupiter and Juno as the triumvirate of justice and wise power. She also controlled commerce and all crafts and is credited with the invention of music. She is often depicted in armour.

Minerva, whose creature is the owl, can be invoked in employment rituals and for the development of skills, retraining and musical ability as well as for truth and justice. Unlike Bellona (see page 70) and the warlike gods, both Athena and Minerva are used in rituals for using legal means or oratory and persuasion, rather than direct action, to overcome injustice.

Thoth

Thoth was the Ancient Egyptian god of the Moon, wisdom and learning. He was also god of time, languages, law and mathematical calculations, who invented the calendar and hieroglyphic writing. He is often depicted with the head of an ibis although he was worshipped as a baboon in Hermopolis.

Appeal to him for all matters of magical wisdom, learning, intellectual pursuits, examinations and better time management.

Wise woman deities

These goddesses are for transformation rituals, for endings that become beginnings and for accepting what cannot be changed.

Cailleach

Cailleach, meaning ' the Veiled One', is the Celtic name for a number of hag goddesses. These are powerful crone goddesses, who have retained their early associations with the winter. For example, the Scottish Cailleac Bhuer, the Blue Hag, manifested herself as an old woman wearing black or dark blue rags with a crow on her left shoulder and a holly staff that could kill a mortal with a touch. She roamed the Highlands by night during winter when her power was at its greatest. Cailleac Bhuer is credited with creating the mountains by flying through the sky dropping stones, and so is said by some folklorists to be the origin of megaliths and stone circles and the nursery rhyme, 'There was an old woman tossed up in a basket'.

Hags are expert shapeshifters and as well as appearing as old women, they may assume the form of lovely maidens, hares, cats, stones and even trees.

Hecate

As well as being a crone goddess, Hecate is a goddess of good fortune, especially but not only of sailors and hunters. As goddess of the crossroads, where offerings were traditionally left to call up her blessings, she is regarded as the supreme goddess of witches and witchcraft and is akin to the Bone Goddess who transforms death into new more perfect life. She can be invoked for all waning moon magic and for rituals for banishing sorrows and bad habits.

Charges

Charges are declarations of the powers of the gods or godesses involved in the ritual, and are in themselves empowering and a way of linking the practitioner's own divine spark with that represented by the Divinity. They are similar to creeds in a Christian religious service.

The Charge of the Goddess

The Charge of the Goddess is a powerful way of focusing on cosmic energies. The Goddess is considered to be both 'transcendent', or above and beyond the created universe (like the traditional idea of God on a cloud, looking down and judging creation!), and also 'immanent', or manifest within every natural object, be it flower, stone, animal or person. The two concepts are complementary rather than contradictory.

Some practitioners feel that charges are an attempt to formalise energies that are beyond definition within a more conventional spiritual framework and that they are therefore artificial and restricting. If you have not used them before, I suggest you try working through the meditation given later in this chapter, to see if it is right for you.

The first and most popular version of the Charge of the Goddess was created by Gerald Gardener's High Priestess Doreen Valiente, herself one of the most influential people in formal magical traditions. Her version of the statement of the unifying principles of the Goddess is widely quoted and often memorised and sometimes adopted as a focus for trance work. (See page 300 for books describing her work.) However, some practitioners, both solitary and those in less formal groups, create their own charges and may alter them as their confidence and experience of magick increase. You can create your own charge at the beginning of some rituals, or use an existing one, even if you do not acknowledge the Goddess as central to your personal spirituality.

You may view the divine force as a more abstract source of light and wisdom, but even so it can be helpful to personify it as a female (anima) and at the same time male (animus) form. Though the Valiente charge includes names of deities of both male and female forms, unless these mean something to you, you may want to exclude them or use names to which you personally relate. You can refer back to the beginning of this chapter, where I listed a number of god and goddess forms, common to magick and drawn from different cultures, that emphasise specific strengths or qualities of the Divinity. However, your own list, drawn from mythology or perhaps your own background, may work better for you. The following is a version I have developed using three goddess forms from the Celtic tradition, my own favourite, which I have adapted for the three phases of the Goddess.

So spoke the Great Mother who has been known in many forms and by many names in countless ages, but is and always will be one and the same. As the Maiden, she is the Celtic Brighid who in early spring softens the Earth with her white wand of fire and so awakens the spring and restores fertility to land and people. As Mother, she is Cerridwen whose magical cauldron of wisdom and inspiration overflows to all who seek and call in need; finally she is Cailleach, the Veiled One, wise woman, healer and bringer of dreams, who in the winter of life transforms the old and outworn into new life to be born with the Maiden in the spring.

'When the Moon is full, you can call on me, goddess, mother, sister, friend, daughter and grandmother of all ages and all places, in joy, for I bring love and plenty. You may also bring me your hopes with the waxing moon and your sorrows on the wane, for I am with you in all states and stages, when you call and when you are silent, when you turn to me as an eager child and when you weep solitary tears in your pillow when your dreams have dissolved into ashes.

'I hold the key to the mysteries of existence and the universe, but these I will share with all who come with willing heart and open mind. For they are not hidden from you, but are all round you in every season. I am in the Moon as she passes through the sky, in the fertile Earth and the mighty waters, for I am them as I am part of you, and you of me, and you too are of the same divine fabric as the Moon and the fertile Earth and the waters, the stars, the sunshine and the life-giving rain.

'I do not ask sacrifice or worship, for I come to you in love as a gentle mother, with compassion, understanding and forgiveness of those things in your heart that you fear to look on in yourself. I am fierce, defending my young and my green places and creatures from all who would do them harm, but I would rather teach than avenge, restore and regenerate.

'I am the great healer of sorrow, pain, loss and doubt. Through me and through my herbs, oils, crystals and sacred waters, you can spread my healing wisdom.

'As I give life, so in death all return to me to be transformed, renewed and born again. I was with you in the beginning and will be with you in the end.

'If you work with honour, love, humility and for the highest good, then you may realise your own divinity and spread light and fertility throughout the Earth. For what you give, will I restore to you threefold and more, time without time and for evermore.'

We are of the circle and we are the circle. May the circle be uncast but never broken.

If you are working in a group, you can each recite different parts of the charge, but best of all, through meditation, alone or as a group, you can work to create your own. If you are a solitary practitioner, you can read or recite your charge into a candle flame or in a wild, open place, and feel the energies resounding beyond and within you. You can also use it before divination or as an introduction to a ceremony for healing or greater understanding.

Meditation can last from five minutes to half an hour or more. In these initial stages, allow your own psyche to guide you as to when the experience is done. If other members of the group are still working, this is not a sign that their experience was more profound. Sit quietly or lie down, enjoying the silence and allowing the images of your meditation to develop quite spontaneously.

If you are working with a group, remain in the circle and pass round a bowl or chalice of pure water. If you are working indoors with candlelight, arrange the candles so they reflect on the water. As each person gazes into the water, they can contribute a series of images about what the Goddess represents to them, which will be stimulated by the meditation. You do not need to use a bowl of water, but it is a way of directing inner images externally to find expression. Some people prefer to pass round a crystal ball or a large piece of uncut crystal. A crystal is helpful if you find it difficult to retrieve images from meditation or if you find meditation unproductive, as the living energies provide a direct route to your unconscious wisdom.

After your meditation, if you are working alone, surround a clear bowl of water with white candles and, looking into it, begin to speak. You may like to record your words on cassette to make them easier to recall. If you do not consciously try to formulate poetic expressions, profound poetry and rich images will emerge almost from another place. This is the deep pool of collective wisdom speaking.

If you are in a group, the images can be set down by your scribe as a collective charge that can be changed over the months. Working on your charge can be a fruitful activity every six weeks or so as it reflects and stimulates the group consciousness.

Copy a version of your charge into your Book of Shadows. It is good to read if you feel afraid or alone at any time when you are not doing magical work.

The Charge of the God

For some practitioners, this charge is less important, but I believe that the male polarity or energies are an integral part not only of the seasonal Wheel of the Year (see page 246), but also of human experience, whether you are working alone or as part of a coven. It is one I have found helpful, but you can create your own through a god meditation by visualising a god form that seems relevant to you. Again I have used Celtic god forms:

These are the words of the Father, who is son and consort of the Great Mother, born in the beginning of She who created the universe from her own body, from her smiles and tears and ever-fertile womb.

'I am He, the wild untamed power of the hunt, the horned beasts and the woodland, that offers food, shelter and protection to people of all races, clans and creeds. I am Cernunnos, horned Lord of Winter; as Master of the Animals and Lord of the Corn, I offer willing sacrifice for the land and people; as King of the Dark Places beneath the soil, in the nurturing womb of the Mother, like all creatures who have entered the gentle Earth, I grow strong again, resting but never slumbering, until I hear the call at the darkest and coldest hour to be reborn as Lugh, radiant son; at that hour I bring the promise that the Sun will not die, but as the wheel turns bring lighter days and the promise of spring as the mid-winter yoke is conquered once more.

'I bring power, strength, courage and nobility to defend the weak and the vulnerable, and to give of my life blood to maintain what is of worth and just and lovely. Mine is not the path of ease, but of ecstasy in the wild wood where the untamed instincts bow only to natural law and natural justice; as the fruit of the sacred vine, Lord of the Dance, the young stag who masters the old; as the Barley King, I dance and laugh and sing of the spirit that never can be broken, of the potency of the life force coursing through my loins to bring increase and abundance, as fields and the animals and humankind are made fertile by the sacred coupling beneath the may bowers and blossoming trees.

'Birth follows death, plenty follows dearth, creation follows necessary destruction, and so renewed, I dedicate myself to the sanctity of all life ruled by the highest of intent and in humility in the hour of my greatest triumph.'

A Goddess meditation

You can use this to create your personal or group Charge of the Goddess.

Find a quiet, safe place for meditation where you will not be disturbed and can fall asleep without coming to any harm, if you naturally drift from a meditative to a sleep state. Choose a time when you are not too tired and before you begin, have a bath to which a few drops of sandalwood or ylang ylang oil are added for heightened psychic awareness.

For the meditation, use a focus, for example a bubbling fountain or water feature, fragrant herbs or flowers, such as lavender or roses, or a scented candle of jasmine, apple blossom, lilac or neroli. (You can easily make a water feature by setting up a very small electric pump in a deep container in which you place crystals, greenery, perhaps a tiny statue and some plants.) You can work either alone or as a group, sitting in a circle round the focus, so that you can see it without moving your neck or head. Experiment until you get the height of the table and the distances right. For group work, you can light a circle of candles.

If you are working indoors, and there is no natural harmonious sound, such as the water, you may like to play softly a CD of rainforest or ocean sounds, birdsong or dolphin calls.

❀ Light incense sticks of frankincense or myrrh.

❀ Sit either cross-legged on the floor on a rug or blanket with your hands supporting your knees, in the lotus position if you are skilled in yoga, or on a chair with both feet flat on the floor. If you wish, support your back with a pillow and have arm rests on the chair for your elbows. Relax your arms and hands, with palms uppermost. It is important to be comfortable and not to be distracted by worrying about keeping in a particular 'approved' position.

❀ Visualise yourself surrounded by a circle of warm, protective light or, if you are using a candle, gaze into the flame.

❀ Take a slow, deep breath through your nose, inhaling the light. Hold it for a count of 'One and two and three' and slowly exhale darkness through your mouth.

❀ Let the circle of light expand and enfold you so that you are bathed in the light. You may find it easier at this point to close your eyes and to see the light with your inner vision.

❀ Within the sphere of light, allow the goddess form to build up quite naturally. It may be a familiar figure or a composite of many different female power icons of beauty, wisdom and grace. She may be old, young, wise or challenging, according to the qualities you are attracting to meet your as yet, perhaps, unformulated needs. In different meditations you may see different goddesses and so adapt the charge accordingly to emphasise particular strengths and qualities they evoke.

✤ Let words flow about the Goddess and her relationship with the world, nature and the cosmos.

✤ Do not attempt to hold or recall them, but allow them to ebb, form again and disperse, like waves or ripples on a pond.

✤ You may experience colours, lights and fragrances unconnected with the stimuli: sounds of wild animals or the wind through the trees, a sensation of warmth or coolness.

✤ When you are aware of the sounds of the world beginning to return and the light fading, gradually move away from the goddess form, letting the image fade.

✤ Reconnect with your breathing and allow gentle pink or purple light to radiate within you, leaving you calm and in a deep pool of inner silence. If you have closed your eyes, open them slowly, blinking and stretching slowly, like a cat uncurling after sleep.

CHAPTER 5

Candles, Colours and the Zodiac

I said earlier in the book that you would require tools for your magick. That is not quite true: in fact, you could practise magick with nothing but a candle. A candle is a self-contained magical system, for although it represents the Fire element, it also containing the other three basic elements of magick: Earth is represented by the unburned wax of the candle, Air is the smoke, Fire the flame and Water the melted wax. Thus is created *Akasha*, or Spirit.

For most spells, however, you should have one or two altar candles in white, cream or natural beeswax. A single central candle can be good for times of quiet meditation, but for more focused rituals you may prefer to light one candle to represent the Goddess on the right and another for the god polarity, on the left of the altar.

Any tools (see page 183) and elemental substances (see page 191) that you wish to use, such as salt – which represents Earth in the North – can be set at the four main compass points around them and any symbols set between and in front of them.

These will be the first candles lit in any ritual, either before or immediately after casting a circle. I prefer to light them first, to mark a beginning and an empowerment to the magick and to avoid casting an empty circle, but there are no hard and fast rules.

There is debate over whether you should blow or pinch out candles that you do not wish to burn completely away. The act of blowing out a candle is itself a magical release of power, for, rather than holding the light in a snuffer, you can send it towards all who need it. This is an excellent way of releasing and directing power at the end of a rite.

If you buy candles with two or three wicks, a new one can be lit each day in a three-day ritual. Larger candles can have up to seven wicks and if you need a lot of power, you can light all the wicks during a single ritual. Candles vary considerably in their burning times – the better-quality ones may state the number of hours, but with practice if you always use the same type of candles, you will be able to assess how long they will last. Then you can choose one to match the occasion – either one that will have burned through by the end of an evening in a dusk ritual or one that will last for up to 12 hours for an all-night vigil candle, for example on one of the solstices.

Practitioners of strict ceremonial magick say that you should never use a candle that has been lit for another ritual or purpose and should not use these afterwards for household illumination. However, since candles are so expensive and since you will only be performing positive magick, there is no reason why ritual candles should not be adapted for everyday use. Candles from harmony and healing spells may be used in quiet areas of the home, and candles for energy and success in work or study areas. On the other hand, candles for banishing magick should be left to burn down and any remaining wax buried, or the unused candle be disposed of in an environmentally friendly manner. You can, if you wish, place your banishing candle on a metal tray etched with a symbol of what you wish to remove from your life and bury that.

Both for ritual magick and for your informal candle spells and meditations, you will need a supply of candles in a variety of colours. I will list here astrological significances, the magical colour meanings and the elemental correspondences, so that even if you are new to magick you can begin work at once. If you are an experienced practitioner, some of the ideas may suggest new directions for your personal and coven work.

The elemental candle colours

Each of the four elements – Air, Fire, Water and Earth – is represented by a single candle colour – yellow, red, blue and green. A coloured candle representing each of the elements can be placed at the four main compass points around the circle to mark the quarters – East, South, West and North. You can place the elemental candles either on the edge of the circle in sturdy floor-standing holders, or on small tables or plinths at the compass points. Though each element is represented by a single candle, you can use a second to increase a particular element in its own quadrant of the circle or use the elemental colour in all four quadrants. So, for example, if you were carrying out a Fire spell, you could use four red (or gold or orange) candles and begin the ritual facing South.

Some practitioners invoke Fire to conquer floods and Water to conquer drought but I believe that each element can most effectively counter excesses of itself.

Light elemental candles after the altar candles, after you have cast the circles but before lighting any wish or astrological candle. Begin in the North, with a green candle.

Green

Green is for Earth and the North, midnight and winter. A green candle is placed at what would be the 12 o'clock position on a clock, aligned with magnetic or a symbolic North.

Earth is the element of order, both in nature and institutions such as the law, politics, finance, health and education. It also represents *yin*, the female, nurturing goddess aspect, Mother Earth, the home and family, as well as money and security, and is a good element to invoke when you have matters of property or money that need attention. It is also a focus for all rituals against famine, deforestation and land pollution and devastation through unwise industrialisation or building, and for caring for animals and their natural habitats.

Surround your green Earth candle with grains, berries, fruits, coins or pot pourri. Brown candles may also be used as Earth candles.

Yellow

Yellow is for Air and the East, dawn and spring. A yellow candle is placed at the three o'clock position.

Air represents life itself, logic, the mind, communication, health, new beginnings, travel, learning, *yang* and the male god in the form of Sky deities. It is a good element to invoke if you are seeking change or when communication is proving difficult with either an individual or an organisation, and to clear stagnation of thoughts.

It is also a focus for spells against air pollution, technological devastation and storms, and for the protection of birds, butterflies and insects.

Surround your Air candles with feathers, thistledown, tiny helium balloons, model planes and ceramic or wooden birds.

Red

Red is for Fire and the South, noon and summer. Place your red candle in the six o'clock position.

Fire represents light, the Sun, lightning, fertility, power, joy, ambition, inspiration and achievement and also destruction of what is now no longer needed.

Like Air, Fire represents the yang, male god in the form of the Sun deities. Fire rituals are good when you need power or you have an important issue that needs energy. They are effective against drought, global warming, all pollution caused by burning fuels or chemicals, forest fires and the 'slash and burn' policy in rainforests.

Surround your Fire candle with golden sunflowers or chrysan-themums, tiny mirrors that reflect the light and clear crystal quartz, which is called in the Orient 'the essence of the dragon'.

Blue

Blue is for Water and the West, dusk and autumn. A blue candle is placed in the nine o'clock position.

Water represents love, relationships, sympathy, intuition, reconciliation, harmony, healing and the cycle of birth, death and rebirth, natural cyclical evolutions from one stage to another as opposed to changes made consciously under the auspices of Air. It is also potent for fighting floods, cleansing seas, lakes and rivers of pollution, in campaigns to provide fresh water in arid places, in all initiatives towards world health and the care of whales, dolphins, seals and endangered sea creatures.

Like Earth, Water represents the yin, female goddess in the form of the Moon Goddesses.

Surround your Water candles with silver objects, sea shells and pieces of coral or, for the lunar goddesses, mother of pearl and moonstones that grow brighter as the Moon waxes.

Zodiacal candles

Candles etched with zodiacal signs may be used to represent people born during a particular Sun period. They may then be burnt in rituals for different purposes. For instance, you can burn your own zodiacal candle at a time when you need confidence or to assert your identity. Alternatively, you may burn any astrological candles whose strengths you need at a particular time, perhaps the courage of Aries before a confrontation or travelling to an unfamiliar location. You might also use them in a love ritual such as the one on page 102.

Note also the influence of particular groups of signs of the zodiac. The cardinal signs – Aries, Cancer, Libra and Capricorn – are so-called because when the Sun moved into these signs, it marked the beginning of a new season – spring, summer, autumn and winter. People born under a cardinal sign manifest this as a desire to initiate and to take command of people and situations. The fixed signs – Leo, Taurus, Aquarius and Scorpio – are signs entered by the Sun in the middle of a season. People born under them exhibit stability and a tendency to continue in a predetermined path. The mutable signs – Sagittarius, Gemini, Virgo and Pisces – mark the time when the seasons are about to change. Those born under them are correspondingly versatile and ready to compromise.

Zodiacal colours and associations

♈ **Aries, the Ram:** 21 March to 20 April. Colour: red. A cardinal Fire sign, for all matters of the self and of identity, for rituals of innovation, courage assertiveness and action. Ruled by Mars.

♉ **Taurus, the Bull:** 21 April to 21 May. Colour: pink. A fixed Earth sign, for rituals concerning all kinds of material matters and security, also for patience and caution if the way ahead seems hazardous. Ruled by Venus.

♊ **Gemini, the Heavenly Twins:** 22 May to 21 June. Colour: yellow or pale grey. A mutable Air sign, for spells concerning communication, learning, choices, adaptability and short-distance travel. Ruled by Mercury.

♋ **Cancer, the Crab:** 22 June to 22 July. Colour: silver. A cardinal Water sign, for spells concerning the home and family, especially for protection and for gentle love and friendship. Ruled by the Moon.

♌ **Leo, the Lion:** 23 July to 23 August. Colour: gold. A fixed Fire sign, for rituals for courage and leadership, sensual pleasures and love affairs. Ruled by the Sun.

♍ **Virgo, the Maiden:** 24 August to 22 September. Colour: green or pale blue. A mutable Earth sign, for spells to increase efficiency, for bringing order to a chaotic situation, for self-improvement and for healing. Ruled by Mercury.

♎ **Libra, the Scales:** 23 September to 23 October. Colour: blue or violet. A cardinal Air sign for rituals concerning justice and the law, for balancing options and priorities relationships, harmony and reconciliation. Ruled by Venus.

♏ **Scorpio, the Scorpion:** 24 October to 22 November. Colour: burgundy or red. A fixed Water sign, for increasing second sight, for passion and sex, secrets, inheritance and for claiming what is rightfully yours in any area of life. Ruled by Mars in the ancient system, now by Pluto.

♐ **Sagittarius, the Archer:** 23 November to 21 December. Colour: orange or yellow. A mutable Fire sign, for optimism, fresh perspectives, long-distance travel and house moves, creative ventures and expanding horizons. Ruled by Jupiter.

♑ **Capricorn, the Goat:** 22 December to 20 January. Colour: brown or black. A cardinal Earth sign, for ambitions, perseverance, matters concerning officialdom, loyalty and for the acquisition of money. Ruled by Saturn.

♒ **Aquarius, the Water Carrier:** 21 January to 18 February. Colour: indigo or dark blue. A fixed Air sign, for independence, friendship, creativity and for detachment from emotional blackmail. Ruled by Saturn in the ancient system, now by Uranus.

♓ **Pisces, the Fish:** 19 February to 20 March. Colour: white or mauve. A mutable Water sign, for spells to develop spiritual awareness and intuition, and for divination, especially involving water and the fulfilment of hidden dreams. Ruled by Jupiter in the ancient system, now by Neptune.

In magick, it tends to be the old rulerships that are used in spells (see Planets and Angels, pages 226 and 236).

Colour correspondences

Colour is of great significance, both in healing and magick, and colour symbolism is used frequently with candles, and also with crystals, flowers, foods and coloured water, as a way of focusing on and activating the different qualities inherent in the colours.

White

In magic, white represents light, the life force and clear vision and so is helpful where a new beginning or a sudden burst of energy and enthusiasm is needed. White is a good colour for work involving rites of passage, especially for birth, marriage and welcoming new family members by marriage or adoption.

Use white also for protective magick, for replacing darkness with light, in meditation, for Goddess-focused rituals, for increasing spiritual awareness and contact with spirit guides, angels and the higher self.

White contains both solar and lunar energies and is often used for altar candles. You can substitute white for any other colour.

White candles can be used on any day of the week, though they are associated with Monday in the Goddess aspect and Sunday and the Sun for life force magick.

Red

Red, the colour of Mars, the planet and god of war, represents action, power, determination, physical energy and health, courage and determination, sexual passion and potency, survival and change, for careers where danger is involved and the armed forces. It is used as a focus for rituals calling on the power of the gods and for stimulating righteous anger against injustice and inertia.

Because it is a very powerful candle colour, red should be lit for worthy aims only and when you are in a positive frame of mind.

Red candles are most effective when used on a Tuesday.

Orange

Orange is the colour of the Sun, of fertility – both physical and mental – and of creativity with words. Growth, self-esteem, confidence and abundance of all kinds are related to orange, as are independence and asserting your identity if it is under threat or being eroded by the demands or unfair criticism of others. Orange also relates to careers involving people and the arts.

Above all, orange is the colour of joy and also the successful integration of all aspects of the personality into a harmonious whole.

Orange candles are best used on a Sunday.

Yellow

Yellow is the colour associated with Mercury, the winged messenger of the Roman gods. Through his skill and dexterity, he came to rule over commerce and medicine and also became patron of tricksters and thieves.

Yellow candles therefore encourage clear communication and activity of all kinds, improving memory, concentration and learning, and are good for overcoming mental stagnation and blocks in ideas or assimilation of facts.

Use them in rituals when you wish to gain another person's confidence and approval or to win someone round in business or intellectual matters; to sharpen logic; for succeeding in examinations and tests; also for good luck, for short journeys or to initiate a house move within the same area. Yellow is also a healing colour, especially for conditions needing surgery or concerning the mind.

Yellow is good for careers in business, medicine, technology, communication or the media and also for job changes.

Yellow candles are best used on a Wednesday.

Green

Green is the colour of Venus, goddess of love, and so is good for all love and relationship matters, especially partnerships and romance; it is also potent for rites involving the natural world, herbs, gardening and tree magick, for healing the planet and especially the forests and the land.

Green is for peace and harmony, especially within the self. When green candles are used in rituals for wealth, they tend to encourage a gradual increase in profits or resources. As the faerie colour, green is also potent for spells for good luck and increasing magical abilities.

Green candles are best used on Friday.

Turquoise

Turquoise is the colour of Hathor, Egyptian goddess of wisdom, music and dance, whose magical mirror reflected back the true person of all who looked in it (scary stuff if you were just checking your hair).

Turquoise rituals are for integration of heart and mind, feelings and thoughts and the synthesis of wisdom and experience. Turquoise is used for successfully combining different aspects of life or two different career strands; for compassion and altruism; for increasing healing abilities; for maintaining impartiality when making difficult decisions and judgements; and for seeing other dimensions. It is the colour of artists, sculptors, dancers, writers and poets, and can bring inspiration and originality increasing artistic ability.

Turquoise candles can be used effectively on Thursday or Friday.

Blue

Blue is the colour of the Father God and other Sky deities in their external roles as wise judges and rulers and so can be used for this aspect of the god and as a protective colour.

In magick, blue can expand the boundaries of possibility and bring success, confidence and power mingled with altruism, nobility and idealism. Blue is also used for prosperity rituals where this involves advancement or for maximising opportunities, for promotion and expansion of business.

Blue is the colour of long-distance travel and house moves, legal matters and dealing with officialdom. It is also for careers involving justice and leadership. Above all, blue brings calm and the ability to solve problems in the midst of crisis.

Blue candles are best used on Thursday.

Purple

Purple is the colour of Jupiter in his role of wise teacher and keeper of hidden knowledge, and of Osiris, the Ancient Egyptian Father God and Lord of the Underworld, who died each year and was resurrected by his wife Isis. It represents unconscious wisdom and is used for all things of a psychic and spiritual nature and for divination. Purple provides a link with higher dimensions and can bring happiness for all who yearn for something beyond the material plane.

Purple candles aid meditation, work with past lives, scrying with candles and mirrors, and astral travel. They are good for psychic protection and preventing nightmares. Purple can also be used for all rituals where the facts are not clear, for clearing secrecy, for healing the spirit and for banishing what lies in the past, especially failure, and for remembering departed loved ones. Below, I have given sub-divisions for different shades of purple, but in practice they are interchangeable.

Indigo
Indigo is for spiritual healing, for psychic awareness and knowledge of past lives and worlds; it is the colour of the seer.

Lavender
Lavender is for dreams and connections with others, on a telepathic level, for awareness of Devas and other higher nature spirits and for herb wisdom.

Violet
Violet is for clairvoyance, mediumship, spirituality and contact with the evolved self, angelic guides, mysticism and peak experiences.

Purple candles are best used on Thursday.

Pink

Pink is the colour of Venus in her gentler aspects, for family relationships, affection, friendship matters, children and for the growth of new love and trust, especially after betrayal or a setback. Pink rituals are excellent for restoring self-esteem and healing wounded emotions, for letting go of past hurts involving family or childhood, for quiet sleep and for the mending of quarrels.

Pink candles are best burned on Friday.

Magenta

Magenta represents the path of service to others, especially for older women and men in the role of wise counsellor. It can help all in the caring professions and will help anyone transform experiences, both positive and negative, into wisdom that can be offered to guide others.

Magenta candles are best used on Friday.

Brown

Brown is a colour of Saturn, the Roman form of Cronus, god of time. Deposed by his son Jupiter, he was sent to Italy where he taught the farmers, agriculture and engineering and there established a golden age of peace and plenty.

Brown is good for protection, for magick concerning animals and especially household pets, for locating lost objects, learning new skills, for the home, property, practical matters, security and having enough resources for one's needs. It is also the colour of all who work with their hands.

Brown is also the colour of Mother Earth and the Earth spirits and so is good for environmental matters and conservation, especially as an impetus for practical conservation projects. Brown is good for grounding rituals.

Brown candles are best used on Saturday.

Grey

Grey is ruled by Saturn and by Mercury, some say, when he becomes invisible in the sky.

Grey is used primarily for neutralising or erasing negative energies or feelings. It is the shade of compromise and adaptability, of lowering one's profile in times of danger, and offers protection against both physical and psychic attack. It is a colour for keeping secrets and for smoothing down potential conflict and keeping one's counsel when to do otherwise would be unwise.

Grey candles are best used on Wednesday when Mercury cannot be seen and on Saturday.

Black

Another colour of Saturn and also the kings of the Underworld – the Roman Pluto, the bestower of the hidden wealth that lay within the Earth, and the Greek Hades, who abducted Persephone (Proserpine), thus causing winter.

Black is the colour not only of death, but also of regeneration. This belief goes back to Ancient Egypt when the annual flooding of the Nile carried with it black silt, which brought new life to the land each year.

In magick, black is the colour of endings that carry within them seeds of new beginnings. It can be used for banishing negativity, for leaving behind old sorrows and redundant relationships; for acknowledging grief, for rituals of partings, for breaking hexes and for psychic protection. Some people do not like using black candles because of their associations with black magick. If you feel that these associations are too strong for you, substitute dark blue, dark purple or brown candles in rituals.

In a positive sense, black, like brown, is a colour of acceptance, whether of a restriction or of the frailties of self and others, and so it is a candle colour of forgiveness.

Black candles are best used on Saturday.

Silver

Silver is the colour of the Moon and all lunar goddesses such as Diana, the Roman counterpart of Artemis, who, because of her strong association with the Moon in all its phases, was a goddess of fertility as well as love.

It is also used on some altars to represent the Goddess, with a gold candle for the Horned God. Silver is potent in all forms of divination, but especially for candle divination, for awakening clairvoyant powers, telepathic and psychometric abilities, astral projection, for rituals to invoke anima (female) power, for intuition and mysticism. It represents dreams, visions and a desire for fulfilment beyond the material world.

In times of stress and sorrow, silver candles can remove negativity, promote inner stability and bring to the fore your hidden potential. Silver candles are excellent for scrying, especially by the full moon, and for all magick involving the female life and for female fertility.

Silver candles are best used on a Monday.

Gold

Gold is the colour of the Sun and is associated with the solar deities, for example, the Egyptian Ra. In Ancient Greece, Helios, the Sun God, was worshipped each dawn as he emerged in the East and drove his chariot of winged horses around the Sky before plunging into the ocean in the West at sunset.

Gold is potent for worldly achievement, wealth and recognition, for long life, ambitious schemes and money-making rituals that require an instant or substantial return. The colour of male potency and fertility, it represents animus (male) power, energy and change and all rituals with noble or altruistic purpose.

Gold is best used on a Sunday.

Using colour in rituals

You can also use coloured candles as a focus for wishes in a particular area of experience represented by the colour. So you might write a wish for a better memory on yellow paper and burn it in a yellow candle, the colour of Mercury. You could then collect the ash in a heatproof ceramic pot or metal bowl beneath the candle and scatter it to the four winds. For banishing an injustice, you might write about the event on dark blue paper, burn it in the blue candle of Jupiter and bury the ashes.

Around the home, different coloured candles can be burned for different purposes. Scented candles can also amplify the colour energies. See pages 128 and 139 for the meanings of different perfumes.

A black and white candle ritual

This is a ritual for a new beginning after sorrow or loss. You can carry out this ritual for yourself or someone you know who is grieving or unhappy after a betrayal. It is especially healing if you are feeling angry over unjust or cruel treatment, because it can stop any guilt, blame or pain turning inwards and slowing the healing process. You may need to repeat the experience many times. This is an essentially private ritual, but if you are doing it on behalf of someone else, then you might like to invite them to share the experience.

The best time to use this magick is towards the end of the waning moon cycle, late in the evening before the Moon has risen.

✵ Take a small black candle and a large white one and place them side by side in your cauldron, on a metal tray or in a sand-filled, heatproof bowl.

✵ On the black candle, etch a symbol or word to represent your sorrow or anger about a third of the way down the candle. As you do so, send all the negative feelings into the wax.

✵ Light the candle and say:

> *Burn, burn, sorrow turn, melt away, do not stay.*
> *Go in peace, trouble cease.*

✤ Burn pieces of black wool, cut from a large ball with a knife, not scissors, naming each aspect of your grief and watching it burn away, piece by piece.

✤ When you have finished naming the sorrows, sit quietly in the candlelight, seeing the negativity flowing away in the stream of black wax. Make positive plans for the future and write a list of daily actions or short breaks from work that will make you happy. Even if these are of necessity very small, the cumulative effects of a number of minor pleasures can change the balance of your life for the better once a moon cycle has passed.

✤ Once the symbol has melted away, use a taper to carry the flame from the black candle to the white one. This is important, for new beginnings do not come out of nothing, but from the transformation of endings into positive energies.

✤ Once the white candle is alight, blow out the black candle and dispose of it in an environmentally friendly way.

✤ Sit for a few moments, looking into the flame of your white candle, letting thoughts and images appear within either the flame or your mind's vision.

✤ Carry the candle carefully into the bathroom and add to your bath water a few drops of essential oil of rose or lavender for self-love and let the light make pools in the water. Lie in the bath until you feel rested.

✤ When you feel completely relaxed, get out of the bath and swirl the water as it rushes down the plug hole, saying:

Flow far, flow free, flow in peace and harmony.

✤ Spend the rest of the evening in quiet but pleasurable activity, until your white candle is burned down.

✤ Finally, etch in the wax a new symbol of hope and keep it in your special place until it crumbles, by which time it will hopefully no longer be needed.

If the problem is really deep-seated, you can repeat the ritual monthly, each time using a smaller black candle and a larger white one until there are no black energies left.

A candle ritual for love

❀ Scratch the zodiacal glyphs for yourself and a lover on candles of the appropriate colour (see page 94), then light the candles.

❀ Move them closer to each other over a period of three days while speaking words of love and desire to increase the love energies.

❀ For the first two days, blow out the candles, sending the light to wherever your lover is. On the third day, leave the candles to burn down, allowing the wax from the two candles to merge.

❀ In the melded wax, cut the shape of a heart and on this scratch your entwined zodiacal glyphs. Wrap the symbol in white silk and leave it on a window ledge from the waxing to the full moon.

A candle ritual to heal the polluted seas and other bodies of water

This is a ritual to be carried out after dusk. It also has the effect of clearing old hurts and regrets that can hold us back from experiencing joy. A wonderful selection of garden torches and candles are now available, that can be placed in the ground for working out of doors. As you are taking away pollution, work at the time of the waning moon. Blue is the elemental colour of water.

❀ Place four blue candles at the four main compass points in a room or any outdoor area. The four blue compass candles can act as sentinels of light, protecting the four quarters of the circle.

❀ In the centre, place a cauldron or pot. (A three-legged iron pot or any ceramic pot will do. These can often be found in antique shops, at car boot sales or garden centres, as well as in New Age shops. It need not be very large.)

❀ Fill the cauldron with water and float blue candles on the surface.

❀ Light a large blue candle to the West of the cauldron; light the candles in the cauldron from this candle, using a taper.

❀ Surround the cauldron with symbols of the sea, shells and white stones. Prepare a bowl of moonstones, small blue lace agate stones or blue glass nuggets to cast in the water.

❀ Set a tall jar holding wax tapers at each compass point.

If you are working alone, you may need to keep the size of the circle and cauldron quite small, but you can use as much space as you wish. If you are working in a group, four people can light the candles in the four quarters and the scale of the whole ritual can be much larger.

The group can sit or stand in a circle around the cauldron, just inside the four direction candles; traditionally, a magical area extends to a circle about nine feet (three metres) in diameter. However, this can be larger or smaller, according to the size of the group. Circles are usually measured in an odd, rather than even, number of feet, but unless you are casting the most ceremonial of circles, you can estimate the space you will need to work or dance and cast your circle accordingly. (Deities in the cosmos with measuring tapes are remarkably rare.)

✤ Using a taper lit from the candle you placed to the West of the cauldron, light the candle in the West of the circle. If working in a group, this should be done by the person standing by the West candle. As you light the candle of the West say:

I call upon the guardians of the mighty oceans, the inland seas, the straits and the channels between land to protect my/our undertakings and to create this circle of light.
May the circle be unbroken to keep all within from harm.

✤ Re-light the taper if necessary from the West candle. Carry the taper of light to the candle in the North, creating an arc of light. Light the candle in the North. (If working in a group, the taper is given to the person sitting nearest the North candle, who comes forward as the first person returns to sit in the circle.) As the candle in the North is lit, say:

I call upon the guardians of the rushing rivers,
the watercourses and the canals to protect my/our
undertakings and to create this circle of light.
May the circle be unbroken to keep all within from harm.

✤ Re-light the taper if necessary and carry it in an unbroken arc to the East (pass it to the next person, if working in a group) and light the East candle, saying:

I call upon the guardians of the lakes, the still pools,
ponds and marshes to protect my/our undertakings
and to create this circle of light.
May the circle be unbroken to keep all within from harm.

✤ Re-light the taper once again and in the same way make an arc of light to the South, and light the final candle, saying:

I call upon the guardians of the water that flows through or near our homes, the sacred wells and streams, the ditches and the watercourses to protect my/our undertakings and to create this circle of light.
May the circle be unbroken that I now make complete.

❀ Carry the final taper to complete the circle in the West and join it to the burning West candle, saying:

Fire to fire, water to water, so does power increase.

❀ Take a crystal from the dish and cast it into the cauldron, saying:

So ripples the power to cleanse, to heal and to restore life
to the waters of the planet, from whence it has departed.

❀ Say a few words of healing, perhaps naming special waters you know and care about, and areas where there is no clean drinking water. If working in a group, each person can take it in turns to cast a crystal and add a few words of their own.

❀ Blow out the four elemental candles in the reverse order in which they were lit, saying:

May the circle be uncast but remain unbroken.

The floating blue candle and the one next to the cauldron can be left to burn down.

Afterwards, have a simple meal and drink. If you are working in a group, this may be a good time to plan a campaign for furthering your efforts for clean waters in the daily world.

CHAPTER 6

Herbs in Magick

There is a long tradition of using herbs for healing, but they have many other uses. As well as healing rituals, you can place dishes of charged herbs near a bedside in a sickroom or on your healing altar next to a symbol, photograph or the name of the person to be healed. However, they are also excellent for emotional support and spiritual empowerment. For example, if you get stressed on a regular car journey through heavy traffic or on motorways, you may well benefit from a healing or protective herbal sachet in the glove compartment of your car. In fact, herbs may be used to add their strength to almost any kind of ritual and spell.

As they have such a wide variety of uses in magick, you will probably need quite a large supply. Fortunately, herbs are, for the most part, very easy to grow – and very ornamental. If you have a garden you can set aside a small area specifically for cultivating herbs. Alternatively, you can create an indoor garden of herbs grown in pots, so that you have a ready supply of growing energy. Once picked, all your herbs can be used either fresh, for example on your altar, or dried, in healing sachets and poppets.

Each herb has its own natural properties and strengths and they also have the benefit of offering dual purposes. If, for example, you use allspice for a person with digestive or throat troubles, as a bonus both you and the person you heal may experience a gradual upturn in fortune, one of its magical meanings. Though most of the traditional uses of herbs apply to physical and emotional ills and so are most commonly applied to people – and animals, of course – you can also use them for spells concerning places; for example, herbs for soothing wounds, such as lavender, are equally potent in rituals for healing the Earth or reversing the effects of pollution.

Empowering herbs

In addition to their natural properties, you can further empower the herbs, defining their purpose, and adding to the strength they display spontaneously. Empowering herbs can be done in one of two ways. The first method is to use an empowerment ritual, such as the one described on page 109; this is good for herbs to be used in poppets and healing herbal sachets (see below). Alternatively, you can use the method described on page 172 for charging colour-infused water. This is particularly effective for adding extra healing power to a pot of herbs to be placed on your healing altar, as a focus for the need of a particular person.

Herbal poppets and sachets

Traditionally, empowered herbs were used to fill either sachets or featureless dolls called poppets. They were made for love, protection, prosperity, fertility, healing and success and could contain either a single herb or a mixture, depending on the purpose.

Poppets, which are used mainly in love or healing or occasionally in protective magick, are generally kept in a safe place, such as a drawer, rather than carried around. So, for a love spell, two poppets would be tied together and placed in a drawer in a bedroom or left out on the window ledge in the moonlight, especially around the time of the full moon. For fertility, a miniature poppet might be placed in a tiny woven cradle on the window ledge from the new to the full moon. It would then be wrapped in silk until the end of the moon cycle and kept in an enclosed space, for example, a large painted egg made of pottery or wood. The would-be father would make the cradle and the mother would sew and fill the doll.

Some practitioners attach hair from the person to be healed or the object of the love spell to the poppet, but I consider that this is an intrusion of privacy. Instead, I would suggest that if you wish to add extra power, you make your featureless dolls in an appropriate colour.

Herbal sachets are particularly versatile; small ones can be carried around in a bag, pocket or pinned to undergarments, and large ones can be hung over a bed or near the door or in a drawer at work. Traditionally, sachets of empowered herbs were tied with three, six or nine knots of ribbon or twine, these being magical numbers. If you do this, choose ribbon of a colour appropriate to the need – or more than one colour if you wish to add a secondary colour meaning. The number of knots depends on the intensity of the need as knots are a powerful way of concentrating energies. You can, of course, buy ready-made drawstring purses in different colours, which make instant excellent herb pouches, but making herbal sachets is very straightforward (see page 108).

Rather than giving you set formulae for herb poppets and sachets, I have listed a wide range of herbs so that you can mix and match them to your own special needs. I have also given the planetary associations, so that you can, for example, make a Venus sachet by using all her herbs, excellent for healing a broken heart, encouraging the growth of trust, increasing loving energies around you and at the same time strengthening the heart, chest and lungs. Practitioners tend to mingle two or three different herbs to increase the strength of the sachet and you can add a few drops of essential oil for extra fragrance and power (see page 128).

The key is to experiment and be inventive. Keep a note in your healing journal or Book of Shadows of combinations that are especially effective, together with the rough proportions you used. For example, if you were creating a sachet for someone who had suffered a loss in love or a bereavement, you would make a love sachet that emphasised gentleness, using two parts chamomile flowers to one part rosemary. The chamomile is for gentle love, affection and tolerance, and the rosemary would encourage fond and happy memories. Note that some books give other planetary associations, as these do vary under different systems.

The associations for healing and magick are the same whether you use incense, essential oil or the herbal form of a substance. These are just different ways of releasing the energies. Incense, for example, is the best choice if you want an instant response; oil gives a slower but more enduring fragrance; and if your healing spell needs to take effect over days or weeks, then herbs in a sachet would be best. The sachet would act as amulet of protection, but because it was empowered it would also be a talisman, attracting health, abundance or love, according to its composition.

The divisions between healing work and other magical purposes are very slight since every positive ritual automatically releases healing energies. For this reason, I have listed the emotional and psychic as well as the physical healing properties of each herb.

Making coloured sachets for rituals

Making sachets is very simple. If you are good at sewing, fold a rectangle of cloth and stitch the sides together, using a running stitch. Alternatively, just place the herbs in the centre of a square piece of cloth, gather the corners together and tie with three, six or nine knots. The colour of the cloth should be appropriate to the healing need. For a sachet to carry with you, your square of fabric should be about 10 cm by 25 cm (4 in by 10 in). Make it larger if you want to hang it at home or keep it in a drawer. Use a natural fabric, such as felt, wool or cotton. Experiment with different sizes – you can make really tiny sachets to hide in a corner of your bag or in your undergarments or in the lining of a coat, and the size of the sachet has nothing to do with the potency. Even a teaspoon of mixed herbs can be endowed with positive intent to protect, heal and give hope.

Fill your sachet with herbs that have been empowered (see page 109). For extra power, add a small crystal of the same colour as the cloth. If you do not add essential oil in the empowerment, you may wish to add a drop or two of an appropriate fragrance before tying the sachet. You may want to include a herb of protection in sachets made for other purposes, although most herbs do have a protective property along with their main magical use.

Carry sachets until they lose their fragrance. If the sachet represents a long-term objective, replace the herbs regularly. Open the sachet, scatter some of the old herbs to the four winds, burn a few, bury some and dissolve the rest in water.

A sachet for a pet can be hung above its bed. If you are healing absent people, animals or places, then you can wrap the herb sachet with a picture or symbol in white silk and keep it in a high place or put it in a small wooden box on your healing table. Replace the herbs regularly, empowering new ones as before.

You can make herbal sleep pillows containing lavender, hops and aniseed and if you charge the herbs you can drive away bad dreams.

Making poppets

Poppets are a little more complicated to make. Take a piece of white cloth, preferably silk or cotton, and draw the outlines of two doll figures as shown opposite. They should be about 15 cm (6 in) high – any smaller and they become difficult to fill with herbs.

Cut out the two shapes and sew them together using thread of a colour appropriate to the purpose of the spell. Leave a gap at the top of the head so that you can fill the poppet. If the poppet is being used in a group ritual, you may wish to share the sewing, with each member adding a few stitches before passing it on.

Fill the poppet with the herbs, adding a few drops of an essential oil if you wish, and complete the last few stitches to close the gap.

Make a health-giving sachet or doll, empowered with love and good wishes, as a personalised present for a bride or new baby.

A ritual for empowering herbs for healing

All healing herbs must first be empowered. You can use ready-dried and powdered herbs or chop your own and grind them in a mortar and pestle. This method is particularly suitable for herbs to be placed in a healing sachet.

❊ Place your chosen herbs in a small ceramic or glass bowl and run them through your fingers into a ceramic or wooden bowl, repeating an appropriate imprecation, for example,

'Fennel, fennel, give my infant peaceful sleep ',

until you can feel the power rising. (Fennel is excellent magically and medicinally for curing babies' colic and a sachet of fennel and chamomile hung above the cradle is a great soother.)

❊ Add a chant for each herb in the sachet as you put it in the bowl. The chant will become longer until you are naming all the ingredients:

'Fennel, fennel, give my infant quiet sleep,
chamomile, chamomile, bring her sweet dreams…'.

✵ If you wish, add at this stage any essential oil you are using, naming it as part of the cumulative chant.

✵ Place about a tablespoon of the herb or herbs in your ready-stitched sachet, or in the centre of the cloth to be tied. Use more for a larger sachet, but remember that it is best to under- rather than over-fill. As you add the herbs, repeat your chant about the energies you are invoking in the herbs.

✵ Close the sachet or tie the material in three, six or nine consecutive knots of a natural twine or ribbon, seeing your energy and healing bound in the knots. As you tie your bag, visualise yourself – or the person, animal or place that the sachet is intended to heal – fully restored, as you chant:

Three knots I bind, three knots I wind, love, health and tranquillity.
Three more I tie, to Earth, Sea, Sky, for days and nights of harmony,
Three knots to heal, these herbs I seal. In power and joy, so let it be.

(Adapt the chant to the number of knots you are using.)

Herbs for emotional and spiritual empowerment and healing

Agrimony
Agrimony is good for the digestive system, cuts, bruises and throat problems.

It is also effective for psychic protection, to return negative energies to the sender and for peaceful sleep. Use in protective sachets and as part of a sleep pillow for times when you are totally exhausted but cannot rest.

Ruled by Jupiter.

Allspice
Allspice is a herb of healing for all aspects of life, but it is particularly used for the digestive organs, rheumatism and neuralgia.

It is frequently burned as incense to promote good luck and to attract money.

Ruled by Mars.

Aloe vera
Aloe vera soothes wounds and burns, and is effective in treating lack of appetite, bowel and menstrual problems.

As a protective plant, it is popular in the house, since traditionally it brings luck and prosperity.

Ruled by the Moon.

Angelica

Angelica is so-named since it is said to have been revealed by an archangel to relieve plague during the Middle Ages. It is a natural energiser and is good for respiratory and liver problems and for improving circulation.

It is protective, especially for children, when worn as an amulet, and can be grown in the garden to protect both garden and home. It is also believed to give long life and protection against illness.

Ruled by the Sun.

Anise (aniseed)

Anise calms the nervous system and relieves coughs and lung problems. It is a very gentle herb, excellent for skin problems.

It protects against all negative influences, especially in the home, including external hostility, bad dreams. A sachet on the bedpost keeps the sleeper young.

Ruled by Jupiter.

Apple

Apple is good for fevers and nausea. It has all-over powers of rejuvenation and fertility and so is especially used for healing babies and children.

It will also heal relationships, restore youthful optimism and the increase of hope. It increases inner beauty and helps self-esteem, especially if a person is worried or being teased about their appearance. It enhances all forms of new growth and so will restore fertility to gardens and areas of land that have been made barren or urbanised.

Ruled by Venus.

Ash

Ash was a sacred tree to the Celts (as late as the nineteenth century, in Killura in Ireland, a descendant of the original sacred ash of Creevna was used as a charm against drowning). It was used to cure rickets, hernias or wounds that would not heal and toothache (a folklore remedy for toothache was to rub your gum with a new nail until it bled, then to hammer the nail into an ash or oak tree which would take away the pain). The leaves and powdered bark are very effective for all healing and for endowing lasting good health.

It is also effective for protection at sea, while sailing or swimming.

Ruled by the Sun.

Aspen

The aspen was known as the shiver-tree, because the leaves shook even when apparently there was no breeze; by sympathetic magick (see page 35) it was believed that 'like cures like' and so the aspen was said to have the power to cure fevers, agues and illnesses involving shivering or extremities of cold. It is also good for eloquence.

As a protective herb, it can be used in anti-theft and burglary sachets hidden in houses or cars.

Ruled by Saturn, in his most positive aspects.

Basil

Basil reduces stress and clears the mind. It can be used for menstruation problems and stomach disorders including ulcers. It also removes toxins, so is good for anti-pollution rituals. Basil also repels harmful insects and encourages peaceful sleep.

It is a herb of love and fidelity and also attracts abundance and prosperity. As a protective herb, it is good for overcoming fear of flying.

Ruled by Mars.

Bay

Bay can be used for all digestive disorders, for stress and psychosomatic illness.

It offers psychic protection and will heal sorrow. It purifies all forms of pollution and negativity, endows strength and endurance and encourages fidelity.

Ruled by the Sun.

Bistort

Bistort is potent in relieving wounds of all kinds, emotional as well as physical, also throat, mouth and tongue problems, especially when mixed with echinacea, myrrh and goldenseal. It aids fertility, so can be carried by women who wish to become pregnant.

It will repels those who come to a home with malice or ill intent. Bistort also increases abundance and prosperity and psychic awareness.

Ruled by Saturn.

Black cohosh

This herb is particularly associated with older women. For this reason, it is good for problems associated with the menopause.

As a protective herb, it brings courage and love, especially in late-flowering relationships, and the power to make positive change.

Ruled by the Moon.

Borage

Borage is good for lung problems, for lowering temperatures, for relieving problems with the adrenal glands and for speeding recovery after any illness. It was used in Roman times, infused in wine, to relieve depression and on its own to help rheumatism and weak hearts and to purify blood.

It is a herb of courage and protection that can be used in sachets, especially out of doors, or in potentially hazardous places.

Ruled by Mars.

Burdock

Burdock relieves chronic skin conditions and rheumatism and restores balance to bodily energies and organs; it supports the liver and kidneys, especially when mixed with dandelion.

Burdock deters negativity when used in protective amulets and offers protection against negativity; it enhances passion and sexuality and heals loss or betrayal in love.

Ruled by the Moon.

Caraway

Caraway relieves menstrual problems and nourishes nursing mothers. It is effective for all digestive disorders, coughs and bruises, and helps to improve memory.

It is protective against all sources of negativity, especially against theft and vandalism (hide a tiny sachet with valuable items). It is also an aphrodisiac that can kindle or rekindle passion.

Ruled by Mercury.

Catnip

Catnip will help influenza, prolonged fevers, viruses and respiratory problems, especially when mixed in sachets or poppets with elder and yarrow. It is very effective for children (and cats, with whom it forges telepathic links).

It makes a potent love sachet when mixed with rose petals. Around or near a home, catnip attracts good fortune and benign forces. It also enhances inner beauty and domestic joy.

Ruled by Venus.

Chamomile

The most gentle and soothing of herbs, chamomile was beloved of Peter Rabbit in Beatrix Potter's tales. It has many uses, including soothing anxiety, relieving insomnia, and calming hyperactivity in children. It is excellent for all digestive problems, especially in the young (no nursery should be without its chamomile, fennel and lavender sachet as a gift for a new infant), and relieves eye problems in adults and children.

Chamomile is used in charms to attract abundance and prosperity; it is good for meditation and for attracting new love, family happiness and the growth of trust after betrayal and loss, and it is protective and deters those who would do harm.

Ruled by the Sun.

Cloves
Cloves are excellent for relieving tooth pains, circulation problems, back and lung problems and nausea in pregnancy.

As part of an amulet or sachet, cloves will prevent gossip, malice and envy against the wearer and help the user to learn new skills. Cloves are a natural aphrodisiac that both attracts love and awakens sexual feelings. For those who have suffered loss, cloves offer comfort.

Ruled by Jupiter.

Coltsfoot
This is perhaps the best herbal remedy for respiratory problems, especially persistent dry coughs, also bronchitis, asthma, and even emphysema. It also soothes the stomach and combats fluid retention.

It is traditionally used in love rituals and sachets, and to induce peace of mind. It also offers protection to all who travel, and to horses.

Ruled by Venus.

Comfrey
Comfrey relieves burns, cuts, coughs and asthma and speeds healing.

It offers protection while travelling and if placed in a suitcase will guard your belongings from loss or theft. It is a natural bringer of luck and money, and so can be added to abundance sachets if a person has suffered financial or material loss.

Ruled by Saturn.

Dandelion
Dandelion helps to clear obstructions and so is good for the liver, spleen, gall bladder and kidneys. It relieves fluid retention and premenstrual tension, detoxifies the system and encourages circulation.

It promotes psychic awareness, carrying thoughts between lovers. It is commonly used in country love divination to answer questions concerning a lover's fidelity and intentions.

Ruled by Jupiter.

Dill

This is a herb for the well-being of infants and nursing mothers, bringing ease and quiet sleep to colicky, fretful babies and assisting lactation.

It is a herb of love and passion and can also be used in love and protection sachets, especially for homes. It will repel intruders and malice from the home so is a sachet to keep near entrances. Add it to nursery sachets.

Ruled by Mercury.

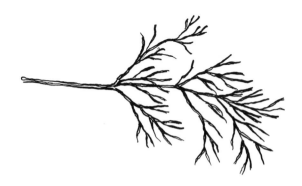

Echinacea (purple cornflower)

Echinacea is a natural antibiotic that also triggers the immune system. It increases the production of white blood cells, and aids the effective functioning of the lymph glands and so is effective for building up resistance in a person who has been ill or is physically vulnerable. It also heals wounds, mouth sores and gum disorders.

Echinacea is a herb of spiritual growth and awareness; it is used where altruism and idealism are to the fore. It also promotes spiritual dreams.

Ruled by Jupiter.

Elder

Elder is beloved of the Romany gypsies as a basis for many different remedies. It is effective as an antiseptic and can be used to treat sprains, wounds, rheumatism, influenza, respiratory complaints, hay fever and sinusitis. It prevents insomnia and brings peaceful sleep.

Elder offers protection from hostility to the user, and to the home from storm damage and other extremes of weather. It brings health, wealth and happiness, and especially marital joy to a new bride or groom.

Ruled by Venus.

Elecampane (elfwort)

Elecampane is effective for all coughs and respiratory complaints, especially in children; it helps asthma and bronchitic asthma, loss of appetite and general failure to thrive.

As its name suggests, it is associated with elves and faeries and is a natural love charm, potent in love sachets, amulets and rituals for attraction. It is protective against all forms of hostility and increases psychic awareness.

Ruled by Venus.

Fennel

From Roman times, this herb has been renowned for its effects on courage, stamina and renewed strength and energy. It is good for improving a sluggish metabolic rate, for reducing all swelling, especially fluid retention, for premenstrual tension, for aiding breastfeeding and for easing an infant's colic and restlessness. It also helps sore eyes and coughs and improves mental alertness.

Fennel brings protection from unwanted visitors and all forms of external hostility.

Ruled by Mercury.

Ginger

Much prized in the East, ginger is still used in China to aid potency and ensure long life. It warms the body, removing pain, especially rheumatism, and it strengthens and heals the respiratory system, as well as boosting the immune system. It is good for throat complaints, and for all sickness and nausea, especially in pregnancy and while travelling, so should be added to travel sachets.

Ginger is also often carried powdered in a tiny sachet in a pocket or purse to attract money, success and also love. It acts as a physical and emotional energiser.

Ruled by Mars.

Holy thistle

Holy thistle is effective for treating all liver, gall-bladder and spleen problems, even helping livers damaged by alcohol or hepatitis. It counters appetite loss and relieves menopausal symptoms.

It is, however, mainly a protective herb, used to keep away all negativity. It is an aid to any spiritual work or contact with the higher self and angels or spirit guides. It encourages altruism.

Ruled by Mars.

Hops

A gentle, safe but powerful sedative, hops are also used in treating insomnia and nervous tension, and internal spasms triggered by stress. Hops will calm the entire nervous system and so can be used to treat coughs, bladder and liver problems aggravated by stress, bowel disorders with an anxiety component, for example irritable bowel syndrome, and skin problems with an emotional cause.

As a protective herb, hops will drive away dark thoughts, doubts and fears.

Ruled by the Sun.

Hyssop

Derived from the Hebrew *esob*, hyssop is mentioned many times in the Bible for its ability to cleanse the body of illness. It relieves coughs, bronchitis, painful throats and viruses, tension and stress-related conditions, burns, and ear pains and problems, especially in children.

It is primarily a herb of purification and will help to banish sad thoughts, despair and doubts, and leave a positive approach. Hyssop removes negativity from the home and from objects that have unwelcoming or sorrowful vibrations.

Ruled by Jupiter.

Juniper

Juniper is a natural antiseptic. It relieves digestive and gastrointestinal inflammations, arthritis and rheumatism, joint and muscle pain and inflammation. It also increases male potency.

Juniper naturally purifies the home from past negative influences and future misfortune – use it especially at New Year. It also acts as an amulet against accidents, theft and illness.

Ruled by the Sun.

Knotweed

Knotweed is a natural antiseptic that helps to heal infected wounds; it will calm nerves and prevent anxiety developing. It relieves tendon problems and is good for general health and improvement of conditions that cause immobility.

A herb to increase emotional commitment and encourage fidelity, it can be used for ensuring promises are kept and for all rituals involving knots.

Ruled by the Moon.

Lavender

Add lavender to any healing sachet, for it has calming and restorative properties and promises a gradual and gentle improvement in health. It is an anti-depressant, a natural sedative and a pain-reliever, especially for tension-related headaches and muscle or joint pains. It also helps digestion. A pillow filled with dried lavender flowers induces peaceful sleep. In a room, it will encourage gentle, positive interactions and reduce hyperactivity in children.

Lavender is a herb of love; it attracts gentle and kind lovers, especially for women. It is good for wish magick.

Ruled by Mercury.

Marigold

Marigold is a good, all-purpose ingredient for healing sachets, especially for all skin complaints and infections. It is effective in the treatment of bleeding, burns, headaches, eye and gall-bladder problems and stomach ulcers. It protects against internal and external infections.

Marigold increases positivity in the home, makes a lover more affectionate, promotes fidelity and helps in all legal problems.

Ruled by the Sun.

Mullein

Mullein is effective for the relief of any respiratory condition, such as bronchitis, hoarseness, asthma and harsh coughs. It can also be used for acidity, skin inflammation and pains of all kinds. It acts as a sedative and a cure for insomnia, guarding against nightmares.

It brings courage and prevents accidents, so is good in travel or workplace protection; it is also very protective against any negative forces.

Ruled by Saturn.

Myrrh

A powerful antiseptic, with anti-fungal and astringent properties, myrrh is good for all mouth and throat problems and for wounds.

It is one of the oldest protective and purification herbs, associated with all healing of mind and spirit as well as body. Myrrh is a good herb to burn as incense for protection and for healing; it promotes higher states of consciousness and so is good for all spiritual work.

Ruled by the Moon.

Parsley

Parsley can be used for enriching the blood and helping all skin conditions such as eczema and acne. It is also good for anaemia and relieves premenstrual tension, kidney, bladder and urinary tract infections, gout, jaundice, and menstrual and menopausal disorders.

A divinatory herb, parsley is said to encourage fertility, love and passion. It is also protective – a poppet or sachet filled with parsley is a gentle but powerful defence against psychological or psychic attack. Plant it on Good Friday.

Ruled by Mercury.

Peppermint

One of the best remedies for travel sickness and all forms of nausea, peppermint is therefore a good herb for anyone who travels regularly. Add it to car sachets for children (make one in the shape of a bear or favourite toy and hang it over a car seat). It is also excellent for all digestive disorders, especially ulcerative colitis and Crohn's disease. It can be helpful in relieving coughs, head and throat pains. Mix with chamomile for insomnia; in larger quantities, it acts as an energiser.

Peppermint can be used for healing and purifying, at home or in sickrooms, to drive away all negativity and illness.

Ruled by Venus.

Rose

An essential ingredient in healing sachets, rose is potent in fighting infections and viruses of all kinds, relieving physical and emotional exhaustion, skin problems, menstrual disorders and hyperactivity.

Use it in love rituals, to attract love and to give meaningful and prophetic dreams. Rose is also a symbol of courage, especially the blood red rose.

Ruled by Venus.

Rosemary (elf leaf)

Rosemary relieves headaches, depression, liver and gall-bladder problems, sciatica and muscular pain. It aids digestion, improves circulation, helps with hair and scalp disorders, improves memory, focuses thoughts and increases energy levels. Put a small handful, chopped, in a muslin bag and add to a bath – this is a medieval prescription for energy and clarity of thought.

A herb of protection, rosemary can drive away bad dreams. Use in love sachets to attract lovers and bring healing to destructive or confrontational relationships. Rosemary is also a herb of remembrance, especially of love, and can bring about reconciliation.

Ruled by the Sun.

Sage

Sage is a popular culinary herb with many medical applications and healing powers; according to tradition, it prolongs life and health. In medieval times it was said: 'Why should a man who has sage in his garden ever die?'. Sage was called *herba sacra* ('the holy herb') by the Romans and was used by the Ancient Egyptians to cure male infertility and by the Chinese to stimulate both yang and yin energies. It is especially good for strengthening the lungs and it boosts the immune system, helping to build up resistance to illness and to speed recovery in cases of debilitating or chronic conditions. Sage eases mental exhaustion and increases the ability to concentrate, so is ideal in sachets for people under pressure from examinations or at work, especially with rosemary. It lifts depression and soothes anxieties.

Sage increases psychic awareness and allows glimpses of past and future; it attracts good health, money and offers protection for the home and family.

Ruled by Jupiter.

St John's wort (hypericum)

St John's wort relieves depression, anxiety, neuralgia, headaches and irritability during the menopause. It is good for relief from pain, helping with fibrositis, sciatica and rheumatism. It is an anti-inflammatory, and so speeds the healing of burns and wounds.

St John's wort is the golden herb of midsummer and symbol of the longest day, the summer solstice and the full power of the Sun. It offers fertility and powers to attract love, especially if picked on the Eve of St John, 23 June, at midnight. Traditionally, it was worn in battle for courage, and it can also bring decisiveness. Use it for protection, especially if combined with dill and vervain.

Ruled by the Sun.

Tarragon

A mild stimulant, tarragon helps the nervous system to overcome restless exhaustion that can stand in the way of relaxation, while also soothing anxieties so sleep comes easily. It is also good for stimulating the kidneys and is a traditional remedy for toothache and digestive problems.

Once associated with dragons and serpent goddesses and the ability to cure snake-bites, tarragon has now become associated with rituals and decisions involving shedding what is redundant, as a snake sheds its skin. It is good for regeneration and helps the user to focus on new targets.

Ruled by Mercury.

Thyme
Thyme brings good health, improves memory and mental abilities and has powerful antiseptic properties.

It is said to aid recall of the past and allow glimpses into the future and to give courage and strength. In a sleep pillow, it keeps away bad dreams and may bring happy, prophetic ones.

Ruled by Venus.

Valerian
Valerian is a relaxant; it reduces tension, anxiety, all stress-related conditions and insomnia, and offers effective pain relief for tension-related conditions including migraines.

A herb of reconciliation, it can be placed in poppets, which are then tied together to bring harmony to a relationship or reunite those parted by anger or circumstance. It was used by the Ancient Greeks to keep away all harm and is still primarily regarded as a herb of protection and peace.

Ruled by Venus.

Vervain
Vervain is a natural strengthener of the nervous system, reducing tension and the effects of stress. It eases depression, especially after illness.

It also offers protection against all negativity; a sachet hung above an infant's bed drives away nightmares, and brings both happiness and intelligence to the very young. A sprig can be exchanged with a friend or lover as a promise of truth at all times.

Ruled by Venus.

Yarrow
Yarrow lowers blood pressure, slows the heartbeat, speeds the healing of wounds and reduces fevers.

A herb of love, yarrow is said to keep a couple together for at least seven years, and so should be given to newly-weds and used in love charms. Married couples keep the herb in a special sachet and replace it just before seven years is over, continuing to do so throughout married life. This can be made into a ceremony of renewal. It also repels hostility and banishes fear.

Ruled by Venus.

Herbal infusions

As well as magical sachets, you can make herbs into infusions. Add one level teaspoon (5 ml) of coarsely chopped dried herbs or two level teaspoons (10 ml) of freshly chopped leaves or flowers to a cup of boiling water; leave it for five minutes and strain. Once the liquid has cooled, you can sprinkle it round rooms, furniture and personal property or add it to a bucket of water for washing floors.

The roots and bark of some plants can be used to make a decoction. Crush and powder two tablespoons (30 ml) of the herb and add to one pint (500 ml) of cold water. Simmer the mixture until the quantity of water is reduced by half and then strain the mixture.

Fresh herbs or flowers can be added to your bath in the following way: place them in a net or a piece of muslin – you could even use an old pair of tights – and hang them under the hot tap while you run a bath. Alternatively, allow the bag of herbs to float in the bath for 10 minutes or add a strained infusion to the water.

Of course, you can always drink herbs as tea or burn herbal incenses or oils. All these are valid ways of getting the medicinal as well as magical properties from herbs, though you should still charge them magically. However you use them, always bear in mind that herbs are very potent so before you begin you should seek the advice of a trained herbalist or homeopath or read carefully a reliable herbal book (see page 299 for a list of those I would recommend). Pay particular attention to any quantities and medical contraindications that are given.

Cautions

It is inadvisable for **anyone** to use any herb in large quantities or over prolonged periods without first taking medical advice to ensure that it is safe. This applies particularly if you are pregnant or breastfeeding, when I would recommend that you avoid the following in any form, including baths, inhalation and teas:

Aloe vera, angelica, anise, autumn crocus, barberry, basil, bay, black cohosh, caraway, cayenne, elder, fennel, feverfew, golden seal, hyssop, juniper, male fern, mandrake, parsley, penny royal, poke rosemary, root, rue, sage, southernwood, tansy, tarragon, thuja, thyme, wintergreen, wormwood, yarrow.

This is not comprehensive list and during pregnancy you should check with a trained herbalist or pharmacist before taking **any** herbal preparation – as you should with any medical preparation at all. **It is advisable to avoid all herbs during the first three months of pregnancy.**

There are many medical conditions that preclude the use of certain herbs. These include asthma, diabetes, high blood pressure, epilepsy and heart disease. Generally, of course, it should be safe to use your herbs in sachets or poppets, but you must avoid inhaling the herbs. Mild herbs, such as rose, lavender and chamomile or hops, are safe options for use in sleep pillows. However, in all cases, you should consult a qualified medical practitioner before using herbs in any form.

A healing ritual for an absent person

This simple healing ritual is for someone who has a virus or other debilitating condition. The virus may be affecting the whole body and not responding to treatment. The ritual incorporates the four main stages of a spell described on page 40 and can work equally well for a solitary practitioner or a group of witches. As the ritual is intended to stimulate the body's immune system, it is best done on the gentle early waxing moon energies (see page 235 for the best hours and day of the week).

Through magick, a concentrated dosage of healing power is offered, based on a particular healing herb charged with the energies of the sender, but without any absorption of the actual substance. So, rather than making a tea or tincture, you use empowered herbs. This is a way of sending herb power to any person or creature without the need to worry about medical exclusions and correct quantities.

Place some echinacea (see page 115) in the centre of your altar in a mortar and pestle. Echinacea, or purple cornflower, is a herb that is taken medicinally to relieve viral conditions. You will also need a ready-cut-out doll shape in white material (see the template on page 109) and a needle and pink thread.

❦ Place on the altar symbols of health: fruit, flowers, seeds and nuts are all full of *prana*, or life force.

❦ Light two white candles, the god candle on the left, then the Goddess candle on other side. If you are working as a group, the person leading the ritual can light the candles.

❦ Call on the person who is being healed, wherever they are, to visualise themselves in a cone of blue light at the time you will be carrying out the ritual.

❦ With feet apart, draw up light through your feet, let it spread through your legs, up your body, your arms and though the crown of your hand (this process is sometimes referred to as raising a light body).

❦ Then cast the circle. Join hands if you are in a group and, beginning with the person in the North of the group, pass the power deosil from hand to hand, chanting:

May the circle be unbroken.

❦ If you are working alone, walk around the outside of a visualised circle of light about five feet in diameter, pointing towards the ground with your power finger (the index finger of the hand you write with) or a wand made of willow, hazel or rowan or ash sharpened at one end. Chant:

*Circle of light, circle of healing, protect me within
and aid this my working.*

❦ Empower the dried herbs by mixing them in a mortar and pestle with a few drops of laurel or eucalyptus essential oil – these are also good for viral infections. As you mix, chant a mantra, such as:

Heal and restore, strength once more.

If you are working as a group, one person should mix the herbs on the altar while the others chant the names of healing deities (see page 77) in ever-rising intensity and pitch, for example:

Brighid, Ganga, Hermes, Thoth, Hygeia, Panacea, Sulis, Iduna!

As you do so, you raise a cone of healing energies over the mortar and pestle, breathing in life from the living fruits and flowers and projecting it as blue healing light that may be mingled with the green of the herbs.

You can adapt the chant if you do not wish to use specific names, for example:

Goddess, Mother, healer, restorer, hear our plea.

✤ Now that you have raised the cone of blue power, it can be directed towards the person to be healed by pointing in the direction of their home, with either your power finger or a wand, and uttering a final cry:

Heal and bless.

Rather than now grounding the remaining power, you can use it to fashion a slower, but equally potent, talisman that will continue the work.

✤ Sit quietly in front of the altar, facing north, and sew a doll-shaped bag, to be filled with herbs (see the template on page 109). If you are working in a group, pass the doll, or poppet, and a needle and thread around the group. Each person can make a few very rough stitches, endowing each with a spoken hope or prayer for the sick person and visualising the stitches filled with light. When only the head is open, the person who made the last stitch should take it to the altar and fill the poppet with the charged herbs, speaking more healing words, and then sew up the head.

✤ Place the poppet between the altar candles where the light can shine on it.

✤ Now uncast the circle widdershins, either from hand to hand or with your power finger or wand, seeing the light returning to the ground and repeating:

May the circle be uncast but remain unbroken.

Any remaining energy can be grounded by sitting on the ground and pressing downwards or standing and returning the power with a stamp of your feet.

✤ Leave the altar candles burning and eat the fruit and seeds and nuts to absorb the magical life force.

✤ Blow out the altar candles (in a group, this should be done by the person leading the ritual) and send the light to the sick person. The person receiving the healing may notice an intensity of blue light when the cone is released.

As soon as possible, give the poppet, wrapped in white silk, to the person to be healed, for them to keep close to their bed.

CHAPTER 7

Oils and Incenses in Magick

Oils and incenses, like herbs, are very versatile. The easiest way of attracting all the good things you want not only for yourself but also for those you love and for those in need, is to burn oils and to release the appropriate fragrances and let them work in their own way. You can choose the appropriate oil for health, happiness, love, success, prosperity, confidence and protection, to name but a few.

Oil magick

You can use oils as part of a ritual. In traditional magick, oils are placed in the West of the altar for the Water element, or the East, if lit, to symbolise the fragrance rising on the Air. But they can equally form the focus of any spell, each oil being charged with its particular purpose before use.

There are many ways you can use oils magically as well as therapeutically: for example, you can burn them in special holders (these are available everywhere from pharmacies, hardware shops and supermarkets); you can sprinkle a few drops on an open fire or on cotton wool; you can pour a little into a saucer and place it above a radiator; you can dispense them in sprays or in any of the variety of condensers and diffusers that are available; or you can dilute them and use them as floor washes.

Cautions

Oils are very potent and should only ever be used in accordance with instructions inside the box from the manufacturer. There are also a number of good books on the market and I have listed a few at the back of this book that will advise on correct dosage.

Generally, oils such as lavender, chamomile, rose, rosewood and geranium are so mild that for an adult you can use up to ten drops quite safely in a bath full of water. However, do not add more than three drops of peppermint, lemon or cedarwood, and no more than four or five drops of other astringent or potent oils such as orange, pine, rosemary, tea tree and thyme to a bathful of water and follow instructions carefully. You can also put a drop or two of the milder oils on a handkerchief or inhale from the bottle, but again follow instructions to the letter.

For children, use no more than four drops of mild oil (lavender, chamomile, rose, rosewood or geranium) in total in a bath; for small children, do not use more than two drops and use only gentler fragrances such as lavender or chamomile (this is excellent for calming children).

Some conditions preclude the use of certain oils; this applies for use in baths, and for inhalations and massage. As with herbs, I recommend that you should always check with your doctor before using any oils.

Epilepsy: Avoid sweet fennel, hyssop, sage, and rosemary.

High blood pressure: Avoid cypress, hyssop, rosemary, sage and thyme.

Pregnancy: It is best to avoid the following oils during any stage of pregnancy.

Angelica, basil, bitter almond, cedarwood, clary sage, clove, fennel, hyssop, juniper, marjoram, myrrh, peppermint, rosemary, sage, tarragon, thyme, wintergreen, yarrow.

Photo-toxic oils

Certain oils, particularly citrus oils, can irritate the skin if they are exposed to the light, and about half of the normal amount of other oils should be used in baths and massage. Avoid direct sunlight for six hours after use. They include:

Angelica, bergamot, ginger, lemon, lime, mandarin and orange.

However, they are ideal for burning and are all energising.

Skin irritants

Some can be an irritant to the skin and so should be used sparingly and well-diluted. They include:

Allspice, basil, cinnamon, clove, fennel, frankincense, lemon, lemongrass and peppermint.

Oils should never be taken internally and except for pure rose and lavender should not be applied undiluted to the skin.

Using oils

To avoid repetition, I have only given a brief reference for those oils whose properties I described in the previous chapter, for the qualities of a substance are the same in any form.

Benzoin: Benzoin reduces tension, stress, and melts away tension, anger, resentment, emotional pain and frustrations. Positively, benzoin increases self-confidence and attracts prosperity, both material and spiritual.

It mixes well with rose, pine and lavender.

Bergamot: Bergamot soothes irritability and lifts depression or apathy, encouraging gentle but honest communication and the manifestation of a person's true potential and inner self.

A citrus oil (see page 127), bergamot mixes well with frankincense and ylang-ylang.

Cedarwood: Cedarwood is a symbol of both spiritual and sexual awakening or reawakening perhaps after a period of loss or stagnation; excellent in meditation, it is an oil of youthfulness and a long and happy life.

It mixes especially well with cypress, juniper and rosemary.

Chamomile: Known as the children's oil and the oil of kindness, chamomile is effective for every childhood problem, including hyperactivity, general restlessness and sleeplessness – it is also good for adults with similar problems.

It mixes well with ylang-ylang, geranium, lavender and lemon.

Citronella: Citronella is an oil of identity and independence, establishing the boundaries of the unique self and repelling those who would dominate or intrude on privacy, whether personally or professionally; it also creates invisible boundaries around the home. Citronella improves mental alertness and dispels exhaustion and inertia. It mixes well with lavender and jasmine.

Clary sage: Clary sage calms and drives away fears and bad dreams in adults and children. It is also an oil of inspiration and positivity and, when problems loom large, replaces doubts with unconsidered options and with an assurance that all will be well.

It mixes well with ylang-ylang, rosemary and lavender.

Cypress: Cypress is an oil of consolation after sorrow or loss, bringing acceptance, healing and the power to move forward. It promotes understanding and compassion towards distress of self and others.

It mixes well with lemon, juniper and geranium.

Eucalyptus: This is an oil of purification of mind, body and soul, driving out negativity and anger, as well as repelling deliberate psychological and psychic attack. Eucalyptus will provide the impetus for action and decisions, especially when people and projects have reached an impasse. The oil also offers clear focus and increased concentration.

It mixes well with cedarwood, clary sage and peppermint.

Fennel: Fennel is the oil of strength, courage and perseverance.

It mixes well with chamomile and eucalyptus.

Frankincense: Frankincense is regarded as the most noble of oils, used in ceremonies and formal celebrations throughout the ages and considered in many cultures to be a gift from the deities, bringing healing and power.

It offers confidence to aim high, attracting abundance of all kinds, money and success, but also granting access to higher dimensions and contact with angels and spirit guides.

It mixes well with cypress, sandalwood and myrrh.

Geranium: Geranium is a harmonising oil, restoring peace and well-being to the home or workplace, encouraging positive, non-confrontational interactions, reconciling quarrels and melting away emotional coldness and indifference in encounters. It relieves tension, depression doubts and despair, replacing them with gentle optimism.

It mixes well with lavender, rose, ylang-ylang, cedarwood and chamomile and indeed most other oils.

Ginger: Ginger is an enhancer of love, passion and money and encourages adventure and innovation.

It mixes well with bergamot, cedarwood and jasmine.

Jasmine: Jasmine is an uplifting oil, boosting both physical and mental potency and increasing love and passion. It deflects potential hostility, transforming it into friendliness and a willingness to compromise.

It mixes with most other oils, especially rose and ylang-ylang.

Juniper: Juniper is a purifying and cleansing oil, protecting against hostility and removing what is redundant.

It mixes well with rosemary, frankincense and cypress.

Lavender: Lavender is a harmoniser and brings love, kindness and reconciliation to any person or place.

It mixes well with almost every oil, but especially geranium, chamomile, marjoram and ylang-ylang.

Lemon: Lemon is the breath of life, bringing energy, clarity, logic and integrity. It is a light-bringer, cutting through secrecy, doubt and dishonesty, and cleansing atmospheres and attitudes.

A citrus oil, it mixes well with chamomile, eucalyptus, lavender and myrrh.

Lemongrass: Lemongrass will clear away negative emotions among family, friends and colleagues, and past resentment and feuds from the past that no longer serve any purpose. It removes also painful memories and helps to leave behind destructive relationships; lemongrass also enhances psychic awareness.

It mixes well with frankincense and geranium.

Lime: Lime brings health and well-being to self and to family and home. It generates enthusiasm and triggers self-healing and regeneration in body and mind. It is protective against psychological and psychic attack and has natural restorative powers.

A citrus oil, it mixes well with eucalyptus and lavender.

Mandarin: Mandarin oil restores confidence self-love and self-esteem, offering protection against the barbs of unfair criticism, spite and gossip. It enhances inner beauty and radiance.

A citrus oil, it mixes well with cedarwood, geranium, and ylang-ylang.

Marjoram: Marjoram is an oil that relieves loneliness and a sense of isolation and alienation, awaking empathy with others. It is an oil of enduring love and fidelity.

It mixes well with lavender and rosemary.

Mimosa: Mimosa is an oil of the night, for secrets and secret love, bringing love and friendship, especially for older people.

It calms anxiety and over-sensitivity to criticism and brings harmony and happiness, melting away opposition and hostility.

It mixes well with bergamot and chamomile.

Myrrh: This is a sacred ceremonial oil, like frankincense, and is burned in healing and purification rituals.

It mixes well with mandarin, pine and patchouli.

Neroli: This is orange-blossom oil, symbol of marriage, committed relationships and fidelity, fertility, sensuality and self-esteem. It prevents moods swings, crises of confidence and panic attacks.

It mixes well with geranium and jasmine.

Orange: Orange is the oil of abundance, joy and fertility, attracting happiness, giving confidence and individuality, and calming anxiety and restlessness in children and adults.

A citrus oil, it mixes well with lavender and ylang-ylang.

Patchouli: Patchouli is the oil of prosperity and is used in money rituals, to bring employment and increase business opportunities. It is also frequently used in ceremonies to heal the planet, as it is a natural restorer of balance.

It mixes well with geranium, myrrh and pine.

Peppermint: Peppermint offers protection against illness, accident, hostility and theft or damage to the home and also attracts money.

It mixes well with eucalyptus.

Pine: Pine is a purifier of all forms of negativity, hostile atmospheres and dishonesty, protecting particularly against emotional blackmail. It is an oil of courage and perseverance under difficulty, of integrity and clear focus.

It mixes well with juniper, lemon and marjoram.

Rose: This is an oil of fidelity, happiness, partnerships and gentle healing, love and especially self-love.

It mixes well with almost every other oil.

Rosemary: Rosemary is an oil for enhanced memory, concentration, justice, career and success.

It mixes well with cedarwood, frankincense and geranium.

Rosewood: Rosewood calms mind, body and soul, creating a setting conducive to peace at home or work, especially if there are difficult negotiations, or potentially hostile visitors or phone calls; it will also clear away existing conflict. Rosewood soothes hyperactive or restless children, and in adults brings acceptance of life as it is and the frailties of others. It is good for energising all forms of natural magick.

Rosewood mixes well with jasmine, neroli and geranium.

Sandalwood: Sandalwood is an oil of passion and sensuality; it also heightens meditative abilities and increases spiritual awareness, offering a path to make contact with the higher self and angelic or spirit guides.

It mixes well with many other oils, especially chamomile, lemon, patchouli and rosemary.

Tea tree: Tea tree is an oil of healing, especially absent healing; it will remove blockages in energy, and banish negativity, replacing it with optimism and channelling restlessness into positive aspects of life.

It mixes with sandalwood, but is usually best used alone.

Ylang-ylang: The oil of poets, ylang-ylang is associated with inspiration and love, especially self-esteem. It counteracts a sense of frustration when things cannot be changed or achieved, and increases confidence and pleasure in possibilities that can be realised within the limitations of the present circumstance.

It mixes well with clary sage, geranium, lemon and chamomile.

An oil ritual to increase prosperity

As I have said before, magick is part of life and there is nothing wrong with carrying out rituals for your personal needs and a little more. However, you must make an effort, when you are financially more secure, to share your good fortune with those who are genuinely in need. As long as you bear in mind the cosmic 'balance sheet', this will ensure that there are sufficient energies to go round.You can, of course, pay in kindnesses and help, as well as in monetary terms.

It is unlikely that you will receive an unexpected cheque in the post the morning after this spell (though I am getting rather good at bewitching one of my financial directors at a firm I work for). Instead, you may suddenly find that you are given the opportunity to earn money through extra unexpected work. Or you will hear of someone who wishes to sell a reliable car or a serviceable computer in a hurry – just at the time when you need one. It would be churlish to demand a computer with a built-in DVD player from the cosmos, but under the psychic exchange system, all manner of good things that are no longer needed by one person can be directed to someone whose old model has just crashed. It goes without saying that you should also remember to redistribute items that are surplus to your requirements to keep the process moving.

Rituals for personal prosperity tend to be practised alone, as group prosperity rituals tend to work better with a more global focus (see page 275 for a mid-winter solstice light and abundance spell).

First, you need to define the purpose of the ritual. In this case that will probably not be difficult if you have been lying awake at night, panicking that you can't pay for a school trip for your child or new tyres for the car.

Once you have established what you require for your needs, find the right oils, using the list above, together with the list of herbs starting on page 110 and the incenses that you may also find in oil form (see page 139).

The ritual is to be carried out over three consecutive nights. Work on the two days before the full moon and the night of the full moon if you can, as this is the best time for energies of increase (see page 233 for magical times and use a diary or check in the weather section of the newspaper). It is also a traditional planting time for herbs and vegetables that grow above the ground.

However, if you need money urgently you cannot sit around waiting for the moon to be right, so burn silver lunar candles on each of the three evenings and picture the lovely ripening Moon we see at this period in the sky, if the weather is clear.

You can carry out the ritual at any time of day, but you should try to choose a time that is quiet. If you can only work during daylight hours, allow the natural light to add to the candle energies or draw the blinds.

You will need:

❧ An oil burner, the kind with a small nightlight underneath.

❧ Three prosperity oils. Good examples are patchouli, peppermint, ginger and sage. If you are pregnant, use frankincense, orange and lavender. (Note that lavender is an all-purpose herb that can be substituted for any other.)

❧ Symbols of prosperity, such as jewellery (golden-coloured for the Sun, and silver for the Moon), and some copper-coloured coins for Venus, planet of growth, to add to your money jar.

(Keep a collection of foreign currency left over from holidays for such prosperity spells. You can often also buy from garage sales or museum shops old or reproduction coins in the traditional metals – such as the US silver dollar – and these tend to have more of the pure metal. Failing this, even metal discs will do.)

❧ Three candles, beeswax, gold or rich blue.

❧ A small pottery jar with a lid to 'incubate' your money. (It is a good idea to collect a selection of jars, small wooden boxes, glass bottles and pots as many spells require a container.)

❧ A small, flat tray or open dish in a silver or gold colour. (Again these are often found amongst unwanted memorabilia. Alternatively, cover an ordinary one with gold or silver foil.)

❀ A crystal pendulum or any crystal pendant that will swing freely.

When you are ready to start the spell on the first night, have a bath, with a few drop of frankincense or sandalwood added, to open your psychic channels. Now prepare yourself for the spell.

❀ Sit in the South of your circle, facing North, the direction of magick and mystery.

❀ Let your body fill with light from your feet right through to your head.

❀ Breathe in the gold and silver colours of the items you have assembled and exhale darkness.

If you are in a hurry, just set up your spell and sit for a few moments drawing up power light and energy through your feet. Extend your hands over your head in an arch, stretching your fingers up so that the powers of the cosmos also enter, as you breathe slowly and deeply.

❀ Place your oil burner in the centre of your altar or on any flat surface, together with your three chosen oils (or you can work with a single fragrance if you prefer).

❀ To the South of it, set your money pot with the lid open and your coins.

❀ Place your symbols of abundance on the tray to the North of the dish.

❀ Arrange your gold, blue or beeswax candles in a triangle (this sacred shape represents the Triple Goddess, the Holy Trinity and the Egyptian Isis, Osiris and Horus). The candle at the apex of the triangle should be in the North, with the other two forming the base to the South, so that the triangle creates a protective enclosure. If you have room, set your candles in holders on the floor or in candlesticks on small tables or chairs at each of the points and have the altar in the centre. This is my preferred method and means that you are within the triangle and can move all round.

❀ On the first night, walk three times in circles around the outside of the altar (or the floor candles if you are using them), moving outwards, and pointing the index finger of your power hand behind you almost horizontally. Visualise a stream of light emanating from your finger. As you circle, chant:

Circle one I cast for the light of the Earth and her store of rich minerals, gold, silver, copper smelted in forges of volcanic fire.

Circle two I cast for the moonlit seas, for silver dolphins, seals and cascading rainbow fish.
Circle three I cast for the sunlit skies, the clouds pure gold and the gilt-tipped eagle soaring high.

❀ Light the candle in the North.

❀ Choose one of your three oils and, holding it in your receptive hand (the one you do not write with), circle over it nine times deosil the crystal pendulum or pendant.

❀ Say three times, faster and faster:

Star, Moon, Sun and candle bright, charge this oil with radiant light, power of ginger [or name of oil] prosper me, enter golden energy.

❀ After the third chant, let your pendulum swing freely on its chain so it spirals round, catching the candlelight and, perhaps, the moonlight.

❀ Add the oil to the burner with a little water and light the nightlight under it.

❀ Take three of the coins from the dish – if possible these should be one gold, one silver and one copper. Place them in the money pot and hold this briefly in the fragrance emanating from the burner, saying:

Venus, Morn and Evening Star, Sun and Moon that shine afar.
I ask in love and not in greed, grant me only what I need.

❀ Place the lid on the pot and leave it in front of the burner, sitting quietly and visualising money coming to you. At this point you may become aware of money-making possibilities you had not considered.

❀ When you are ready, blow out the nightlight, then the candle, sending the light into the cosmos that it may return as money-making energies.

❀ Walk round the circle three times widdershins, beginning with the outer circle of light, drawing the circles back like a thread into your fingers, saying softly:

May the circle be uncast but remain unbroken.

❀ Leave everything in place except for the pot, which you should put in a warm place to 'incubate', traditionally on a kitchen shelf.

On the second night, return the money pot to the south of the burner and remove the lid.

❧ Cast the triple circle as before, then light the candle in the North and also the one at the bottom left-hand corner of the triangle.

❧ Take the second oil and charge it as before. This time you have dual candlelight to reflect in your pendulum.

❧ Add your second oil and then the first one to the burner with a few drops of water. Light the burner.

❧ Take six coins from the dish and add to the pot; if possible there should be two golden-coloured, two silver and two copper. Repeat the chant from the previous night.

❧ Place the lid on the pot, then sit and visualise the money coming towards you and develop your plans to increase your prosperity.

❧ Blow out the candles and nightlight in reverse order of lighting, sending the energies into the cosmos.

❧ Uncast the circles as before and return the pot to its warm place.

❧ On the third night, repeat the ritual, but this time light all three candles and charge the third oil, adding a few drops of each to the burner for the cumulative energies. Add nine coins to the pot, again three of each kind of metal if you have them.

❧ Uncast the circle, but do not blow out the candles. Leave them and the oil to burn through, and only then put the lid back on the pot and return it to the warm place.

❧ Add a coin to the pot every day if you can. To empower the spell even further, you could also place a pot of basil, a herb of wealth, to the East of the burner during the ritual and after the three days, place the charged herbs on a window ledge to attract money.

Do something positive to help a person, animal or place on the day after the third ritual. It need not involve money. You can re-light the oils at any time if energies seem sluggish and repeat the whole ritual a moon cycle later for as long as is necessary. There may be a lot of negative vibes swimming the other way, so persevere and be patient.

Incense magick

Incense has formed a central part of religious and magical ceremonies for thousands of years in lands as far apart as India and North America. It has been used for purification purposes, to invoke angels and to bind or repel demons by medieval magicians. It is said to release specific energies contained in its fragrance and to carry prayers and petitions to the god or goddess figure being invoked.

Since the 1960s, incense sticks, cones and burners have increased in popularity for home use, to create an atmosphere of calm, to induce love and cleanse negativity. Many people use them for meditation as well as for rituals for confidence, health, love, prosperity, psychic protection and success.

Incense is now on sale in floral fragrances as well as the more traditional ones, such as frankincense and myrrh, and these are lovely both for home use and folk spells. Our ancestors would have burned flowers and leaves to create the same effect.

Like herbs and oils, incense can be empowered for specific purposes and can itself form a focus for a spell, as I describe later in this section. In formal magick, incense represents the Air element and is placed in the East of the altar. It is perhaps the easiest and most accessible magical substance and yet it can be a very potent form of magick. Incense burning differs from lighting essential oils, in that the fragrance is transmitted almost instantly on the smoke and so tends to be more concentrated and powerful than the slower-burning oils. It is therefore very effective for rituals requiring immediate action or the same intensity of effort from start to finish, rather than a gradual increase, perhaps of love or prosperity.

There are two kinds of incense. The first is non-combustible incense that is burned by smouldering it on charcoal blocks. This is made from powdered herbs, leaves bark or even pine needles mixed with a gum resin such as dragon's blood and has the advantage of producing clouds of smoke, brilliant for purification or for the climax of a spell. You can buy this type of incense prepared as loose powder, wood chips, granules or special paste, to burn on charcoal blocks or discs.

Traditional practitioners often make their own non-combustible incense, which can be very empowering, but it does take time and can be messy. On page 300 I have suggested an excellent book by Scott Cunningham that describes the process step by step and there are many Internet sites giving recipes and instructions.

To use this incense, place the smouldering charcoal block in a censer or thurible. Until you are experienced you may find it easier and safer to place it inside the censer first, and then light it. (A censer is simply a container for the charcoal. It may be a simple ceramic pot or a much more ornate vessel made of gold or silver. I would not recommend that you use the kind of incense censers on chains used in church services as the incense tends to go everywhere and can be quite dangerous.)

Add your incense gradually, about half a teaspoon at a time, once the charcoal block in the censer is glowing but not releasing sparks. With practice, you will learn to add the right quantity to ensure a steady but not choking stream of smoke as part of the ritual. Many practitioners prefer to light it beforehand and just add a teaspoon of incense as part of the ceremony or spell when they need a billow of fragrance. Incenses with a greater proportion of resin and gum will last longer – hence the popularity of frankincense in religious ceremonies. When working in a group, you can ask one person to top up the censer if necessary during a long rite. If you are alone, make this part of your increasing power actions in a private ritual.

Practise using non-combustible incense before rituals and in time it will become as natural as lighting a candle.

The second type of incense, which many practitioners, myself included, prefer to use, is combustible incense, lit directly in sticks and cones. These are very difficult to make at home but the commercially produced versions are quick and easy to use and the fragrance of the sticks does not alter when burned. Some home-made incenses made from apparently pleasantly scented flowers can smell foul when they are lit!

Sticks and cones are very safe to use: just light the tip, and once it is glowing, gently blow out the flame. This means there is no danger to children or pets who may be around.

Incense is also sold as *dhoops*, pure incense in cylinders attached to long sticky ropes; these come from India and can be burned in a flat dish.

Long, broad incense sticks can be carried when alight if you are careful. There are also many kinds of incense holders available. If you have a holder that collects the ash, you can scatter this to the four winds to carry your wishes on their way.

Whatever type of incense you use, treat it as you would any other substance that is ignited: read the instructions carefully before use and take normal precautions.

Below I have listed some of the most common forms of incense. Some you have met before in herbal or oil form and so I have kept the associations brief to avoid repetition. You may also find a number of these fragrances, especially fruit and floral ones, are available as scented candles. You can use these in your spells to focus on a particular need or quality you wish to attract.

Incenses for magick

Allspice
Allspice is used in spells for money, strength and action.

Apple blossom
Use apple blossom for love, fertility, optimism, inner beauty and youthfulness. It is particularly good in rituals concerning babies and children.

Avocado
Use avocado incense for desire, increase of beauty in oneself or the environment.

Basil
Basil is used in rituals for fidelity and prosperity.

Bay
Use bay for healing, prosperity, protection and marriage.

Benzoin
Benzoin is used in rituals for money; it increases mental powers and concentration.

Bluebell
Bluebell is used for faithfulness in love and betrothals.

Carnation
Carnation is used for strength, healing and family devotion.

Cedar/cedarwood
Cedar and cedarwood are best for healing and cleansing redundant influences and negative thoughts.

Chamomile
Like its herbal counterpart, chamomile incense brings money, quiet sleep and affection, and is used in spells to do with all matters of the family.

Cinnamon
Cinnamon is for spirituality, success, healing, psychic powers, money, love and passion.

Cherry
Cherry brings new love and divinatory abilities.

Cloves
Cloves are used in spells for love and money; they repel hostility and improve memory.

Copal
Use copal for protection and purification; it is especially good for cleansing crystals.

Cypress
Cypress is for times of transition to a new phase, letting go of sorrow.

Dragon's blood
Dragon's blood is used for love and protection, passion and male potency.

Fern
An initiator of change, travel and fertility, fern will also bring hidden wealth, maybe in terms of potential.

Fig
Use fig for wisdom, creativity and creation, fertility, harmony and balance.

Frankincense
Use frankincense for courage, joy, strength and success.

Freesia
Freesia increases trust, especially after loss or betrayal; it also brings belief in a better tomorrow.

Gum arabic (acacia)
Use gum arabic in rituals for dreams, meditation, psychic protection and development.

Heather
Heather is used for passion, fidelity in love and good fortune; it maximises opportunities and is particularly effective in weather magick, especially rain-making.

Honeysuckle
Honeysuckle is used for money, psychic powers and protection.

Hyacinth
Hyacinth assists in overcoming opposition in love; it brings happiness and desire for reconciliation.

Hyssop
Hyssop is used for making a love commitment, for healing and all forms of protection, especially from psychic attack.

Ivy
Ivy is effective for fidelity, married love, permanent relationships and constancy.

Jasmine
Jasmine is used in Moon magick and prophetic dreams. It brings sensuality, money and passion.

Juniper
Use juniper for protection from psychic attacks and physical theft; for cleansing, healing and house moves.

Lavender
Lavender is particularly good for love and reconciliation,

Lemon/lemongrass
Both repel spite, protect against malice and gossip; they bring passion and increase psychic awareness and are good for those who travel.

Lemon verbena
Lemon verbena will break a run of bad luck; it brings love and protection against negativity.

Lilac
Use lilac for all domestic matters, acceptance of the frailty of self and others, and to ease nostalgia; lilac cleanses negativity.

Lily
Lily is for purity and breaking negative influences in love; it is frequently used in Mother Goddess magick.

Lily of the valley
Lily of the valley increases mental abilities, brings happiness and restores joy.

Marigold
Marigold is used for dreams and guarding against infidelity. It is effective in rituals concerning legal matters, luck and money.

Mimosa
Use mimosa for protection, love, prophetic dreams and purification.

Mistletoe
Known to the Druids as the all-healer, mistletoe is for healing sorrows, overcoming injustice and finding what is lost. It is also good for male potency.

Moss
Moss is used for good fortune, prosperity, money and permanence, whether in work or relationships. It frequently appears in water magick and divination (use with candles on water).

Myrrh
Myrrh is good for healing, peace, protection and inner harmony.

Myrtle
Sometimes mixed with other fragrances, myrtle is used in spells concerning fidelity in love, marriage and mature love. It may also be used in matters of property and security.

Nutmeg
Use nutmeg for fertility and healing, especially of the environment; it will also bring a gradual increase of wealth.

Orange blossom
Beneficial for marriage and permanent relationships, use orange blossom also for restoring trust and increasing confidence and hope.

Pine
Use pine for healing, fertility, purification, protection and money; it also returns hostility to the sender.

Poppy/opium
Poppy may be used for divination, fertility and making oneself less visible in danger; it also brings luck and sleep.

Rose
Rose is for gentle love, attraction, dreams of love and reconciliation.

Rosemary
Rosemary is used for love and happy memories; it also improves memory and concentration.

Sage
Use sage in rituals for health, enhanced mental powers and wisdom.

Sandalwood
Sandalwood is effective for spiritual and psychic awareness and healing; use it also in matters of sexuality.

Strawberry
Use strawberry for innocent love, friendship and happiness.

Tamarind
Tamarind is for love, especially new love, and the rebuilding of trust.

Thyme
Thyme is used in rituals for courage, divination, health, love, money and purification.

Vanilla
Vanilla brings passion and enduring love; it also increases mental powers.

Vetivert
Use vetivert for love. It can also break a run of bad luck and bring money. It is protective against theft and all kinds of negativity.

Violet
Use violet for secrecy, modesty and uncovering hidden talents.

Combining incenses in rituals

As well as the single fragrances, there are many commercial products that combine several basic fragrances to evoke a particular mood, for example morning dew, raindrops and emerald. You can experiment with these and find those that seem right for your life or, if you make your own non-combustible incenses, you can combine a number of single fragrances to your own personal recipes.

But it is quite possible by using a number of individual fragrance sticks in the same ritual to combine their energies and, more importantly, create exactly the proportions of specific energies you need for a ritual. For example, you might burn a rose incense for love with a cinnamon incense to add passion and energy to that special, loving relationship. The amount of incense used for each quality determines your priorities, so, in this case, if loving energies were the prime focus, you would burn two rose incense sticks or cones and one cinnamon. You can also do this with your oil mixes.

A six-incense ritual for love

Six is the number of Venus in her morning star aspect of love. You can use this ritual for attracting love, for deepening a relationship, consummating it or strengthening it during a difficult period, perhaps when everything appears to have got into a rut. You can alter the focus of the ritual by varying the number and type of each fragrance you use, for example whether your primary concern is to increase trust, passion or encourage fidelity (use the incense list on page 139).

This ritual is best carried out early in the moon cycle, any time from when you can see the crescent in the sky.

In the ritual, I refer to a pentagram, a magical symbol that can be used for attracting energies or closing them down in ritual magick. Its uses can be varied according to the way it is drawn. However, in this ritual, it is the shape that is important, so just imagine the shape as illustrated overleaf, with its single point at the top. Arrange five of your incense sticks as though on the points of this invisible pentagram and put the sixth in the centre as the combination and synthesis of the different powers.

First, gather together the tools you will need.

- A candle of the appropriate colour for the type of love you wish to focus on: pink for new love, green for increasing commitment and faithful love, or red for passion and the consummation of love.

- A gold or silver ring or, if you prefer, one made of copper, Venus's own metal.

- A small white cushion or piece of white cloth.

- Six incense sticks of appropriate fragrances and separate holders to catch the ash.

- Ivy or any green fronds; if you cannot obtain any, green ribbon will do. (Ivy is a plant associated with fidelity and permanent relationships.)

Now begin your ritual.

- Place your ring in the centre of your altar, on the white cloth or cushion.

- To the left of it (towards the West, the direction of love and emotions), place and light the candle.

- Take your incense sticks one by one, and light each in the candle, reciting:

> *Incense of love, incense of power, thus do I charge thee,*
> *now at this hour.*
> *Incense of faithfulness, incense of truth, bring love*
> *that will last, in age and in youth. In sickness and sorrow, in*
> *health and in joy, in wealth and in dearth, may nothing destroy.*

- Beginning at the single (top) point of your invisible pentagram, light your first incense, saying:

> *I light this incense to bring love into my life and the one*
> *who is right for me.*

✥ Moving deosil, light and place the second incense on the next point of the invisible pentagram, saying:

> *I light this incense that I may give love where*
> *it will bring joy and bear fruit.*

✥ Continuing deosil, light and place the third incense at the next invisible point, saying:

> *I light this incense for the increase of that love and for*
> *mutual fidelity and respect.*

✥ Light and place the fourth incense, saying:

> *I light this incense for the marriages of mind and soul as*
> *well as body, in a union that is beyond any legal bonds.*

✥ Light and place the fifth incense, saying:

> *I light this incense that love will always be willingly given and*
> *received and never become possessive or manipulative.*

✥ Light and place your final incense to the East of the ring, saying:

> *I light this incense that love will be compassionate, ever supportive,*
> *accepting of frailties and based on love of the real person, not*
> *worshipping the ideal of loving, nor demanding the perfect lover.*

You can adapt the pledges according to the focus you give the ritual and even rewrite them entirely to express your purpose.

✥ Take the ring and pass it through the six incenses in turn, saying for each ring of faith:

> *Love I pledge, truth I offer, care and kindliness. Ring of promise,*
> *love I ask, truth I seek, into eternity if right may it be.*

✥ Return the ring to the centre, and bind it with six loose knots of ivy or ribbon, saying:

> *Do not bind, join heart and mind,*
> *Hold safe we two, till life is through,*
> *Love without end, my dearest friend.*
> *I call you – [name the person, or say 'love unknown'].*

Again you can adapt the words. A pledge of fidelity is actually a very potent way of attracting a new lover – perhaps someone who works close to you whom you have not thought of in a romantic way.

✥ Let the candle and incense burn through and then collect the incense ash in a pot or jar with a lid.

❧ Sleep with the ring and ivy next to your bed on the cushion and in the daytime surround it with white flowers.

❧ When you have time, take the ash to the top of a hill or any windy place and scatter it to the four winds, saying:

Go free in love and return in joy.

You can carry out the spell on a larger scale by placing the ring, the candle and one large incense stick on your altar in the centre of the invisible pentagram. Place the other large incense sticks on small tables, chairs or blocks at the other points and work within the pentagram. You could even use garden incense and carry out the ritual in a sheltered spot out of doors, maybe even picking your ivy and white flowers during the ritual.

A ritual for harmony

This ritual can be used when, for example, a colleague, family member or friend is intruding in your life, but you do not want to hurt their feelings. It can be very successful if you have received one too many phone calls or visits at inconvenient moments from a friend or neighbour. It may help to ward off constant interference in your projects by your boss or a colleague at work, or possessiveness that is not malicious but comes from loneliness in a close relative, a child or even your partner. You can carry it out before going to work or when you anticipate the arrival of the person. It is much kinder than a traditional binding spell as it preserves the positive aspects of the relationship.

❧ Light deosil a circle of lavender and rose incense sticks for love and kindness.

❧ Fill a pot or a small cauldron, or any heatproof dish, with sand and in it stand a single orange candle for independence.

✻ Take a long piece of red thread and tie nine loose knots around the base of the cauldron to represent the tangled emotions, saying as you tie the knots:

Bind and wind nine times through, bonds that stifle, tangle,
twine, bind unwilling me to you.

✻ Cut through the knots one at a time, using a knife (not scissors), saying:

Ties so binding,
Cut right through,
Guilt unwinding,
Freedom finding,
Loving you,
Not what you do.

✻ Light your candle, saying:

Light of self, burning true, I am me and you are you.
Light of friendship, light so kind, free in heart and soul and mind.

✻ Now burn each of the knots in the orange candle so they drop into the sand, saying:

Free to live in harmony
Caring still, but separately.

This is also a good ritual if you are separating or divorcing from a partner but need to maintain friendly contact, perhaps because you work together or have joint family or financial responsibilities.

CHAPTER 8
Crystals and Protective Magick

Whether you are carrying out spells, rituals or divination or are simply feeling anxious, vulnerable or under attack from inner or external forces, psychic protection can enclose you in light and keep out all that threatens your harmony. It is a very positive form of magick that for everyday use requires a basic ritual or visualisation that takes only a minute or two. Some people carry out routine psychic protection when returning from work and in the morning as naturally as taking off their work clothes and having a bath, to shed the pressures of the day.

You can also with practice learn to cast protection round those you care for: a child who is being bullied or an animal or bird that is endangered, an area of natural beauty under threat from developers or a group of people who are being unfairly targeted.

Of course you can't save a rainforest single-handed because there will always be a vast tide of despoiling vibes flowing in the opposite direction. But as has been shown by events such as World Days for Peace and the experiments on the power of prayer, if enough individuals send out positive intentions, followed by peaceful action, then people power really does make a difference. There is, as ever, just one proviso: you must remember the Wiccan Rede, 'An it harm none, do what you will', and apply it rigorously.

I am often asked to carry out protective spells for people who feel that they are the subject of unfair scrutiny, jealousy, anger or resentment. This may be manifest as deliberate malice, a muttered curse or a declaration of some vengeful intent. But more usually the origins are more obscure, perhaps coming from someone gossiping or lying in bed at night, fuming over an achievement or good fortune enjoyed by their supposed enemy. A whole tradition of 'evil eye' superstitions and antidotes grew out of such envy and bad wishing. If you are to help counteract this kind of bad feeling, without causing harm in return, it is best to resort to some kind of protection. Note that you do not have to identify the sender of bad vibes in order to protect the victim. You will usually know who it is, as in most cases there is a likely candidate, and very frequently the wrong-doers give themselves away as they cannot resist the satisfaction of checking the effect of their unpleasant actions. Don't be tempted into direct retaliation, however – remember the Threefold Law.

The same tools and methods of protection can be used whether you are protecting a cat from an aggressive, stone-throwing neighbour or whales in a distant ocean from marauding fishermen. These include herbs, oils and incenses, made into sachets and poppets used in rituals (see Chapters 6 and 7). Salt, sacred water and wax amulets may also provide protection. One of the most potent methods of protection is through the use of crystals.

Crystals

All crystals have innate protective qualities as well as healing and empowering properties and so can offer instant harmony and energy even in the most draining situations.

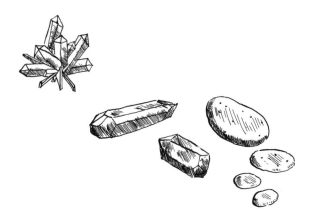

Collecting protective crystals

Certain crystals have, over the millennia, from Ancient Babylon, Egypt and the Orient, acquired the reputation of possessing strong protective qualities and are also usually potent in strengthening and healing. These include amber, black agate, amethyst, bloodstone, carnelian, garnet, jade, black and red jasper, jet, lapis lazuli, tiger's eye, topaz and turquoise. However, as you work with crystals and stones, you may discover that a particular crystal or even a stone from the seashore fills you with calm and confidence; if you carry or hold this at times when you feel vulnerable, it will increase in power the more you use it.

Build up a collection of small protective crystals with which you can ring your bed for quiet sleep or place around your home or workplace to absorb the negativity of others. Buy or make a dark silk or natural fabric drawstring bag or purse in which you can carry a single protective crystal, or your crystal pairs (see below), whenever you leave home. Place them in the four corners of a room that always seems dark or inhospitable. Set crystals at the four corners of the table where you are carrying out divinatory or psychic work to act as a psychic shield from negativity or debilitating emotions.

Balancing the energies

Crystals can be used in pairs to balance energies and restore equilibrium to a person or situation. This little piece of magick is particularly useful when you are under stress. Simply hold a dark crystal, such as a smoky quartz or apache tear, in your power hand and a clear crystal quartz or a golden citrine in your receptive hand, and close your eyes. You will feel the adrenaline surge and panic flowing away, leaving you calm and protected, able to deal with any situation.

I always keep a couple of suitable crystals in my hand luggage for difficult moments when travelling – crowded trains, delays, especially late at night when I feel very vulnerable, and even small enclosed lifts, which I hate, having become stuck in one when I was heavily pregnant. You could also buy and wear a pair of small, jewelled pins containing crystals, or two lapel brooches fastening the two sides of your scarf, or odd cufflinks with balancing crystals. (Who knows, you may even find you start a trend…)

Experiment, using the list on page 153, to find which crystals offer balanced energies for you; you may well find some work better than others in particular situations. For example, my friend Jenny, a 40-year-old sales adviser, found that gentle green jade in her power hand and malachite, a rich green and black stone good for strengthening teeth and bones, in her receptive hand, made her feel protected when her aggressive area manager visited her. Soft rose quartz in her power hand and a glowing reddish orange carnelian in her receptive hand helped her to avoid the loss of self-esteem she always felt when she went home to see her critical mother.

Cleansing crystals and gemstones

You should always cleanse your crystals before and after use in protection, healing and empowerment.

When you obtain a new crystal, cleanse it before charging it with your own personal energies. In this way you can remove all the energies, not necessarily negative, of those who have prepared, packed and sold the stone. If the stone was a gift, however, you may wish to accept the loving energies with which it was offered and rely on your innate defensive powers to filter out any unconscious negativity left from the previous owner's life.

You will also need to wash your crystals, and your crystal pendulum (see page 163), if you use one, regularly in running water to keep their energies clear.

If you have been in touch with a particularly negative influence, first wash the stones, then sprinkle them with salt and pass over them an incense stick or oil burner in a fragrance such as lavender, pine or rose. Finally pass them over the flame of a purple, silver or pink candle; in this way your crystal absorbs the healing energies of all four elements.

Leave the crystals to dry in natural light, then wrap them for a few days in a dark cloth with a large piece of unpolished amethyst wrapped separately so it will not scratch the smaller crystals. Amethysts have great powers of healing for other crystals, but they need frequently to be rested and anointed very gently with diluted lavender oil or a lavender infusion (see page 118).

You can also cleanse crystals by leaving them in a rainstorm or burying them in a pot of lavender, sage, chamomile, rosemary or other herb of love and harmony. Leave them for 24 hours and, if necessary, wash off any remaining soil with running water. The result will be a new vibrancy, especially in the case of rutilated quartz, jade and moss agate (the last two are called the gardener's crystals). For more methods of cleansing, empowering and crystal protection, see my book *Psychic Protection Lifts the Spirit* (see page 301).

Charging your crystals with positive power

All crystals contain power as well as protective qualities and cleansing is itself empowering. However, if you are being subjected to stress or harassment of any kind, you might like to charge your crystal, so that when you touch or look at it, you will be enclosed in its radiance and stimulate your own innate self-protective power. Your charged crystal acts as an amplifier for your own inner radiance and self-confidence and will repel any hostility.

My own favourite method is to wrap the crystals in white silk and take them to a sacred place of ancient power, such as a standing stone, an old stone circle or one of the ancient healing wells. These wells were formerly dedicated to the Mother Goddess but were Christianised and rededicated to St Bride, the Virgin Mary or other Christian, often Celtic, saint.

Go as early in the morning as possible and place the crystals on a flat surface, either on one of the stones or close to the water. Sit near to the source of power, touching it with your two hands so that you create a circuit of energy parallel to that being absorbed by the crystals and so empower your own auric field (the area of psychic energy that exists around our bodies). Auric fields contain different colours; they can be seen spontaneously by clairvoyants but anyone can, with time and practice, interpret auras, which change according to a person's mood and the influences on it. After about ten minutes you may detect a slight luminescence around yourself as well as the crystals. Your crystals will now be charged and can be placed in their drawstring bag.

When under stress, touch your chosen crystal for strength and protection. Keep it on your desk at work, place it between you and an adversary or next to your bed if you are troubled by bad dreams or fear psychic attack or malevolence at night. People living in areas with high rates of robbery and violence may wish to put a power crystal, such as turquoise, red jasper or carnelian, as a protective buffer near external doors and windows. In less extreme circumstances, charged rose quartz and amethyst are excellent for sleep and relaxation problems, for charging simply accentuates the innate calm energies of the crystal.

With the gentle crystals (such as amethyst, rose quartz or smoky quartz), you will experience a gentle warmth and enclosing light of pink, green or purple according to the colour of the crystal. But with the power crystals (such as clear crystal quartz, citrine or carnelian), you may see with your psychic vision sparks of gold emanating and enclosing you in a protective shell. Anyone who approaches in a confrontational way may stop and back off. The crystal is not hurting them, it is just strengthening your own boundaries against intrusion.

If you cannot visit an ancient site to charge your crystals, hold a crystal pendulum up to bright sunlight, or in front of a fibre optic lamp, and swirl it so that it catches rainbows. Hold your pendulum in your power hand. With your other hand, hold the crystal beneath the pendulum so it catches the light, and turn your pendulum over the crystal nine times deosil to absorb power.

Another method is to take your crystal out into the light of the full moon (the two or three nights leading up to the full moon are also powerful). Hold your crystal up so that the light of the Moon shines on it. Alternatively, fill a bowl with water and place it in the open air so that the Moon is reflected in it. You can then bathe your crystal in empowering moonlight and leave to dry.

You can also bathe a crystal in sunlight; I find the Moon method more gently empowering for crystals that are primarily intended to act as guardians. But experiment, as Sun water may be best for you.

As these are personal crystals, ask the Moon or Sun in your own words to lend their power; alternatively, you may prefer to remain silent and let these ancient forces work in their own way.

You can also use this method for empowering amulets and lucky charms or St Christopher medallions. St Christopher is patron saint and protector of all travellers.

Protective crystals

The following crystals are those that I, in my personal work, and people with whom I have held healing workshops or teaching sessions have found especially protective. They will absorb negative energies emanating from both fears and doubts, and repel external attack, replacing darker feelings with positive emotions and intentions.

To benefit from the protective powers of a crystal, you can carry or wear it, or keep it close to you at work, at home or when you travel. You can also add a crystal to your bath water. Alternatively, you can soak it in pure spring water overnight and drink the crystalline water in the morning or carry it in a small bottle to splash on your face and wrists at stressful times.

Agates

These bring stability, security, emotional and physical balance and acceptance of self and others as they are. Agates are said to be good in all colours for reducing effects of harmful rays, pollution and all forms of psychic, psychological and physical attack.

Black agate absorbs negativity, repels psychic attack, irrational thoughts and words, and promotes acceptance and tolerance of differences in others.

Blue lace agate is a natural peace-bringer and protects against harsh words spoken by self or others.

Moss agate (clear with green, moss-like tendrils) is the stone for protecting against pollution and deforestation. Plant a circle of them in the soil of a tropical plant and each day visualise healing rays being sent to the rainforests. Moss agate also protects against food cravings and obsessions.

Amber

Known as the honey stone, because of its great antiquity and soft, warm touch, amber is said to contain the power of many suns and has the power to absorb negativity and protect the user from harm. It will also melt any emotional or physical rigidity.

In the Chinese tradition, the souls of tigers pass into amber when they die and so it is also a gem of courage in the face of unfairness or hostility. Above all, it protects children, especially from falls and bullying, and increases their self-esteem (coral also does this).

Brilliant for soothing anxiety and creating a golden shield of protection that mingles power with kindness and a sense of perspective, amber is said to protect wearers from pollution, both industrial and technological.

Amethyst

Amethyst is one of the best healing and protective stones. Egyptian soldiers wore it in battle so they would not panic in dangerous situations and so it is an ideal crystal to calm children and adults and to keep away night terrors. The Greeks believed that amethyst prevented the wearer from drunkenness – *amethystos* means 'not drunken' – and so it protects against excesses not only of alcohol, but of those who seek to dominate through greater strength or status, at work or socially. Worn during sleep, it prevents insomnia, and when carried throughout the day, it reduces anger and impatience in self and others.

Apache tears (obsidian)

These small black globules are so-named after a tragic incident in Arizona. A group of Apaches were ambushed by soldiers. Many were killed and the rest threw themselves over a cliff, rather than be taken prisoner. The women and maidens of the tribe wept at the base of the cliff for a whole moon cycle and their tears became embedded within obsidian crystals in the rock.

Apache tears protect against treachery, deep sorrow and are especially potent in protecting persecuted minorities whether these are people, endangered species or places. They ease and release physical and mental pain, loss, sadness and anger, allowing the user to move forward. Apache tears are particularly powerful for protection against one's own fears of frailty, mortality, loneliness and loss of any kind.

Beryl

A crystal of the Sun, beryl drives away inner fears and repels external threats and malevolence, increasing confidence and a sense of well-being. In its golden form it is excellent for creating a shield of golden sparks around you in difficult situations where there are too many factors or conflicting demands to assimilate and you feel overwhelmed.

Deep blue beryl is used for crystal balls. It offers inner peace and the courage to stand against bullies and autocrats, but allows you to be generous to the petty-minded.

Pink beryl (morganite) offers gentle protection for children and animals and encourages compassion towards our enemies.

Bloodstone (heliotrope)

The red spots of bloodstone were, according to legend, formed from the blood of Christ as it fell on green jasper at the crucifixion and so it is traditionally used in icons and religious carvings. In Ancient Babylon, bloodstone was used in amulets for protection against enemies and has been carried by soldiers in many cultures to overcome fears, to prevent wounds or stop bleeding. It is good for deflecting cruelty, spite and malice and for situations in which the fears are real and the opposition great. Travellers may carry this stone to protect against accidents or attack.

Carnelian

Though most usually a translucent, vibrant red or orange, carnelians can also be yellow or brown. In any shade, carnelians have traditionally been regarded as the stones of courage and self-confidence of leaders, and those who wish or need to be leaders should wear one around the neck or in a ring. They are powerful against all forms of malevolence and danger, repelling envy in others. Most of all, carnelians protect us against ourselves and our own weaknesses.

Coral

Coral is an organic gem, usually pink, red or orange, and is known as the protector of children. Coral has been a children's stone from the time of the Ancient Greeks when Plato wrote that it should be hung around children's necks to prevent them falling and to cure colic, and rubbed on the gums to help painless teething. It is good for all children's fears and against threat to their person or self-esteem. It is also protective for adolescent girls, pregnant women and new mothers, and invokes kindness and gentleness in others.

Garnet

Usually a deep, clear red, garnets are the ultimate protective stone. Eastern European peoples used the garnet against illness, night phantoms and all forms of manifest evil, including the mythical vampire. In medieval times, garnets were engraved with a lion's head for health and safe travel; however, being a brittle stone, this was not easy and the few that did not shatter were highly prized. It is still regarded as a stone to be carried by travellers, especially for protection against attack. Like the emerald, it will change colour if danger is near. Garnets also provide energy for difficult tasks when rest is not possible.

Avoid using garnet when you are feeling angry, as it will amplify these feelings.

Jade

A stone that protects against ill-health and poverty, jade is another very gentle stone that is said to contain great deal of the undiluted life force. It connects the user with Earth energies and offers protection from injury and accidents, especially during travel. It is a good stone for rituals to heal the planet.

Jasper

Jasper is, like agate, a powerful grounding and earthing stone and protects against fears as well as external danger.

Black jasper is protective against all negative sources and especially the user's own repressed feelings. It is good for absorbing anger.

Brown jasper offers stability in turbulent times; it is good to use after rituals.

Green jasper protects against jealousy, increases empathy with others' difficulties and soothes bad dreams.

Red jasper is naturally defensive against external hostility and danger.

Jet

Jet is, like amber, an organic gem of great antiquity. It is actually fossilised wood that has been turned into a dense form of coal. Travellers and fisherfolk benefit from its protection – in past times, the wives of sailors would keep a jet amulet safe at home so that their husbands would return safely from the sea. It protects all who travel by night, alone or in lonely places, and older people in all aspects of their lives. It guards against bad dreams and endows the wearer with the emotional strength to face the ending of a natural phase.

Lapis lazuli

Known as the eye of wisdom and the stone of the gods, lapis lazuli jewellery is mentioned in an Ancient Egyptian papyrus dating from over 3,000 years ago as having healing powers. The Sumerians believed it contained the souls of their gods and goddesses and as such would endow them with magical powers, and the goddess

Ishtar was famed for her beautiful necklaces of this crystal. In Egypt, lapis lazuli was first used in a powdered form for eye make-up as protection against the evil eye.

Lapis lazuli counteracts insomnia and the inability to communicate, and is a powerfully protective stone against all pettiness, spite, injustice and unfair officialdom. It offers the courage and clarity to win through, however seemingly powerful the opposition, but it demands nobility of purpose in its users. Lapis lazuli is good for healing both air and water pollution and for world peace.

Malachite

A purifier and energiser, malachite will replace negativity with positive energies. It cleanses the auric field around people, animals, plants and places. Malachite will absorb pollution and, it is claimed, harmful rays from computers and televisions. It is especially effective if a crystal is placed in the corners of a room where white electrical goods are being used.

Because it is so powerful, malachite should be cleansed at least every two days.

Rose quartz

Rose quartz is the stone of gentle healing and protection. It is known as the children's stone because it is so gentle in soothing away childhood ills and sorrows that may haunt us into adulthood. It is good for protecting families, the home, pets and anyone who is ill or vulnerable.

It promotes family love and friendship, and brings peace, forgiveness, emotional harmony and the mending of quarrels. It heals emotional wounds and heartbreak, grief, stress, fear, lack of confidence, resentment and anger. Rose quartz will keep away nightmares and night-time fears. Cleanse and recharge it frequently, especially if the colour begins to fade.

Smoky quartz

This is traditionally associated with removing negative influences on the user. It can promote physical health and galvanise our shadow side, transforming anger and resentment into positive action, rather than leaving us to deny negative feelings or project them on to other people. It is a powerful stone to use when one's survival, either professional or personal, is an issue. Smoky quartz also counteracts self-destructive impulses.

Tiger's eye

A brown or red translucent stone (the green and blue versions are cat's, falcon or hawk's eyes), tiger's eye combines the powers of the Earth with the deep instinctive ability to survive life's challenges.

Throughout the ages, tiger's eye has been a talisman against the evil eye. Roman soldiers would wear engraved stones as protection from death and wounding. Tiger's eye is also associated with practical aspects of life and enhances the five senses. Thus it can alert us to physical danger as well as potential malice. It is effective in tackling gossip, backbiting and spite in a firm but creative way, and is perhaps best of all for creating a sparkling shield of protection.

Topaz

Topaz is the Sanskrit word for 'fire'. Topaz increases power as the Moon waxes, being at its greatest potency at the time of the full moon. Perhaps because of this, topaz was said to be proof against nightmares, night terrors and phantoms and malice of the night as well as violent emotions. Water in which a topaz has been soaked is a cure for insomnia if drunk an hour before bedtime.

A natural energiser, golden topaz is especially good for alleviating work anxieties, especially in the caring professions, and should be kept in the workplace.

Turquoise

Mined by the Egyptians in Sinai more than 6,000 years ago, turquoise and imitations of it have been discovered in graves from around 4000 BC. It is the stone of horsemen, warning them of danger, and will prevent horses from stumbling if placed in a saddle or on a bridle. So it is the stone of all travellers, especially those who travel far by air or sea. In modern times, a small turquoise can be attached to pets' collars and to the mirrors of birdcages to protect them. It can also be plaited into horses' manes to prevent their being stolen or harmed, using the following method. Soak the turquoise in sacred water for 24 hours, then charge it with power by sprinkling salt on it and passing it through the smoke of a powerful incense such as cedar, then through the flame of a pink candle and finally with the sacred water. Finally, bind the turquoise with three hairs from the animal.

Turquoise is a power stone and is good in global rituals, to protect persecuted groups and for healing the sea and air. It is particularly effective in whale and dolphin conservation work.

A protective crystal ritual

This ritual is particularly effective for anyone feeling anxious about travelling or moving house. You will need a map of the journey involved. You may like to work by candlelight, in which case light a yellow candle for a journey of a short distance or duration and a blue one for major travel. You can also adapt this ritual for a house move, burning a brown candle for a move to or within a town or city and green for a rural or more isolated location.

❧ Spread five or six protective crystals across the map from your home to your destination.

❧ Prepare a circle of protective incense sticks or cones, such as copal, juniper or lemon verbena, alternated with fern or frankincense incense for travel. Use holders or burners wide enough to collect the ash. (Incense combines the qualities of the Earth in its substance and of the Sky when lit and so is a very balanced form of magic, combining the Sky Father and Earth Mother, animus and anima energies, or yang and yin in the Oriental tradition.)

❧ As you light the incense, say:

Far or near, guard my home, guide me safe o'er hill and foam,
In darkest night, though apart, my home I carry in my heart.

❧ While the incense is burning, make positive plans for your journey and focus on the most pleasurable aspects.

❧ When the incense is burned through, collect any ash and sprinkle a little over the crystals you placed over your home and destination.

❧ Wash the crystals in sacred water or any source of running water and allow them to dry naturally.

❧ Take your home crystal on the journey with you and give the destination crystal to a loved one. If you live alone, bury it in a plant pot near the door to await your homecoming.

❧ For a house move, bury the 'new home' crystal near the front door of your present property to create a happy atmosphere for the new owners or tenants. Bury the 'old home' crystal in the ground near your new front door when you move, to transfer positive energies with you and make the new home instantly yours.

Amulets

Very potent protection can be provided by amulets. These are charms that have been marked with a symbol to indicate the power they contain. This could be a protective god or goddess, or a sign of the zodiac or a planet that you feel has the power you need. Alternatively, you might simply write the name of the person to be protected and surround it with a circle to keep out ill-wishing. You can make an amulet in any shape you wish, out of candlewax or clay, or you could use wooden discs, cut from an old broom handle. The symbols may be engraved, using a sharp knife, or painted on. You can add decorations if you wish. Amulets may be carried in your pocket, or you could drill a hole and thread a ribbon through an amulet and hang it around your neck. They may also be placed in a house to offer protection against danger and illness. Protective crystals (see page 153) also make good amulets and empowered herbs of protection (see Chapter 6), carried in a purse or bag are potent in the same way.

Traditionally, the week before the midsummer solstice is the time for making protective amulets, so that they can be passed through flame or held up to the Sun on the solstice day at noon.

Salt

Salt has always been central to religious and magical practices because it is an absolutely pure substance. It is powerful for psychic protection but also in money-making and in healing rituals. Centuries ago, it was regarded as precious because it was the main preservative of food through the long winter months for early settlers around the globe. In formal magick, it represents the element of Earth.

In modern protective and banishing rituals, a salt circle is created to keep out harm. Many of us still adhere to the old practice of throwing a pinch of spilt salt over our left shoulder, 'into the eyes of the Devil'. Salt was also added in the making of Holy Water to ward off evil and increase physical strength as well as powers of fertility. Salt is still added to water in casting a triple circle in more formal magick (see page 51).

On a less formal level, small quantities of salt can be empowered and used for all kinds of domestic protection. To empower salt, pass a clear quartz or crystal pendulum over it deosil, chanting the purpose, for example, 'Salt, salt, protect me from all danger'. Keep them separate from other condiments in a watertight container and then you can build in the specific need, perhaps protection for a traveller, purification of a house or comfort for a child unhappy at school. Twists of salt in silver foil hidden in the corners of a room at home or work can offer protection, as can salt in a drawstring bag carried while travelling to guard against illness, accident or harm. You can also scatter a circle of salt around a schoolbag, travel bag or briefcase, around your desk or on the threshold, to create a protective shield.

You can charge pepper in the same way to make a salt and pepper floor wash for floors (this is an old Afro-Caribbean tradition). As you scrub or sprinkle, create the empowerment charm, for example 'Salt of Earth, pepper of Fire, guard my home and cleanse away all harm'. Pepper also works wonders for keeping away the office vamp or Adonis and if you think your partner is at risk from temptation, add the empowered condiment to a salad and they will absorb the protection.

A protective ritual with empowered salt

❋ Place the salt in a small ceramic dish on your altar and light a pure beeswax candle at the four main compass points around the edges of the altar. Beeswax has a long tradition in magick: it was sacred to the Mother Goddess and later the Virgin Mary. Demeter, goddess of the grain, was called Queen Bee and Aphrodite's symbol at her hive-shaped shrine in Eryx was a gold honeycomb. Her high priestess was always called Melissa, Latin for bee.

❋ Beginning at the North of your circle, light your elemental candles. At each quarter of the circle say:

Demeter, Aphrodite, Melissa, pure mother bee, charge with thy light this salt, to enfold my home (workplace/journey) with thy golden mantle of protection.

You may wish to leave out the goddess names or substitute a Mother Goddess or religious icon of your own. Perhaps surprisingly, many witches do ask the blessings of Mother Mary and I believe that if you work in love, then you should use your own focus. If you prefer, just say:

Benign light, charge with honeyed fragrance this salt, to enfold –
[insert the name of the person to be protected].

❄ Next enclose your dish of salt in a square of small protective crystals such as jade or tiger's eye and one or two amber if you have any in your collection. (Rose quartz or glass nuggets in smoky brown and yellow make good substitutes.) Begin in the North and make sure the crystals are touching. The square is a sacred geometric form symbolising time and space and so is good for all protective rituals. The square should be just inside the candles. Some practitioners create a symbolic square by placing just two crystals in the centre of where each side would be, and you can do this if you prefer. As you create the square, say:

Safe within, nought to enter, nought to harm, nought within but this benign light of love. Thus do I build, thus enclose – [insert the name or place to be protected] in light and protection.

❄ Now create a circle of golden petals, pollen, leaves or pot pourri. The circle should almost touch the candles, so that they can stand sentinel round it, and should enclose the square or crystals and the salt. The circle represents the spirit and so encloses the space and time square. As you scatter the petals or pollen, say:

Circle of gold, shield from malice, danger and stranger, enter the salt and empower this sphere with a shield of gold.

❄ Leave the candles to burn down, making sure they are in broad-based holders so wax does not fall on the petals.

If you are working with other people or wish to have a more active ritual, place the dish of salt in the centre resting on the altar or on a rock. Set tall candles in floor holders a short distance away and make an invisible square with frankincense or sandalwood incense by walking round the square and then scattering your golden petal, herb or pollen circle.

If you cannot obtain beeswax candles, use plain white candles and place a tiny dish of honey to the right of the salt. Since the honey will also be empowered, you can absorb the protective magick by using it in a drink or sandwich.

❄ When the candles have burned down completely, clear away the crystals and wash them under running water.

Water

Because water is vital for life, it has become associated with rebirth and healing through the washing away of sins and disease, and so with protection from ills of all kinds.

Water for rituals must first be consecrated. You can use either pure spring water or tap water left for 24 hours in a crystal or clear glass container. Cover the water with mesh in the waxing or full moon and then leave out of doors to absorb the light of the Moon and the Sun for a full 24 hours. The full moon rises around sunset, so you can follow the old Celtic day (see the chapter on Planets and Angels). Even if you cannot see the light because of cloud, the energies are still potent.

In formal magick, consecrated water is placed in the West in a special bowl. In the home, it is good to keep a supply of sacred water ready for use at all times: purify objects and areas by sprinkling it, add it to your bath, drink it, put it in your pets' bowl and use it to water your plants.

One way of unobtrusively absorbing the protection of sacred water is to keep some in a mineral water bottle so you can dab it on your wrists and temples at times of stress or take a drink if you feel worried or under threat from a person who exudes hostility.

Add a little to the cup when making tea or coffee for an adversary. You are not giving away your power but, by the Threefold Law, creating harmony in the source of the trouble. Sacred water can also be poured on earth that has become barren or spoiled and into polluted seas and rivers.

A ritual for consecrating water

If you are carrying out a special healing or protective ritual, you might wish to use this slightly more complex method of creating sacred water. It is possible to buy or obtain water from holy wells, usually in return for a donation towards the upkeep of the well, and some commercially bottled spring water comes from sacred wells. For example, the healing water from Prime's Well, in the Malvern Hills, where the hero in Langland's poem *The Vision of Piers the Plowman* received his vision, is now piped and bottled as Malvern Spring Water, without which Queen Elizabeth II will not travel.

Use the following ritual to consecrate your bottled water, or, if you are in a hurry for your rituals, pass a pendulum nine times widdershins over it to remove any influences added in the bottling and nine times deosil to energise it. (A pendulum is made by hanging a crystal, or a piece of wood or metal on a chain and can be used to transmit answers to questions by its movements. Crystal pendulums are also used to catch the light of the Sun or Moon, thus adding the energies of these light forces.) Use a crystal or clear glass jug or decanter, if possible, in which to keep your water. The kind used for wine, with a stopper or lid, is best.

✿ Wash a clear, round crystal quartz (a stone used in many cultures to energise and purify water) under running water to remove any impurities introduced by the modern world. Place it in the bottom of your jug or decanter.

✿ Pour mineral water, from a sacred source if possible, into the jug. Some practitioners, following the ancient Celtic tradition, use water that has been boiled with nine quartz crystals added.

✿ Leave this water out of doors in a circle of white flowers or blossoms for 24 hours, where it will absorb the complete light cycle. If the Moon is not visible, because of clouds, burn a white candle or nightlight behind it.

✿ Pass a twig from one of the protective trees, such as rowan, ash, palm, thorn or olive, over it nine times widdershins to remove any lingering negativity.

✿ Finally, pass the twig over it nine times deosil to empower it, saying:

Water of the goddess, flowing from the Earth, filled with
lingering moonbeams, healing bring to birth.
Water filled with sunlight, crystal light empower, floral life
force entering, blessings on us shower.

Keep your sacred water on a special shelf in a cupboard and when it is almost empty pour what is left into a pond or lake and wash out the jug or decanter under running water.

Revitalising rainwater for use in rituals

Before the days of acid rain, practitioners of magick would use rainwater collected in a container before it touched the ground as sacred water. Nowadays, you may find it necessary to revitalise the rainwater you use with a few drops of flower essence. There are many brands available: Agrimony from Dr Bach's Flower Essences; Goatbeard from the Pacific Flower Essence Remedies; Coconut Palm from the African and Amazonian Essences; Alaskan soap berry; Deva Fig Tree or Morning Glory; and Findhorn rowan, all of which seem to work as purifiers for me. Flower and tree essences are created from the living energies of the plant and this spirit water is especially good for protective baths. (See pages 299 and 304 for further details.)

A protective water ritual

This ritual is particularly effective for removing the effects of spite or unfair criticism or a destructive encounter that has shaken your confidence.

It is based on an old custom whereby a rag was dipped into a holy well and the water rubbed on the body part that was causing pain. The rag was then left on a tree overhanging the well to dry and take with it the illness or pain, after which the rag was left to decay, so ensuring a permanent or long-term cure. These wells, called cloth or 'cloutie' wells in the north of England, are still a focus for protection and healing in many parts of the world, surrounded by ribbons and flowers.

You will need a large crystal or glass bowl for this ritual. Such bowls, frequently used in magick, are often obtainable cheaply from car boot or garage sales.

❀ Pour sacred water into the crystal bowl so that it is about half-full.

❀ Pass over the bowl three times deosil a silver coloured knife, or a traditional tool related to Air, saying:

One, twice, three times, by this blade of Air, by the mighty winds and the boundless sky, thrice thus do I charge this water with power and protection against all who would do or wish me harm.

❀ Dip a small piece of white cotton or flannel into your sacred water, saying:

Wash away the sorrow, wash away the pain, Father Sky and Sister Water, let but peace remain.

❀ Tie the cloth to a healing tree, such as ash, birch, aspen or willow (failing this, any tree or large plant in your garden or home will do) and leave the cloth to dry naturally. As you tie it, say:

As the sacred water returns to the sky to fall as life-enhancing rain, so may my – [name your unhappiness] be dispersed and transformed into joy and reconciliation.

Place a coin in a special pot every time you use your sacred water, so that when it is full you can buy a present for someone you love, a person who is lonely or ill or to give to a favourite charity.

CHAPTER 9
Healing Magick

Herbs have been used for healing since time immemorial in cultures all over the world. In herbal medicine, the herbs whose properties alleviate a particular illness or state of mind are taken internally or applied to the physical body externally. However, in healing magick, light and healing energies are transmitted through colour, crystals, herbs, oils and incenses and used as a focus for transferring healing energies to trigger the body and mind's own immune system, through visualisation and telepathic waves. In this way, healing magick is akin to spiritual healing.

By directing the natural restorative energies of the Earth, nature and the cosmos towards a sick or distressed person, animal or place through mind or soul flow, we can stimulate and amplify their self-healing powers.

A number of witches are formally trained in the healing arts, using both conventional methods, such as surgery, and alternative therapies, such as chiropractic, aromatherapy and Reiki. Witches may also be members of healing associations, and conventional medicine is increasingly recognising the value of alternative and much older methods.

But many witches without any formal training in either conventional medical treatment or spiritual healing follow the tradition of the wise men and women, the Wicca. These practitioners passed their craft down over centuries, from one generation to the next, but we also all have an innate ability to heal, which tells us how to soothe a loved one's headache or a child's distress. If you do wish to learn more of the craft see pages 299 and 305–7 where I have listed books on herbalism and aromatherapy and healing organisations. Unlike some modern physicians or surgeons, who sometimes regard the prolonging of life as the major purpose of their work, regardless of the quality of that life, many witch healers, like other spiritual healers, accept that sometimes decline and death are inevitable. So they work to ease the parting and the passing over, knowing that this life is not the end. Magical healing has a very gentle tradition.

You can carry out healing with the sick person present, by directing the light and energies towards them. This can be done, for example, through a candle flame set between you. Alternatively, you can circle a pendulum over their head, widdershins to remove pain for whole-body healing or to ease a painful place, and deosil to restore energies. If the subject is absent, you can visualise them and send healing light across the cosmos. Healing magick can also be used with your pets, and for more general purposes, such as healing a particular place or the planet (for example the water ritual to heal the polluted seas, given on page 102).

Do note that I am not claiming that the methods of magick healing given in this chapter will always effect a complete cure; if you suffer from a chronic or acute condition that does not quickly improve, you should consult your conventional doctor or registered alternative medical practitioner. However, magick has successfully been used in speeding healing, partly, it would seem, by stimulating the body's own self-healing system, operating through the close connection between mind, body and spirit in a way that the medical profession is only now beginning to understand.

Creating a healing sanctuary

Many practitioners use their magical altar for healing work and because each piece of work is related, this adds to the positive energies already concentrated there. However, if you have room, you might like to set aside a corner specifically for healing.

You can use a table or any flat surface for your altar. On it, you should keep a single, pure beeswax or white candle; this is a symbol of the unity of all life and the one divine source that flows through every natural being, whether it is male or female, god or goddess, animal, bird, fish, tree, plant or stone. You will also need your special healing crystals, perhaps arranged in a circle around the candle and a clear crystal sphere or crystal pendulum for directing sunlight and moonlight. The crystals could include gentle rose quartz and amethyst for healing all ills and bringing harmony, moonstone for female and hormonal disorders and for fertility, citrine for energy and lifting depression, and agates for balancing energies. Later in this section I have listed some healing crystals I use under their different colours, as these are related to healing properties. You can also refer to the list of crystals in the previous chapter on psychic protection.

You can also keep here pots of healing herbs, seasonal fruit, flowers, nuts and seeds that will be empowered by the healing energies. These can regularly be given to anyone feeling tired or anxious – not forgetting yourself.

A covered jar of empowered salt (see page 161) and a bottle of sacred water (see page 163) are also important. However, you might like to bless them before use, in the name of the Goddess, a healing deity (see page 78) or simply the powers of goodness and light, by passing them three times over the healing candle flame.

You will also need somewhere to keep all you need for your healing work that you can also use in more general magical work with a healing focus. You might have a box at the side of the altar, or, if you adapt a cupboard for your altar, you could use the space inside it. In this place you would have your dried herbs, healing oils and incenses, favourite flower essences, coloured bottles containing empowered water and small crystals or glass nuggets. You could also collect twigs or small carved artefacts from healing trees, such as ash, olive, rowan, palm and aspen. (See page 139 for details of incenses and page 128 for information on oils.)

On the table in front of the candle you could keep a special healing book in which you could write the names of people or places you know who need healing. These could include pets, a hospital or hospice with which you have connections, sanctuaries for injured creatures, threatened species and places. It is better to have this separate, rather than as part of your Book of Shadows, but if you prefer you can use your Book of Shadows for both areas of work.

You might also like to keep a special 'Loving Connections' section for the names of friends or family members who are away from home and may be feeling lonely, and also anyone from whom you are estranged.

A bound journal with blank pages is good for this kind of work or you could buy a leather loose-leaf binder and insert blank pages with dates. If you work in a group, one member can be responsible for regularly updating the book.

A ritual for creating healing magick

Each evening or morning – or whenever you have time – light your healing candle and hold one of your special crystals and your crystal sphere or pendulum and focus on of the names in your book, sending the candlelight reflected though the crystal to wherever it is needed. The traditional healing hour is ten o' clock at night, but what is more important is that the time is one where you can be quiet and are not pressurised by other demands. Begin by holding a healing crystal and focusing the energies through the candle flame; you can then extend this ritual for specific healing purposes.

You will need a photograph, newspaper cutting or symbol of the person, animal or place to which you are sending healing energies.

❀ Take a dish of sacred water and place it near the candle.

❀ Hold the symbol of the person to be healed between your hands and speak a few words of love and reassurance as though they were with you. If you have already created for the sick person a herb poppet (see page 108) or sachet (see page 106), hold that between your hands and repeat the original herb empowerment or sit in silence recreating the ritual in your mind. You can add words of healing as above. If the object of the healing is a place, such as a lake or woodland under threat, imagine that you are in that place.

❀ Circle your crystal pendulum or a pointed healing crystal over the symbol (or sachet or poppet) nine times widdershins, saying as a mantra:

Go, pain and sorrow, change to star or sunbeam, transformed in joy and in tranquillity.

❀ Plunge the pendulum into the water and hold it to the light so the drops of water fall off and scatter as rainbow light beams all around the symbol. You can also create the light beams by angling your candle or hanging rainbow crystals in your window. It is not cheating, but directing natural forces for a purpose and infusing physical light beams with spiritual energies. Mirrors are another good way of reflecting light beams.

❀ Now circle the pendulum nine times deosil over the symbol, saying:

Sunbeam, star beam, rays of light, replace, restore, renew, rejoice.

❀ Blow out the candle, sending the light to the sick or sorrowing person, saying:

Go, light of healing, radiance of love and friendship, to where you are needed most this night, with – [name the person, animal or location].

May blessings fall, darkness and doubts recede into nothingness.
So may it be in the name of all that is good and loving and pure
[or 'in the name of the Goddess', if you prefer].

If you are feeling ill, worried or afraid you can go to your healing place and light the candle, holding your favourite crystal and expressing softly your needs and fears. However, the more healing you carry out for others, the more harmony will fall on you under the Threefold Law.

If you are working with friends or in a group, after showering it with light beams, pass the symbol round to each person, adding individual blessings. Give each person a small, white candle to set before them so that they can personally send light and blessings.

The words can be spoken as a joint mantra or chant.

A short ritual for absent healing

This can be carried out once a month for those who regularly need your help and support. Use natural candles such as beeswax rather than paraffin-based for this ritual if possible.

* Light your healing candle and burn rose or lavender incense or a healing oil, such as chamomile or rosewood.

* Read through all the names in your healing book, adding any new ones to the list and giving thanks for any who have recovered.

* Speak your own prayer or mantra to your god, the Goddess, or any healing deities who seem appropriate. You may call upon an Archangel (see page 236) or the benign powers of Light and Love, if this seems more meaningful. Each person present can again add blessings.

* Leave the candle and incense to burn away and bury any ash or wax afterwards in the earth beneath a tree.

A healing ritual with sunlight and moonlight

This is a very magical form of healing and can be carried out either alone or as a group activity. Quartz crystal balls were traditionally used medicinally to concentrate the rays of sunlight upon a diseased or painful area of the body or in the direction of some internal organ. This clear crystal stone has always been associated with energising powers and with healing. In its spherical form of completeness, it is perhaps the ultimate healing and magical stone. You can buy tiny spheres quite cheaply and these work just as well as a large crystal ball.

Sunlight is good for energising and improving physical health and vitality, encouraging regrowth and regeneration, and for matters of the mind where clarity and optimism are needed.

Moonlight is potent for removing illness or pain and for all problems concerning emotions, hormones or fertility and is especially effective in healing women, children and pets.

❈ Direct the sunlight or the light of the full moon into your crystal sphere, so that it shines on the person you are healing, or their photograph or other symbol. If you are using sunlight, be careful that the crystal does not become too hot and of course do not look directly at the image of the Sun.

❈ Stand in a circle in the open air and in the centre, place a dish of pure spring water. Use a golden coloured bowl for sunlight, and a silver bowl for moonlight.

❈ Into the water, drop tiny clear quartz crystals (if you are working in a group, each person adds one crystal). As you cast the crystals, make a wish for healing the sick or distressed person.

❈ Hold a crystal pendulum and swirl it on its chain to catch within it either rainbows or sunbeams, or the silver light of the Moon.

❈ Cast the beams into the water, calling:

Go forth with love and healing.

You can, if you prefer, create your own words.

❈ Pour the water into a clear glass bottle with a stopper and send or give it to the sick person. They may drink it or use it in a bath.

❈ Return the energies to the cosmos by placing yellow flowers or seeds in a pot for the golden energies if you used sunlight, and white flowers for the Moon.

Colour healing

Colour has long been believed to have the power to influence not only our moods, but our physical well-being. The Babylonians called the healing power of light 'the medicine of the gods'. Healing colours have been used for thousands of years in Chinese treatments and in Ayurveda, an ancient Indian medicine. The Ancient Egyptians wore amulets of coloured stones: red to treat disease, yellow for happiness and prosperity, and green for fertility.

Colour healing is not just a fancy: we know for a fact that each beam of coloured light has its own wavelength and is absorbed by the body through the skin and the optic nerves. This triggers complex biochemical changes. Each of the seven primary wavelengths or vibrations of light visible to the human eye focuses on different parts of the body, evoking in them both a physiological and psychological response. Red has the longest wavelength of visible colour and violet the shortest. The colours that we can see make up only a very small segment of the electromagnetic spectrum and lie between the infra red and ultra violet rays.

Methods of using colour for healing

You can use specific colours to charge water with magical healing energies. You can then drink this water or pour it into your bath, to absorbing the essence of the colour. You can also place one of the appropriately coloured healing crystals listed below in water for a few hours to increase its life force.

Coloured candles may also be used: light a candle in the appropriate colour, then breathe in the specific colour energies and exhale the darkness. This can be practised alone either for your own benefit or to direct the colour energies towards a sick person.

Colour breathing, which is used to create a cone of power (see page 40) is another healing method. You can also co-ordinate healing breathing within a group, again directing the energies to where they are needed.

Healing with crystals and colour

The healing colour associations listed here are drawn from a variety of traditions and my own experience. You may find that for you the colour correspondences are different – this is the reason there are so many alternative systems. I have included the key colours here, but you can also refer back to the colour correspondences that I mentioned from page 90 onwards in the section on candles.

White/clear

White is for limitless potential, clarity of vision, the life force, integration, seeking what is of worth.

White can form a focus for all kinds of healing since it is the synthesis of all other colours. It promotes health and healing, integration of mind, body and soul. White light is a natural pain-reliever, and can help to protect against cerebral disorders, increase breast milk in nursing mothers, speed the mending of broken bones and relieve calcium deficiency and toothache.

Clear crystals include diamonds, clear crystal quartz, zircon and pure white stones, especially those from the sea.

Red

Red is for power, courage, energy and vitality.

Red restores energy levels and is good for raising blood pressure and improving circulation, promoting cellular growth and activity; red crystals are used in healing blood ailments, especially anaemia. Red light is linked to reproduction and fertility and relieves sexual dysfunction especially impotence; it also helps with pains in feet, hands and bones.

Red crystals include agate, jasper, pyrites and garnets.

Orange

Orange is for confidence, assimilation of knowledge and experience, personal desire and needs, the boundaries between self and others.

Orange, like red, is a colour of energy and warmth, easing arthritis, rheumatism and increasing the pulse rate, relieving gall-bladder and kidney pains and stones, menstrual and muscle cramps and allergies, and lifting exhaustion. Orange is also used to strengthen the immune system.

Orange crystals include amber, agate, coral and carnelian.

Yellow

Yellow is for happiness, the mind, intellect, communication and will-power.

Yellow stimulates the nervous system, improving memory and concentration, easing eczema and other skin problems; it also promotes a healthy metabolism and calms anxiety and stress-related ailments that may affect the digestive system adversely.

Yellow crystals include jasper, topaz, calcite and citrine.

Green

Green is for the heart, emotions, peace and balance and all gentle regrowth.

Green lowers high blood pressure, acting as a restorative for the heart, lungs and respiratory system and fighting infections and viruses, especially influenza, bronchitis, fevers and colds. It also counters panic attacks, addictions and food-related illnesses. Green is a good healing colour because it stimulates tissue and cell growth and general body regeneration.

Green crystals include jade, malachite, olivine (peridot), emerald and cat's eye.

Turquoise

Turquoise is for tranquillity, empathy, altruism and wisdom.

Turquoise strengthens the immune system, soothes inflammation and calms the nerves. It helps to relieve asthmatic and general respiratory difficulties and skin complaints such as eczema, swellings and thyroid problems.

Turquoise crystals include aquamarine, malachite, opal and turquoise.

Blue

Blue is for ideals, the expansion both of perspective and physical horizons and authority, and for allowing what is not of value to be gradually replaced by higher purpose and direction.

Blue is called the healing colour because a blue aura is often seen around healers. It is a soothing and cooling natural antiseptic, relieving burns, cuts, bruises, insomnia, inflammation of the skin and mouth, sore throats and childhood rashes and teething pains; blue also lowers high temperatures and high blood pressure. All shades of blue, such as violet and indigo, reduce migraines and headaches.

Blue crystals include sodalite, lapis lazuli, sapphire, blue lace agate and turquoise.

Purple

Purple is for inner vision, psychic awareness and spirituality, the colour of the evolving soul.

Purple is cleansing and uplifting, counteracting doubts and negativity.

Within the range of purples, specific shades are good for certain areas of the body, though in practice they are usually interchangeable.

Indigo helps to ease eye, ear, nose and skin problems and migraines, and soothes the nervous system. It aids healing of deep tissue and bones and is a natural sedative.

Lavender increases the power of all herbs, oils and flower and tree essences used in healing.

Violet is effective for treating allergies, asthma, sleep disorders and stress-related illnesses.

Purple crystals include amethyst, sugilite, sodalite, peacock's eye (bornite) and purple kunzite.

Rose

Rose (or pink) is for unconditional love, reconciliation and gentleness and for soothing loss.

Rose is the gentle healer, promoting restful sleep, pleasant dreams and optimism. Ear, eye and gland problems, head pains and psychosomatic illnesses fall under its auspices, as do disorders relating to children and babies, especially fretfulness and hyperactivity.

Rose crystals include pink kunzite, rose quartz, tourmaline and coral.

Magenta

Magenta is for spirituality expressed in the everyday world, for originality of vision and for a path of service to others.

Magenta is good for all matters concerning the mid-life crisis, menopause and anything that blocks physical or spiritual fertility.

Magenta crystals include sugilite, rhodonite and rhodoschrite.

Brown

Brown is for nurturing powers, for acceptance of frailty in oneself and others, and earthing power. Brown heals stress, restores physical energy and gives the strength to go on under difficulty. It aids the healing of the feet, legs, hands, skeleton and large intestine. It also heals the Earth and its animals.

Brown crystals include rutilated quartz, tiger's eye, fossilised wood, desert rose and leopardskin jasper.

Grey

Grey is the colour of compromise, adaptability and the ability to merge into the background, and keep one's own counsel.

Grey is good for healing the immune system and for calming stress and fears, giving peaceful dreams and helping the subconscious mind to work though conflicts. It is also good for bones.

Grey crystals include smoky quartz, apache tears and grey-banded agate.

Black

Black is for transitions, regeneration, acceptance of life as it is, the positive confrontation of mortality and an awareness that we are all ultimately alone.

Black heals the feet, legs and bones, and helps to heal trauma and leave behind old stresses and anxieties. It encourages rest, cures insomnia and assists in working through loss. It is used only rarely in healing, followed by the infusion of light as, unless used carefully, it can bring out dormant depression. Breathing out black and darkness and breathing in light and colour is very restorative.

Black crystals include jet, apache tears, smoky quartz and onyx.

Silver

Silver is for meaningful dreams, visions, a desire for fulfilment beyond the material world and hidden potential.

Silver alleviates hormonal problems in men and women, regularises and heals the female menstrual and reproduction system and assists in all matters of fertility. It eases water retention and nightmares.

Silver crystals include moonstones, whose colour deepens as the Moon waxes, haematite, mother of pearl, snow and milky quartz and rutilated quartz.

Gold

Gold is for perfection, immortality and peak experiences, visions and the achievement of major life goals, especially those that change the world.

Gold is especially potent for overcoming addictions, obsessions and compulsions and relieving depression. Gold is the most powerful healing colour of all, associated with long life and immortality, and will give a surge of healing energy in any chronic or debilitating illnesses.

Gold crystals include amber, golden tiger's eye, topaz and citrine.

A colour healing ritual with candles

Candles of specific colours can help in the healing process. If you are not certain of the root of a problem, you can use a white or pure beeswax candle, plus, if you wish, one for the perceived area of pain. For your monthly major healing sessions, this ritual can be used after the names have been read, working with pink or white candles to include everyone in the book who is sick or sad. It is especially good for chronic conditions or when healing may take some time. This is a gentler method than creating a cone of colour. Early evening just after dusk is a good time to work.

 Choose a candle of the appropriate colour. Extinguish all other lights.

✤ If the person to be healed is present, they can work with you in building up the energies. Sit on cushions on either side of the candle, allowing room for movement.

✤ Place a dish of small dish of dried rosemary or lavender for general healing next to the candle. If the healing is for yourself or for someone who is absent, light the candle. If you are working as a group, sit in a circle, each person holding their own coloured candle (you can make rainbow with different colours round the circle if you wish), with a large white candle in the centre. Each person will also need a small dish of herbs.

✤ Gaze into the flame and if there are others present, ask them to do the same, gently drawing in the coloured light and exhaling darkness or pain.

✤ Breathe in and take in the light, as you do so saying in your mind:

Welcome, light.

✤ Hold the breath while you mentally count 'One and two and three', then send out the healing energies, saying silently:

Farewell, pain [or sorrow, darkness, etc.].

✤ Continue to breathe and visualise the colour entering and radiating and the darkness or pain fading away. If you are working in a group, one person can sit near the central candle and speak the words or drum the rhythm of the breathing. You may hear clairaudiently (in your mind) the collective voices rising and falling. After a time, you will see with your mind's eye that the same colour breath is being inhaled and exhaled by each person, and at this stage the healing energies are balanced.

✤ Gently circle your arms over your head and sway from side to side, either sitting, kneeling or standing, while scattering gently your healing herbs like a gentle shower of rain (your hair will shine wonderfully when you next wash it). At the same time, chant softly:

Go forth, increase and multiply, cosmic light intensify, healing Earth and Sea and Sky.

✤ When the energies feel right, add to the last chant a final long melodious *'Heal!'* and extinguish the candle(s), letting the light and sound fade into the silence.

✤ Press your hands and feet gently to the ground and let the energies flow back into the Earth, saying softly:

We thank you, Mother Earth, for healing blessings soon to be received.

Healing with water and coloured glass

Spring water placed in glass bottles of the appropriate colour will absorb the colour energies and can be used in rituals of all kinds, magical as well as healing. They can be further empowered by adding crystals of the same colour as the bottle to the water. If possible, work out of doors. You can use this method for endowing living energies into any symbol of healing, such as an amulet, popper, sachet or even a photograph of the person to be healed. Use bottles with stoppers or corks (these can be obtained from most household shops or from antique stalls). Build up your collection so that you have a bottle of the correct colour for every need. Although the water retains its clear colour, some people are able to detect a faint glow of the colour.

As before, the water can be drunk or added to a bath, in order to benefit from the energies. You can also add water to an animal bowl or a place in which wild birds come to drink, use it for plants that are failing to thrive or pour some in a polluted water source or on barren land. Look back to the list on pages 172–76 to find the correct coloured glass to use for each occasion. You will remember, for example, that water from a pink or indigo bottle will bring harmony and gentle healing calm. But more specifically, a drink in a teenager's lunch box made with pink water will heal any hurts and fears a sensitive youngster experiences in the outside world. Clear water to which a quartz crystal has been added is an instant energiser, transmitting the life force in concentrated form.

You can use the colour-infused water in rituals to send healing to a species, people or place far away by sprinkling a circle of water around a picture or symbol.

You can empower a larger quantity than you immediately need, and pour it into small bottles of different colours, preserved in your fridge for future healing work when they are needed. By combining the magical and healing colour associations of the different colours, you can adapt your empowered waters for almost any need.

Water made in a soft blue bottle empowered with a blue lace agate softens harsh words: use it for making coffee if difficult relatives come to call. A darker blue, perhaps empowered in a deep blue bottle with a sodalite crystal, is calming and so the infused colour would help to alleviate panic experienced when flying. Just moisten a small cloth with it, take the cloth on to the aircraft and dab it on your temples and pulse points on take-off and landing or at other times when you feel panic rising.

Healing the body is only one small part of health and so you should experiment and note any uses you find for your infused waters. Take some colour-charged water to work or to a difficult social event in a mineral water bottle. In my on-going struggle with my weight, I have found that orange water in which a carnelian has been soaked is wonderful for restoring balance and self-esteem and so preventing food binges.

A healing ritual with coloured glass

This method of healing is one of the oldest in traditional folk magick, using the equivalent of the ceremonial elemental substances that I wrote of in Chapter 6. Folk magick was originally based on substances that have comprised the diet of ordinary people for thousands of years. They are all infused symbolically as well as actually with the life force.

🌸 Empower your water, if you wish, and pour it into the chosen coloured bottle. Close your bottle and surround it with a circle of fruits, unprocessed food, flowers or crystals of the colour to be used. Leave space between the bottle and the edge of the circle.

🌸 Inside the circle, to the North of the bottle, place a large golden, white or orange vegetable, preferably grown under or close to the ground. This represents the fruits of the Earth, born of the Earth Mother.

🌸 In the East of the circle, place some seeds or nuts that represent the source of new life and potential.

🌸 In the South, set a small dish of honey, which is considered as sacred as salt in many traditions and is especially associated with healing.

🌸 Finally, in the West, place a seed roll or bread, representing the cutting down of the corn, so completing the cycle.

❀ Take a twig or a wand from a healing tree, such as ash, or a long frond of greenery and walk round the circle deosil. Infuse each of the magical foods in turn with circles of the wand deosil, saying:

Fruits of the Earth, born from the womb of the land, give life and healing, health and joy from your ever-replenishing store.

❀ Touch the vegetable with the wand and then lift the wand in a high arc before lowering it to touch the bottle of water in the centre.

❀ Now move to the East and circle the wand deosil over the seeds, saying:

Seeds of potential, from the loins of the Father, give growth and power, possibility and regeneration from your limitless treasury.

❀ Touch the seeds with the wand and raising it in a high arc as before, project the energy into the bottle.

❀ Go now to the South and circle the wand deosil over the honey, saying:

Melissa, Mother Bee, bring abundance, warmth, sweetness and nourishment from your ever-replenishing hives.

Touch the dish and transfer the energies as before to the water.

❀ Finally, go to the West and circle the wand over the bread, saying:

Corn Father, willing offering of the life-sustaining bread, bring an ease to sorrow and suffering and the peace and fulfilment of healing harvest home.

❀ Touch the bread with the wand and transfer the energies as before to the water.

❀ Finally, pass the bottle of water over the vegetable, seeds, honey and bread, saying:

Fruit and seed, nectar and corn, enrich, empower and endow this water with your healing powers and the life force that flows though our lives and through all creation.

Eat the empowered food to boost your own energies and to spread calm or healing.

CHAPTER 10
Ritual Magick

Ritual magick is no different from any other activity that you may carry out in a systematic way. Yes, it is true, it is more formal than folk magick: you are using special tools and following a series of pre-ordained steps based on traditional practice. But this does not mean that it has to be so complicated as to be beyond the capabilities of any normal person. You do not need special powers; and the preparation is just the same as you would do if you were redecorating a room, servicing your car or preparing your annual accounts. When you decide to do any of these tasks, you set out the necessary equipment in advance, so you are not constantly dashing off to find what you need. You check that it is all in working order and you probably consult a reliable reference book, computer software or calculator to clarify the necessary stages and finer points of the method. And that is exactly what preparing for ritual magick is like.

First, you need to collect any relevant information; for example, you must find out which tools, herbs, candle colours, etc. you may require. Then you must check that your magical tools are charged with power. You must check whether the hour and the day are well chosen to benefit from the energies and are most aligned to the focus. If you are working with a group, you must decide in advance who is to carry the salt and other elemental substances round the circle, who will perform particular parts of the ritual, such as welcoming the Spirit Guardians.

This preparation is important, although, as I have previously said, many of the words and actions in the best rituals remain spontaneous within the basic framework. You do not even need to belong to a coven to create beautiful rituals. Indeed, practising alone, you will find that as you increase in confidence, the natural rhythm of the ritual cycle will amplify your own innate powers and you will feel angelic or devic forces joining with you as you walk around the circle and hear their voices mingling with your chants.

You should not allow yourself to be overawed, as I have been in the past and still occasionally am, by books and practitioners who vaunt their knowledge of obscure magical phrases, measure their circles down to the last millimetre and insist that only their form of working is authentic. What matters is the actual connection you make in your ritual with the storehouse of natural and higher energies – and that can be done with a kitchen candle if the need is great and the intention pure. Ultimately, the power is within you, and as you become skilled with magick, you may find that the external form becomes less important.

However, formal magick does have its place, for a special need or for raising spiritual awareness, or for focusing magical energies through the accumulated power of tools charged and regularly used for positive purpose. Some people believe also that in ritual you tap into the energies of all those before you who have created circles of power and protection, and within them have raised and called upon the elemental qualities to bring desires and needs from the thought to the material plane.

The aims of formal rituals

Rituals and spells at all levels cause a positive change or effect, whether for oneself, a loved one or the whole ecosystem, as they bring healing, peace, reconciliation or whatever is needed in the spell-caster's life. But over and above all these is the purpose of raising one's own levels of awareness so that perhaps for a few moments you feel connected to a higher power, perhaps even the source of divinity, and this is best expressed though the more ceremonial forms of work. The awareness you attain may be experienced as a sense of deep peace, of being filled with golden light, of floating through clouds or a certainty of being loved and protected, perhaps even as a glimpse of a Divinity.

Formal rituals do not have to be focused on a particular aim, however. Sometimes, you may wish to carry out a ritual without having any specific purpose in mind. In this case, you can simply cast a circle and raise the energies gently through a natural focus of herbs, flowers or fruit, allowing wisdom to be channelled through you and then giving thanks for blessings received as you close the circle.

The tools of ritual magick

Formal ritual magick requires its own special tools. These may be real or symbolic.

The list I give here is intended only as a guide: some of these may not be relevant to your own way of working. I have listed the areas of the circle in which each tool is traditionally placed. There are many sources of magical tools and, as I mentioned in the section on spells, you may already have a number in your home. You do not need to spend a great deal of money unless you wish, but I would suggest that you take time in finding the right items. Even if you work in a group, you may like to build up a set for your own personal work.

Some people prefer to make their own magical tools and this certainly does endow them with energies. I have suggested books that tell you how to make your own candles for special ceremonies and even your own knife. Woodcarvers are an excellent source for small staves suitable as wands and will often make items to order. In time, you will build up a collection of items and by personalising and charging them, you make them not only powerful, but also your own.

Keep your magical tools in a special place, separate from your everyday household items, wrapped in a natural fabric. You can buy excellent hessian bags and may wish to keep fragile or items that will scratch in separate ones. You can also use silk. Secure your bags with three protective knots.

You may have heard various warnings about needing to destroy charged tools on the demise of the owner, and the dire consequences of their being touched by any outsider. This is real late-night-cinema stuff. But common sense dictates that you should not leave knives, sharp wands, etc. where children might harm themselves and on the whole it is better to keep magical items away from the curious and the sceptical.

There is really no reason why you should not use your kitchen knife for cutting vegetables and then, after a quick purification in water or incense, chop herbs in an impromptu spell, or open your circle with it. But on the whole it is better to keep a separate knife for your special ceremonies.

I believe that even formal tools are like electrical devices that are lying unplugged and unused: they contain the potential to help or harm only if misused. What is more, without your personal vibes, which act as your password, the power cannot flow; you have not created an independent life form.

The following tools are commonly used in formal magick.

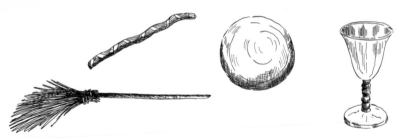

The athame

An athame is, quite simply, a ceremonial knife. It is one of the ritual tools that entered the tradition through the influence of magicians and witches who set out the wisdom, mainly at the beginning of the twentieth century and in the upsurge of covens during the 1950s. Gerald Gardener, one of the founding fathers of Wicca, considered ritual knives and swords of prime importance in modern formal witchcraft.

You can obtain an athame from a specialist magical shop (see page 303), but as I said before, any knife – even a letter-opener – will do, although it should preferably have a silver-coloured blade. Athames are traditionally double-edged and black-handled, but a single-edged blade is better if you are new to magick, to avoid unintentional cuts.

There is a vast array of scouting and craft knives available, with black wooden handles on which you can engrave magical symbols such as your zodiacal and planetary glyphs (see page 93) with a pyrographic set obtained from an art shop. You can also paint moons, stars, spirals, suns, or crosses with silver paint. I use a curved-bladed knife with a silver engraved scabbard, which I bought from a souvenir shop in Spain.

The athame is set in the East of the altar and represents the element of Air. Like the sword, it is traditionally used for drawing magical circles on the ground and directing magical Air energies into a symbol. When you are casting a circle, you can point your athame diagonally towards the ground, so that you do not need to stoop to draw (which is not very elegant and bad for the back). With practice, the movement becomes as graceful as with a sword.

The athame can also be used as a conductor of energy, especially in solitary rituals, being held above the head with both hands to draw down light and energy into the body. This uses the same principle as that of arching your arms over your head to create a light body as described on page 124. One method of releasing the power is then to bring the athame down with a swift, cutting movement, horizontally at waist level, then thrust it away from the body and upwards once more to release this power. If others are present, direct the athame towards the centre of the circle. After the ritual you can drain excess energies by pointing the athame to the ground.

An athame may be used to invoke the elemental Guardian Spirits by drawing a pentagram (see page 203) in the air and for closing down the elemental energies after the ritual. With its cutting steel of Mars, it is effective in power, matters of the mind, change, action, justice, banishing magick, protection and for cutting through inertia and stagnation. The athame is sometimes also associated with the Fire element.

If you don't like the idea of a full-sized athame, there are some lovely paper knives in the shape of swords or with animal or birds' heads.

Some covens give each of their members a tiny athame, to be used for drawing down energies during ceremonies. The main athame is used by the person leading the ritual who may draw the circle, open all four quarters and close them after the ritual.

An athame with a white handle is used for cutting wands, harvesting herbs for magick or healing, carving the traditional Samhain jack-o'-lantern, and etching runes and other magical or astrological symbols on candles and talismans. Some practitioners believe that you should never use metal for cutting herbs but instead pull them up, shred them and pound them in a mortar and pestle, kept for the purpose. Pearl-handled athames are considered to be especially magical.

The sword

Like the athame, the sword stands in the East of the circle as a tool of the Air element. Swords are the suit symbol of Air in the Tarot and are also one of the Christian as well as the Celtic Grail treasures. Each of the Tarot suits and the main elemental ritual items in magick, represented by these four suits, is associated with one of the treasures of the Celts. The treasures belonged to the Celtic Father God, Dagda, and are said to be guarded in the Otherworld by Merlin. There were 13 treasures in total, but four have come into pre-eminence in magick and Tarot reading. These four main sacred artefacts – swords, pentacles, wands and cups, or chalices – have parallels in Christianity and were associated with the legendary quest of the knights of King Arthur, who attempted to find them. The Grail Cup was the most famous of these. The Christian sword of King David, identified in legend with Arthur's sword Excalibur, appears in Celtic tradition as the sword of Nuada whose hand was cut off in battle. With a new hand fashioned from silver, he went on to lead his people to victory. According to one account, the Christian treasures were brought in AD 64 to Glastonbury in England by Joseph of Arimathea, the rich merchant who caught Christ's blood in the chalice as He was on the cross and took care of His burial after the crucifixion.

Some present-day, peace-loving witches, myself included, do not really like the concept of using swords, even though they are pretty spectacular for drawing out a circle on a forest floor, and swords are rarely used in home ritual magick. If you do want to use one, however, you can obtain reproduction ceremonial swords.

The sword is the male symbol to the female symbol of the cauldron, and plunging the swords into the waters of the cauldron can be used in love rituals and for the union of male and female, god and goddess energies as the culmination of any rite. However, the chalice and the athame, or wand, tend to be used for the same purpose, unless it is a very grand ceremony.

The bell

The bell stands in the North of the circle and is an Earth symbol. It is an optional tool and can be made from either crystal or protective brass. Best for magick is the kind that you strike.

The bell is traditionally rung nine times at the beginning and close of each ritual; the person ringing the bell should stand in the South of the circle, facing North. (Nine is the magical number of completion and perfection.) It is also rung to invoke the protection of angels or the power of a deity and in ceremonies to welcome departed members to the circle. You can also sound the bell in each of the four elemental quadrants, before creating the invoking pentagram (see page 203), to request the presence of each elemental guardian. It can also be sounded as you pass your chosen symbol around each quadrant of the circle. However, you should not use the bell to excess – it is better under-utilised.

The broom

The broom, or besom, was originally – and still is – a domestic artefact. It represents magically the union of male and female in the handle and the bristles and so is a tool of balance. Brooms have several uses in magick. A broom is sometimes rested horizontal to the altar to add protection, and couples jump over one in their handfasting ceremony. Most important, you should use your broom to cleanse the ritual area before every ritual.

Brooms are easily obtainable from any garden centre (you want one in the traditional 'witches' broomstick' shape, not an ordinary brush). Brooms made with an ash handle and birch twigs bound with willow are traditionally recognised as being especially potent, being endowed with protective and healing energies. Some practitioners carve or paint a crescent moon at the top of the handle, others decorate theirs with their personal ruling planetary and birth sign glyphs entwined.

When cleansing the area for rituals, you might like to scatter dried lavender or pot pourri and sweep it in circles widdershins, saying:

Out with sorrow, out with pain, Joyous things alone remain.

(See the spring-cleaning ritual on page 254).

You can also sweep areas of your home such as uncarpeted floors, patio paths and yards to cleanse the home of negativity. Remember to sweep out of the front door, away from the house and eventually into the gutter, or if in you live in a flat, you can collect the lavender and dust in a pan and send it down the waste disposal unit.

You may also wish to cleanse the area further by sprinkling salt and pepper dissolved in water after sweeping. If you are working on carpet, you can use a very soft broom (some modern witches even hoover in circles widdershins and sprinkle the area with water in which a few drops of a cleansing flower essence, such as Glastonbury Thorn, has been added).

The broom is an Earth artefact.

The cauldron

The cauldron is the one ritual tool that is positively charged by being the centre of domestic life and can replace the altar as a focus for less formal magick spells. If you can obtain a flameproof cauldron with a tripod, you can, on special occasions such as Hallowe'en, light a fire out of doors and heat up a brew of herbs and spices in the cauldron. When not in use, you can keep your cauldron filled with flowers or pot pourri.

If your circle is large enough, you can place your cauldron in the centre. Then, if you are working in a group, form your circle of power around it, so that the altar is within the outer consecrated circle and you make a human inner circle with the cauldron as the hub. If you are working alone, you can have your altar in the centre with the cauldron in front of it. Alternatively, you can have a small pot or cauldron in the centre of the altar.

Experiment with the different positions both for group and solitary work and walk or dance your way around to work out the logistics. Some practitioners do not use a cauldron at all.

In your rituals, you can light a candle in front of the cauldron, fill it with sand in which to stand candles, or surround it with a circle of red candles to represent Fire. Wishes written on paper can be burned in the candles. Water darkened with mugwort may be placed in the cauldron, especially on seasonal festivals such as Hallowe'en and May Eve, and white candle wax dripped on the surface to create divinatory images that offer insights into potential paths.

You can cast flower petals into the cauldron water to get energies flowing. For banishing, add dead leaves and tip the cauldron water into a flowing source of water. You can also burn incense in the cauldron if this is the focus of a ritual.

The cauldron is a tool of Spirit or *Akasha*, the fifth element.

The chalice

The chalice, or ritual cup, used for rituals is traditionally made of silver, but you can also use crystal, glass, stainless steel or pewter. The chalice represents the Water element and is placed in the West of the altar. Like the sword, it is a sacred Grail treasure (see page 185) and is a source of spiritual inspiration. The Grail cup is most usually represented as the chalice that Christ used at the Last Supper, in which His blood was collected after the crucifixion. As such, it signifies not only a source of healing and spiritual sustenance, but also offers direct access to the godhead through the sacred blood it once contained. Tradition says that the original Grail cup was incorporated by Roman craftsmen into a gold and jewelled chalice called the Marian Chalice after Mary Magdalene. In Celtic tradition, it became the Cauldron of Dagda (see page 68). In rituals, the chalice can be filled with pure or scented water with rose petals floating on top. I have also mentioned its ritual use with the athame in male/female sacred rites, as the symbolic union of god and goddess that has in many modern covens replaced an actual sexual union (that now tends to occur in privacy between established couples only).

The chalice is also central to the sacred rite of cakes and ale that occurs at the end of formal ceremonies – the pagan and much older equivalent of the Christian holy communion. The offering of the body of the Corn God is made in the honey cakes on the pentacle, or sacred dish, and the beer or wine in the chalice is fermented from the sacrificed barley wine. In primaeval times, actual blood was used to symbolise the sacrifice of the Sacred King at Lughnassadh, the festival of the first corn harvest (see page 264). The rite goes back thousands of years.

The cakes and ale are consumed by the people acting as High Priestess and Priest in a dual energy rite or by those initiated in those roles. Crumbs and wine are first offered to the Earth Mother or poured into a libation dish (a small dish for offerings). Then the priestess offers the priest a tiny cake and then takes one herself and he offers her the wine before drinking himself. The dual roles work just as well in a single-sex coven. The cakes and ale are then passed round the circle and each person partakes of the body and blood of the Earth, offering a few words of thanks for blessings received.

In some groups each person has an individual chalice set before them, but everyone still drinks one after the other, offering thanks, unless there is a communal chant of blessing before drinking.

The chalice can be filled with wine or fruit juice or water, depending on the needs and preferences of the group.

The cakes and ale ceremony and the male/female chalice rite can both be easily incorporated into a solitary ritual.

The pentacle

The pentacle is a symbol of the Earth and is familiar to users of Tarot packs. It is placed in the North of the altar.

It consists of a flat, round dish or disc, engraved with a pentagram within a circle, (see page 203 for an explanation of the pentagram and how to draw one). The pentacle has been a magical sign for thousands of years. The five-pointed star of the pentagram within it is a sacred symbol of Isis and the single top point is considered by many to represent the Triple Goddess.

You can place crystals or a symbol of the focus of the ritual or charged herbs on the pentacle to endow it with Earth energies. It can then be passed through the other elements or empowered by passing over the pentacle incense for Air, a candle for Fire and burning oils or water itself for the Water element. The pentacle can be moved to the centre of the altar once the symbol on it has been fully charged.

It is very easy to make a pentacle of clay, wood, wax or metal, and on it mark a pentagram with the single point extending upwards. This is what you might call the all-purpose pentagram – drawn this way it always has a positive influence.

You might also like to make a larger pentacle for holding the tiny cakes for the cakes and ale ceremony. You can find special recipes for these cakes in books I have suggested on page 301, but any tiny honey cakes will serve well.

The wand

The wand is a symbol of Fire and should be placed in the South of the altar.

The wand is sometimes represented by a spear. Both the wand and spear, like the athame and sword, are male symbols. The spear, another Fire symbol, is not used in magick, except occasionally in the form of a sharpened stick in sacred sex rites, when it is plunged into the cauldron or the chalice as a symbol of the sacred union of Earth and Sky, Water and Fire.

The wand is traditionally a thin piece of wood about 50 centimetres (21 inches) long, preferably cut from a living tree (some conservationists disagree unless the tree is being pruned). After a strong wind or in a forest where trees are being constantly felled, it is often possible to find a suitable branch from which the wand can be cut. It should be narrowed to a point at one end and rubbed smooth.

You can make a series of wands from different woods for your ceremonies.

Ash is a magical wood, associated with healing and positive energies.

Elder wands are symbols of faerie magick and so are good for any visualisation work.

Hazel comes from the tree of wisdom and justice and is linked with the magick of the Sun. The wand should be cut from a tree that has not yet borne fruit.

Rowan is a protective wood and so is good for defensive and banishing magick.

Willow is the tree of intuition and is said to be endowed with the blessing of the Moon.

You can also use a long, clear quartz crystal, pointed at one end and rounded at the other, as a wand. In its crystalline form, especially, the wand is used for directing healing energies from the circle to wherever they are needed.

The wand is used for directing energies and for making circles of power in the air – hence the image of the faerie godmother waving her wand – deosil for energies to attract energies and widdershins for banishing. It can be used to draw pentagrams in the air at the four quarters and it can also be used for drawing an invisible circle when you are working on carpet or another fabric that cannot be physically marked.

In some traditions, the wand is a tool of Air and so this and the athame, or the sword, are fairly interchangeable. However, the wand seems more effective for casting and uncasting circles, invoking quarters and closing power. It is also particularly good for directing energies in rites of love, healing, fertility, prosperity and abundance.

Symbols of magick

Although you can carry out rituals using absolutely anything, you may like to create a special set of symbols for a variety of rituals. These you can keep in a separate box within your main store of magick artefacts so they do not get scattered or broken.

You may include a thimble to symbolise domestic affairs, a tiny padlock for security at home, a wooden toy boat for travel, a silver locket for fidelity, a key charm for a house, tiny painted wooden eggs for fertility in any venture – just to suggest a few. You can also use small fabric dolls to represent people, for example in a love spell.

Tarot cards also provide excellent symbols for magick: the Emperor for power, the Empress for fertility, the Ten of Pentacles for prosperity, the Lovers for romance, the World or the Eight of Wands for travel, Temperance for harmony, Justice for matters of law, etc. Even if you do not use Tarot cards for divination, a brilliantly illustrated pack, such as the Rider Waite or the Morgan Greer, will by their pictures suggest all kinds of images for your work. My book *Tarot Talks to the Woman Within* (Quantum, 2000) contains many examples of Tarot spells and in spite of its title, the book is very male-friendly. The Tarot is also very portable.

You may also find a supply of white clay useful for creating impromptu symbols and if the clay is soft you can empower it with written words or symbols. I am not suggesting you create waxen images of the kind you see in B-movies, and I certainly don't want you to collect nail clippings or hair in an attempt to harm anyone in any way; this is merely a representation of a person or desired object. It may be possible to find a natural source of clay. A beach near my home provides me with an abundant supply. You can also buy the natural, untreated potters' material. After using the clay in a ritual, you can return it to the soil. Clay is especially good in binding spells or banishing spells when the actions to be bound or the destructive habit are to be re-absorbed by the Earth. It is also excellent in group rituals as a number of people can mould into it their collective energies (see the ritual on page 205 for restoring employment to a community).

The substances of magick

The substances of magick for formal rituals are the same as those used in informal magick. I have already described their magical associations in informal spells and in ritual magick the correspondences in colour and fragrance are exactly the same. Each is set in its own quarter of the circle and used to charge the focus of the ritual with power. They can also be used for empowering and cleansing your ritual tools.

If you make your own candles or incense for your rituals, you can endow energies by chanting the purpose for which they are being made. Some practitioners prepare their ritual substances the day or the evening before the ceremony, at the right planetary or angelic hour for its purpose. But you do not need to do this – the days of apprentices and long hours devoted to a single ritual are gone and even the most complex ceremony need take no more than an hour, many much less.

Salt

Salt rituals are among the oldest forms of magick and salt can form the focus of magick for health and prosperity ceremonies as well as for psychic protection. The kind used is most usually sea salt and represents the Earth element. It should be kept covered and separate from domestic salt and it must be empowered before use (see page 161).

The salt should be placed on the altar to the left of your Earth ritual tools, in a small ceramic dish with a silver spoon. Use new salt for each ritual and tip any remaining into flowing water, watching it carrying away your wishes to fruition.

A very simple crescent moon ritual for attracting money involves piling magically charged salt in a central cone, surrounding this with coins and filling them all with power. Then take the empowered coins and leave them in an open jar in the moonlight until the full moon. On the day after the full moon, spend them on giving happiness to others.

After the ritual, dissolve the salt in sacred water and tip it into a flowing source of water to get the money energies moving.

In a formal ritual for the same purpose, focus the energies by casting a formal circle, inviting the guardians of the elements (see page 200) to lend their power to the endeavour. Pass the elemental tools, incense, candles and water over the salt and money, thus concentrating the energies. Dissolve and tip the salt away in a tub of water that has been swirled nine times to get the power flowing as the climax of the ritual. The difference is one of degree of intensity.

Incense

I have already described in detail the different kinds of incense and how to use them, starting on page 139.

Incense is placed in the East of the altar to the left of the ritual tools.

Incense is, as well as an elemental substance, an easy but powerful way of marking the boundaries between the everyday world and the magick. Frankincense, myrrh or sandalwood is sometimes burned on the altar before a ceremony to purify the area, especially if the room is used for other purposes, and to raise the vibrations from the mundane to the more spiritual. If you are using the granular kind you burn on charcoal, you will need a censer, but a bowl containing sand will serve for incense sticks or cones.

As the incense is burned, so the energies are released.

Candles

All rituals and spells use a number of candles but they are particularly significant in formal magick. I will repeat very briefly the basic information you need for a formal ritual, but you might like to read through again Chapter 5, as candles are such an important part of magic.

You will need one or two altar candles in white, cream or natural beeswax. From the altar candle(s), you will light all the other candles used in your rituals. If you have only one, it will stand in the centre. If two, they are usually placed symmetrically to the right and left of the altar, the god candle on the left and the goddess candle on the right.

You will also need four elemental candles, to represent Fire, Air, Water and Earth, in appropriate colours (see page 90), though if you are carrying out a ceremony in which the power of one element predominates, you could use four candles of this same element. If you are working entirely on the altar, these can be small candles, placed in a line nearer to the perimeter. More usually, however, the candles mark the outer perimeter of the circle at the four compass points. You can, place these on small tables or plinths, or have floor-standing candle-holders.

Green is for Earth, midnight, winter and the North. Place the candle at the 12 o'clock position on a clock, aligned with magnetic North (use a compass if necessary).

Yellow is for Air, dawn, spring and the East. Place the candle at the three o'clock position.

Red, orange or gold is for Fire, noon, summer and the South. Place the candle in the six o'clock position.

Blue is for Water, dusk, autumn and the West. Place the candle in the nine o'clock position.

Light elemental candles after the altar candles if they are within the circle, but before any wish or astrological candles, and begin in the North. If you wish, you can light each candle as its Guardian of the Quarter is invoked (see page 200) and thus called in the ascending flame.

You may also use a candle to represent the petitioner in the ritual. This may be yourself or the person for whom you are performing a ritual. The candle should be in the appropriate zodiacal colour according to the petitioner's birth date (see page 93) and one the colour of the need (see page 94).

In love rituals, light two candles, one for each lover, and place them slightly in front of the altar candle(s): the male lover's candle should be placed next to the goddess candle and the female's by the god candle, if applicable.

If you have a central cauldron, you can stand any candles of need or petitioners' candles in it.

Empowering candles
Usually candles are so powerful that they are already full of magical energies, However, in more formal and elaborate magical ceremonies, you may wish to inscribe or anoint those candles representing a need or person with either olive oil or a ready-prepared, fragrant, anointing. In my book, *Candle Power* (see page 298), I have written in detail about making your own candle oils and ways of inscribing candles with magical alphabets.

Inscribing candles
Carving your wishes and intentions into a candle endows the candle with your special energies and as you etch each letter or symbol, these energies become concentrated.

If you anoint a candle, you should engrave it afterwards, although you may feel that inscribing it is sufficient. Engraving candles is not difficult, but you must use a very light touch and choose good-quality candles. Beeswax is not so easy to inscribe, but because it is very malleable, you can push tiny symbols, such as coins, etc., into the wax or you can buy sheets of beeswax and even if you do not fashion your own candles, you can add tiny beeswax symbols. You can also buy beeswax candles – and some ordinary ones – in different shapes, for example entwined lovers for a love ritual, or a beehive for abundance.

Anointing candles with oil

You can anoint, or dress, candles with scented oil or use candles that have fragrance already added. When you anoint candles with oils, they become more flammable, so you need to be extra cautious about sparks. For safety, stand your candlesticks on a fireproof tray.

Generally, the anointing is performed in silence. You can use virgin olive oil for dressing candles for any need. Some people add a pinch of salt for purification and life-giving properties.

Before beginning, pour a small quantity of the oil into a clear glass or ceramic dish and gently swirl it nine times deosil with a ceramic or glass spoon, visualising light pouring into it and endowing it with healing and magical energies. You need use only a small quantity as the anointing action is symbolic. Rub the oil into the candle in an upward motion, starting in the middle of your candle. Use a previously unlit candle as this will not have absorbed any energies apart from those with which you endow it. Rub in only one direction, concentrating on the purpose of your ritual. See the qualities of your oil and your need entering the candle. Then, starting in the middle again, rub the candle downwards, again concentrating on your goal. A few practitioners will rub from base to top for attracting magick and from top to bottom for banishing magick; it is also usual to use a white candle for attracting energies and a black for banishing.

By physically touching the candle with the oil, it is said that you are charging the candle with your personal vibrations so that when it is lit, it becomes an extension of your mental power and life energy. If the candle represents another person and they are present, ask them to anoint their own candle.

If you light a candle for a formal ritual on successive days, you should re-anoint the candle each time, visualising the partial completion of the goal.

Water

Water represents its own element and stands in the West in a dish to the left of the chalice. See page 163 for instructions on how to make and empower sacred water. You can also use water to which rose petals have been added or you can float lavender or rose essential oil on top (this water should not be consumed internally).

Charging and cleansing your tools

Once you have prepared your elemental substances, you can charge your tools ready for use. If they have been bought, whether new or second-hand, you might also like to cleanse them first. You can also cleanse them after a formal ritual or when their energies seem depleted.

If the ritual is important or arduous, you can recharge the tools before each use, but usually this is not necessary, as the cleansing from a previous ritual will automatically restore the energies. However, as you polish your candlesticks or athame before putting them on the altar, you may wish to focus on the intention of the ceremony and visualise light entering the tools.

Charging with power

You can charge your tools separately as you obtain them. Alternatively, group them together on a table before their first use in ritual and create a circle of light around them with small purple candles at the eight main compass points (North, North-east, etc.). Start at the North candle and end with the North-west candle.

✤ First create a circle of salt round the tool(s), beginning in the North, to offer the tool(s) the protection of the ancient Earth element, saying:

Mother Earth, charge with the power of the ancient stone circles and the wise ways of the ancestors this – [name the tool(s)] of magick and healing, that my work may be rooted in what is possible and help create abundance and prosperity for others and the land, as well as for my own needs.

✤ Next, draw a circle of smoke deosil in the air around them, using a frankincense or myrrh incense stick, saying:

Father Sky, charge with the power of the mighty winds and the limitless potential of the cosmos this – [name the tool(s)] of magick and healing, that my work may be focused, filled with energy and bring positive change to ever-widening horizons.

✤ Now, using a golden or scarlet candle in a broad-based candle-holder, mark an inner circle of fire in the air, around the artefact(s), saying:

Brother Fire, charge with the power of ancient ritual fires and the brilliance of the Sun, this (these) tool(s) of magick and healing, that my work may be filled with light and inspiration and purged of all self-seeking and negativity.

✿ Finally, sprinkle sacred water or rainwater that has not touched the ground before collection on top of the circle of salt saying:

Sister Water, charge with the power of mighty oceans, wide rushing rivers and deep still pools this (these) tool(s) of magick and healing, that my work may release stagnation and bring fertility and peace, not only to myself and my loved ones, but to people whose lives are blighted by polluted places and, especially, water.

Cleansing using the forces of nature

Leave your artefact(s) on a piece of white silk in a sheltered, safe place out of doors or near an open door where children, pets or the curious cannot reach them. Begin at dusk where they can absorb the light of the Sun, the Moon and the stars, for 24 hours. This will be effective even if you cannot see any of these heavenly bodies in the sky. Charge at the time of the waxing moon to the full moon if possible; if not, let them stand for 48 hours. If the Moon is waning and so not good for energising, create a circle of alternate moonstones and crystal quartz for the powers of the Sun and Moon, and leave the tools within this circle for the full 48-hour cycle.

Sprinkle the tools with nine drops of sacred water that was collected under the full moon or rainwater that has not touched the ground, saying a variation of this old magical rhyme whose origins are unknown:

One for joy, two for gladness,
Three and four to banish sadness,
Five and six do life renew,
Seven, eight, nine bring power anew.

Few of these old chants are great poetry, but that was not their purpose – they were created in the days before widespread literacy as a way of remembering magical rituals. If you prefer, you can substitute your own, composed by you or a coven member who may have a gift for such work. The rhymes served like simple mantras to build up power – some people recite the chant several times, very fast, while sprinkling the water slowly.

Cleansing using a crystal pendulum

Hold a clear crystal pendulum over the tool(s) and make nine circles widdershins.

Plunge the pendulum in cold running water to cleanse it, shake it dry and circle it nine times deosil over the tool(s) to restore energies. You may need to repeat this several times if a tool seems lifeless or after you have been carrying out a banishing ritual.

The four elements

The four elements – Earth, Air, Fire and Water – play an important part in all kinds of magick. Plato, the Greek philosopher who lived around 360 BC, was the first to identify these elements as the components that made up the whole universe and right until Elizabethan times people still believed that our nature was influenced by our elemental composition. Indeed, Jung, the twentieth-century psychoanalyst, used this concept in his personality types, renaming them as Earth/sensations, Air/thinking, Fire/intuition and Water/feelings. Jung also thought that we each had a predominant element, a secondary one and a shadow one that we denied or projected on other people whom we then unconsciously disliked because they mirrored our faults.

In formal magick, the four elements are seen as providing natural energies for transforming wishes into reality. Together they combine to form the fifth element – Ether, or *Akasha* – that represents pure Spirit, or perfection. Medieval alchemists attempted to create this elusive substance, called the philosopher's stone. It was said to turn base metal into gold and, as an elixir according to the Eastern tradition, to cure all ills and offer immortality.

These elements form the basis for raising power in formal magick and in less formal spells too and are represented by Devas, the Guardians of the Watchtowers or the four main Archangels.

Earth

Earth represents midnight, winter and the quarter and direction of the North. It is the most magical of directions.

Earth is the realm of the actual and material, where magical wishes and intentions find expression and so it is very important. It is also the element invoked for abundance and in prosperity rituals, as well as matters concerning your home and family. It is also used for magick concerning animals, all who work with their hands, especially in agriculture, horticulture and environmentalism, in finance or maintaining law and order, for banks and financial and legal institutions. Earth can thereby form a focus for rituals where justice and authority are an issue.

Its elemental creatures are gnomes, with their stores of hidden treasure, wisdom and, above all, common sense. They are a reminder that what is of worth does not necessarily offer excitement or instant results.

Earth's colours are green or brown. Its zodiacal signs are Taurus, Virgo and Capricorn.

Air

Air represents dawn, spring and the quarter and direction of the East. Some practitioners open their circles facing this direction, rather than the more usual North.

Air is the realm of potential of new beginnings, change, action, travel, house or career moves, knowledge and learning, communication, the media and technology. It can therefore be used for magick concerning all who work in commerce, medicine, teaching, the retail trades, the media and science and all who are studying. It also can be used in rituals for health.

Its elemental creatures are sylphs, gentle spirits of the air who can be seen fleetingly as butterflies, offering ideas, ideals and a reminder to enjoy happiness while you can.

Air's colour is yellow and its zodiacal signs are Aquarius, Gemini and Libra.

Fire

Fire represents noon, summer and the quarter and direction of the South.

Fire is the realm of light, the Sun and lightning, and so forms the focus of magick for fertility, power, joy, ambition, illumination, inspiration, achievement, all creative and artistic ventures, poetry, art, sculpture, writing, music, dance, religion and spirituality, psychic powers and mystical experiences, passion and sexuality.

It can be invoked by those who work in the arts and those who seek or are required to be leaders and for those in all dangerous professions, especially involving fire, furnaces or metalwork. It is also potent for destruction of what is now no longer needed, for binding and banishing and so for protection.

Because it is the most powerful of the elements, it must be used only with care in a pure, calm frame of mind and for a positive purpose.

The elemental creature of Fire is the salamander, the mythical lizard that lives within Fire (the name is nowadays given to a species of amphibious newts). The salamander offers an understanding of mystical processes and visions to inspire future paths and ventures.

The colour of Fire is gold, orange or red and its zodiacal signs are Aries, Leo and Sagittarius.

Water

Water represents dusk, autumn and the quarter and direction of the West.

It is the realm of love, relationships, sympathy, intuition, healing and the cycle of birth, death and rebirth. Water can form the focus for rituals of purification, healing, all water and sea magick, Moon magick, reconciliation and peace, harmony in oneself and with others, restoring balance, unconscious wisdom and divination, especially scrying. It is also potent for overcoming stagnation and inertia and for moving forward after an impasse, for friendship and for travel by sea. It is linked with work in the caring professions and all healers, with those who work in the psychic arts, sailors, people who live or work on or near water and for those in the hospitality industry.

Water's elemental creatures are undines, spirits of the water. The original undine was created without a soul, but gained one by marrying a mortal and bearing him a child. However, she also lost her freedom from pain and her immortality and so she is a reminder that love may have a price, but that without it life does not have meaning.

The colour of water is blue and its zodiacal signs are Cancer, Scorpio and Pisces.

The four quarters of the circle

Every magical circle is divided into four quarters that are in ceremonial magick called the Watchtowers. The higher essences who protect the quarters are invoked as the Guardians, who control and direct the elemental powers. Sometimes they are called Kings, sometimes Devas, or they may be pictured as the four main archangels, Michael, Gabriel, Raphael and Uriel.

How you perceive your guardians in the ritual circle is up to you. As with all magick, there are disagreements about which archangel represents each element. This is because angels are found in a number of different traditions and religions and so may serve different functions under similar names.

Previously, I have associated Raphael with the North and Uriel with the East, seeing Raphael in his aspect as a healer and protector, and Uriel as the fiery dawn in the East. However, recently I have started to use a more traditional association of Raphael as the messenger in the East and Uriel as sentinel of the North and I have found that this works better. Do read about angels and experiment to see what suits you. I have listed source material on pages 201–2 and you can find more information on the Internet. Use the elemental candle colour to represent the angel you want. You can also use angels in the four quarters to invoke protection in less formal magick by lighting candles in the four quarters when you feel afraid or alone.

I have also seen Michael listed as archangel of the dawn and East, but I think he is better placed as archangel of the Sun in the South. If you feel uncertain, simply refer to each guardian as 'Archangel of the North', etc., then the celestial being can reveal itself in the form that is right for you.

The angelic colours I have given vary slightly from the elemental ones and if you are carrying out a personal angelic ritual of protection or meditating on the archangels, you can use the archangel colours for your candles.

Some practitioners do not greet the Guardians of the Watchtowers at all, but instead light each elemental candle in turn, visualising golden energies pouring from each direction into the circle.

Uriel

Uriel, whose name means Fire of God, is associated with earthquakes, storms and volcanoes and is the archangel of salvation. He is sometimes linked with the courage of Mars. He warned Noah of the impending flood and led Abraham out of Ur. Believed to have given alchemy to mankind, he also imparted the wisdom of the *Kabbalah*, the book of sacred writings, to Hebrew mystics. He stands as wise protector and keeper of the sacred mysteries, hence representing the direction of magick and initiator of all who seek the mysteries.

Uriel stands in the North and his colour is the deep blue or purple of midnight.

Raphael

Raphael is the healer and travellers' guide and is often associated with Mercury, the messenger of the dawn. He is the angel who offers healing to the planet and to mankind and all creatures on the face of the Earth and in the skies and waters and the promise that tomorrow really is another day.

He is also guardian of the young. He is depicted with a pilgrim's stick, a wallet and a fish, showing the way and offering sustenance to all who ask.

Raphael stands in the East and his colour is yellow.

Michael

Archangel of the Sun and Light, Michael is the warrior angel. He appeared to Moses as the fire in the burning bush and saved Daniel from the lions' den. As commander of the heavenly hosts, Michael, with his flaming sword, drove Satan and his fallen angels out of the celestial realms; as Angel of Judgement, he also carries a scale for weighing the souls of the dead. According to the *Koran*, the cherubim were created from Michael's tears.

He offers power to overcome any obstacles and challenges, and brings wisdom and illumination as to the right path.

Michael stands in the South and his colour is gold.

Gabriel

Archangel of the Moon, the messenger archangel and the heavenly awakener, Gabriel appears many times in the Bible. He visited the Virgin Mary and her cousin Elizabeth, mother of John the Baptist, to tell them that they were to bear sons who would lead mankind to salvation. It was Gabriel who parted the waters of the Red Sea so that the Hebrews could escape from the Pharaoh's soldiers.

Gabriel is usually pictured holding a sceptre or lily. To the followers of Islam, Gabriel is the spirit of truth who dictated the *Koran* to Mohammed.

Gabriel brings wise words of truth and the clear voice that speaks of hope and a new purpose in life, but also compassion and the acceptance of the weaknesses of oneself as well as others.

Gabriel's protection can be felt with each new moon, especially on the day before the crescent is visible in the sky.

Gabriel stands in the West and his colour is silver.

Pentagrams

The pentagram, as I have already mentioned, is one of the most sacred geometric forms in magick. Some witches wear a gold pentacle, a pentagram in a circle (see page 189), on a chain as a sign of their craft.

Each of the five points of the pentagram represents one of the five elemental powers, so that the uppermost single point is symbolic of Spirit, or *Akasha* or Ether. It is dedicated to the Goddess in her triple aspects. It is the realm of spirituality and the divine spark within all life.

The top left point of the pentagram symbolises Air and the fixed sign of Aquarius, representing logic, intelligence and the conscious awareness that enables us to reach beyond the material and follow steps to knowledge of what is hidden.

The top right point is the element Water and the fixed sign of Scorpio. It represents the feelings that endow magick with purpose, desire whether for love or spiritual development and the compassion and empathy that make us care about ourselves, others and the world we live in. It forms the interconnectedness of all life.

The bottom left point of the pentagram symbolises the element Earth and the fixed sign of Taurus. It connects with the Earth Mother, ecology and the basis from which we explore spirit and also the material plane in which ideas are manifest.

The bottom right point in the pentagram symbolises Fire and the fixed sign of Leo, flaming ever upwards, the impetus and illumination that transforms thought into action and enables us to see potential, not least our spiritual potential.

These positions correspond with the zodiacal positions on an astrological wheel.

On another level, the pentagram is seen as representing the human body with the four limbs outstretched and the head touching the clouds.

Drawing a pentagram

Pentagrams are remarkably easy to draw. They are created in one continuous line, moving from point to point, and ending where you began. In ritual magick, pentagrams are drawn in the air at each of the four compass directions of the circle, either with an athame, a wand or the index finger of your power hand. It is best to draw really big, strong pentagrams.

Pentagrams can be drawn either to attract the elemental guardians (invoking, or attracting pentagrams) or to close their energies (banishing pentagrams).

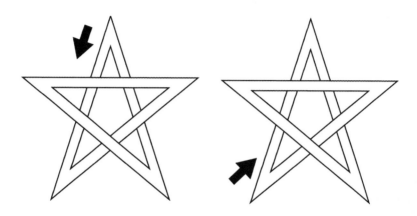

There are various rather complicated ways of drawing pentagrams, but I suggest you use the basic methods given on the previous page for attracting when opening your four quarters and banishing when closing. If you wish to find out more, I recommend you read Dion Fortune's *Applied Magick* (see page 300). If you do not wish to draw pentagrams at all in your circle work, you can instead call the Guardians in the candle flame.

Preparing for ritual

Preparation for ritual is important. Despite this, even magick has to conform to the needs and customs of the modern world, and so witches today often do not fast for 24 hours or abstain from sex for the same period. But you should try to slow your activities down in the hours before a formal ceremony, eat only a light meal and turn off all phones, faxes and computers if you are working from home.

Make sure you have all the basic tools and ingredients for the ceremony and that the room is ready.

About an hour before the ritual, prepare yourself, by having a bath in which a sprinkling of sacred salt and a few drops of cleansing oils, such as pine or eucalyptus, have been added. Light purple or pink candles in the bathroom and allow all your daily concerns to flow out of your body into the water, to be transformed by the candlelight. When you are ready to get out of the water, swirl the reflected light three times widdershins and as you take out the plug, say:

Go in peace, flow in harmony to the sea of eternity.

Wear something light and loose for the ritual. You may like to keep a special robe for your magical work, ready washed and pressed. Though some witches work skyclad, in groups this can result in self-consciousness and sometimes unnecessary emotional complications that can detract from the magick. Also, in Northern climes it is usually too cold! But the choice, of course, is yours.

Next sweep out and cleanse the area you will be working in and set up the altar, either in the North or the centre of your circle. Practitioners who work from the East of the circle may want their altar there. The position of the altar really does not matter. (See also page 42 for working in the southern hemisphere.)

If the altar is placed centrally or in the North, you follow the tradition, as I do, of working from the North; this means that you cast the circle from the North and enter the circle from the South so you are facing the North. If, however, you work with the altar in the East, you will cast from the East and enter from the West, facing the East. A central altar will work for either direction and it also means a group can easily circle it. After all, for most of us space is at a premium, and sometimes it is a question of marrying metaphysics with logistics.

Creating a temple

Before you begin a formal ritual, you must cast an astral or spiritual temple above and surrounding the circle and the location. In your mind's eye, visualise your own temple, perhaps one from the ancient world, resplendent with gold and jewels, with a statue of a deity in marble, gold or silver. The roof of the temple may form a crystalline pyramid or be open to the stars. (Readers of the late Dion Fortune's occult novels will have no difficulty in forming images of such splendid edifices.) Or you may create a grove of oak or olive trees or one of the ancient stone circles as your working place or a castle room whose battlements are lashed by a stormy sea. The altar in your temple may be pure gold, ornate stone or beaten copper, and the candles may be set in ancient lamps. With practice, you may find that a particular temple form automatically creates itself in your mind's vision, but if this is not helpful, then concentrate on the magick that exists your own very special working place.

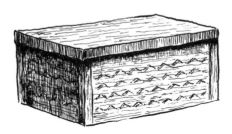

Let us go through a formal ritual. I have created this one for a solitary practitioner, but it adapts well for a group.

A formal ritual to restore prosperity

Such a ritual could be used, for example, to boost employment in a town that has become an urban wasteland.

🜨 Set four floor candles in the elemental colours in the four main compass points of what will be the circle. The altar is in the centre.

🌑 Place a single large beeswax candle in the centre of the altar. Arrange your tools and the four elemental substances, also on the altar, to form a square around the central candle: salt in the North, frankincense, fern or cinnamon incense in the East, a gold candle in the South, for abundance, and a jug of water and two small dishes in the West.

🌑 Set the pentacle containing a honey cake in the North, and place the athame in the East, the wand in the South and the chalice of juice or wine in the West.

🌑 Place a ball of clay or dough within the elemental square, on a dish in front of the candle so that light shines on it.

🌑 Facing North, light the altar candle.

🌑 Take the salt from the North and stir it deosil with your athame, saying:

> *Power of new life, power of healing, power of regeneration,*
> *enter this salt, I ask, mother and father of light and love.*

You can substitute the names of gods and goddesses associated with success, prosperity, fertility and renewal into the ritual if you wish.

🌑 Take next the water from the West and pour some into one of the dishes. Stir it deosil, saying:

> *Power of growth, power of fertility, power of prosperity, enter this*
> *water, I ask, mother and father of abundance and increase.*

🌑 Now take the salt to the water and tip a little in it, stirring it once more with the athame, saying:

> *Dissolve and disperse, flow far and free to attract rebirth to –*
> *[name the town] and its inhabitants.*

🌑 Now cast the circle around the elemental candles, with your wand, starting from the North in a single unbroken movement, visualising as you do a stream of light emanating from it that encloses you above, around and beneath. (If you are working with a group, they can stand or sit within a circle while you cast around them. This is better than slowing the ceremony by having people entering the circle separately after it is cast and then having to close the circle after each one.) Say:

> *I cast this circle of light, of power and of protection. May the*
> *circle that is cast always be unbroken. Bless my workings this night*
> *[or day], O mother and father of rebirth and renewal, unified and*
> *yet two, and all that is and has been and shall be, creative spirit of the*
> *universe, the cosmos and the smallest blade of grass.*

✤ Pick up the bowl of salt water and sprinkle a second circle deosil around the perimeter of the first, saying:

Salt and water, enclose, bless and protect you who have sustained life from the beginning and will so to the end.

If others are present, a second witch or the High Priest then sprinkles all present individually with the water, saying 'Bless and protect'.

✤ Light the incense in the East (or add to it if it was lit before the ritual).

✤ Create a third circle around the perimeter, saying:

Breath of life, bring purity, clarity and focus, force of life itself that flows alike within plant, tree, bird, animal, human and stone. Bless and protect.

You are now going to light the elemental candles, and as you do so invoke the Guardians. Re-light the taper from the central candle as necessary.

✤ Light a taper from the central candle and carry it to the North, saying:

Lord [or Lady] of the Northern Watchtower, I call upon your strength and persistence to restore the prosperity and stability to this town where new industry and investment are so badly needed.

✤ Light the green candle of the North.

✤ Go to the East, saying:

Lord [or Lady] of the Eastern Watchtower, I call upon your swiftness and clarity of purpose, to bring technologies and opportunities into this town to attract new kinds of work, perhaps from overseas.

✤ Light the yellow candle of the East.

✤ Go next to the South and say:

Lord [or Lady] of the Southern Watchtower, I call upon your cleansing fire and spirit of inspiration to purge what is redundant and corrupt and to bring hope and energy to this town where decay and despair have taken root.

✤ Light the red candle of the South.

✤ Go finally to the West and say:

Lord [or Lady] of the Western Watchtower, I call upon your healing and restoration to heal bitterness and divisions between the people who have experienced such hard times and whose town has become ravaged and neglected.

❋ Light the blue candle of the West.

Now you are going to empower the clay. If working as a group, once the clay has been empowered with the ritual substances, you could pass it round for each person to fashion it and add their energies.

❋ Take the salt and sprinkle a few grains on the clay, saying:

Make new buildings rise, new industries grow, new houses and parkland, schools and health centres be created, that this town may be a worthy home to those who work in it.

❋ Take the incense and circle the clay nine times, saying:

Bring retraining, new investment, government grants, new technology and new equipment so that the town may become a hive of activity and generate ever more opportunities into the next century and beyond.

❋ Light the gold candle in the South (in this case it will be different from the candle of the southern watchtower) and pass it over the clay so that single drop of gold wax falls on it, saying:

Bring gold of prosperity, gold of abundance, fire of inspiration and creativity so that this town may be rich in opportunity, in the arts and in culture, as well as in material wealth.

❋ Finally, sprinkle the clay with a single drop of water from the jug or a second dish, saying:

May the lifeblood of the town be restored and fertility course through the veins of the people that their children and grandchildren may know happiness and lives unclouded by sorrow and anxiety for their livelihood and their dwellings.

❋ Taking the clay between your hands, begin to mould it, using a marking tool if you wish, to make a tool, such as a wheel, or a figure, a bridge, a loaf, a house or a flower, or any abstract symbol that represents the rebirth of the town through its people. Endow it with your wishes, visualising the place growing and prospering, perhaps reciting:

Go forth, increase and multiply,
or
Rise again from the ashes, rise anew, rise glorious, rise, rise again.

Chant faster and faster until at last you toss the ball into the air and catch it, saying;

Go far, go free, bring life to thee.

In a group, you could pass the endowed clay round a second time, tossing it from person to person while chanting.

❧ Return the clay to the altar and take your honey cake on its dish.

❧ Hold it over the central candle, saying:

Bring abundance to those who need it, enough for their needs and a little more, joy and hope.

❧ Bite into the cake and scatter a few crumbs on the clay, instead of in a libation dish .

❧ Take the athame and plunge it into the chalice, saying:

God to goddess, join thus thy power and give power to thy people who are in need this hour.

❧ Drink from the chalice and instead of dropping some wine in the libation dish or on the ground, let a drop fall on the clay, saying:

Fruit of the vine, harvest gathered and transformed, transform likewise what is barren to what is fruitful and living.

If you are in a group, you can pass the cakes and wine round and each person can contribute a positive thought or perhaps voice any personal worries they may have about employment and ask for blessing.

❧ Sit in the candlelight, seeing the new town rising from the old, and if you have any special fear about your own job security or those of loved ones, let these too flow away as the released energies multiply. Allow any excess energies to drain back into the Earth, by pressing with your hands, feet and body.

❧ Beginning in the West, blow out the candle, saying:

Lord [or Lady] of the Western Watchtower, I thank you for your healing and your harmonising light. Go now in peace.

❧ Move next to the South. Blow out this candle, saying:

Lord [or Lady] of the Southern Watchtower, I thank you for your inspiration and your cleansing light. Go now in peace.

❧ Move next to the East. Blow out this candle and say:

Lord [or Lady] of the Eastern Watchtower, I thank you for your clarity and your life-restoring light. Go now in peace.

❧ Move finally to the North. Blow out this candle and say:

Lord [or Lady] of the Northern Watchtower, I thank you for your grounding power and your protecting light. Go now in peace.

- Take again your wand and, starting from the North and working widdershins, close the circle just once, saying:

May the circle be uncast but remain unbroken, may light and love and healing still remain and fall on whoever needs their blessing.

- Leave the clay and allow the central and elemental Fire candle and the incense to burn away. When they are burned through, clear them away and bury the clay beneath a living tree or in a large plant of lavender or basil.

There are many other things you can add to a formal ritual, for example, ringing the bell or drawing pentagrams. In this ritual, you could also have passed the elemental tools over the clay to give it additional power. Ceremonies are really a glorious mix and match and this is just a sample of how you can combine the tools and the forms to create the ceremony you want.

You may like to record in your Book of Shadows those rituals that work well and others that did not seem so potent, together with any reasons why you think this is so. In time, you will develop perhaps three or four basic ritual 'templates' for coven or personal work, and with practice the preparations and stages will become almost automatic. As your energies ever more creative and spontaneous, they will, within a formal framework, become incredibly potent.

CHAPTER 11

Moon Magick

Moon magick is one of the oldest forms of ritual, rooted from the earliest times in the observations of humankind, of the changing phases of the Moon. These associations have passed into modern magick and it is by reconnecting with the natural energies that we can use the ebbs and flows of the lunar cycle, not only to amplify our own powers for magical purposes, but also to harmonise with them, rather than fighting against our bodies and spirits in our everyday lives.

Rituals throughout the ages have tapped into the prevailing lunar energies that, like the tides, are affected by the different cycles. In this way, magical intentions can be carried on either the outflowing or inflowing psychic tide to give them the impetus to manifest themselves in the physical world.

To go against the Moon cycles in magick or in life is a bit like swimming against the flow: quite possible with practice, but involving unnecessary effort.

The Moon Mother

The Moon was regarded as the mother of all long before written records existed, for she was seen to give birth to a new moon every 29 days. Because the old moon apparently died, it was believed that that she took the souls of the dead back into her womb and gave them new life. In the same way, the three main lunar phases gave rise to the concept of the Triple Goddess who has been worshipped in cultures from palaeolithic times where early cave art displayed crescent moons that have been identified as Goddess symbols. The evolved Triple Goddess of the Celts, which reflects the lunar cycles of maiden, mother and crone, is an icon also seen throughout the classical world. (see page 72).

Moon time

The earliest calendars were based on the lunar cycle and Moon time is still used in the modern world in both pagan and religious rituals: the Chinese New Year is a lunar festival and the Chinese ritual year follows the Moon and the Native Americans calculate their months by the Moon. The Coligny Calendar of the Gallic Druids, which runs from full moon to full moon, was named after the place in France where it was discovered in 1897, engraved on bronze. Similar calculations were inscribed in stone at Knowth, one of the sacred ancient megalithic sites in Ireland.

Many of the original lunar calendars were based on the natural and agricultural world and helped in establishing an agricultural calendar, noting times in the cycle when crops were planted and ripened and when birds migrated, as well as the coming of the herds among hunting peoples. 'Blue moons', where more than one full moon occurs in the same calendar month, have always been regarded as especially potent. In the Further Reading chapter, I have listed sources where you can find these older calendars.

In modern magick, old Moon names are a good way of connecting with the powers of nature that, unlike seasonal energies operate on a monthly basis, but magically are strongest on the actual eve and night of the full moon and the days before and after the full moon. So Moon names can give a focus to magical purposes at the right time in the yearly cycle, as they emphasise the prevailing energies that different peoples have interpreted according to their own seasonal trends. Sadly, we no longer top up our psychic batteries in the same way, and the further we move from nature, the harder it gets to access these helpful powers.

The night of the full moon is good for solitary practitioners and groups as well as formal covens, to tune into the full force of the monthly energies. If you have coven business, leave it to another night – it is a shame to waste all that time on mundane matters, when you could be riding high on the cascading powers. You can carry out more than one full moon ritual on the same night, opening the circle and perhaps following an energetic spell with a gentler rite, or vice versa, before closing the circle. The one I have suggested on page 222 would easily form part of a more complex full moon rite. Alternatively, you could perform it privately, perhaps the evening before or after the full moon. You can, if you are working alone, spread your full moon rituals over three nights, with the major one on the night of the full moon and the others on the preceding and following nights.

I have started the full moon calendar on page 214 with the moon that is nearest to the Celtic New Year on 2 November, the moon that the Celts called Samnios, the 'falling of the seeds'. In Native American lunar calendars, the full moon around this period was often known as the 'hunters' moon' or the 'trading moon', because the trading of goods was carried out in preparation for the needs of the coming winter. You may find that each of the full moons corresponds with a personal event or prevailing mood in your own yearly life cycle. You may even give it a personal name and create your very own Moon calendar or devise one based on your own region. The passing of the urban year can equally be a focus or you can use goddess/god names to reflect the different moon energies.

There is a great variety of translations of the Celtic and Native American names. For example, I always call Samnios 'Going Home for the Winter' because this is the time of year that coincides, like the Celtic herdsmen returning from the hills, with the closing of the small caravan site where I spend so many of my spring and summer days, working and taking my youngest child to play by the sea. It is for me a time of sorrow, but also of realisation that the site has become muddy and cold and I am spending more and more time huddled within over the small heater. I know that it really is time to put away the picnic bench outside the van where I eat, read and carry out rituals in the sunnier times.

To the Celts, this moon carried the hope of seeds that would take root to burst through in the early spring. As I close the van, I too look forward to returning in spring, maybe having weathered the storms I know are gathering round me emotionally as well as physically.

I have listed the 12 moons that correspond to the 12 months of the year. However, because some years have 13 moons and lunar months vary slightly in length, a thirteenth magical month, Ciallos, the month of no time, is added every two and a half years. There are fairly complex rules for its insertion, but a good lunar almanac will keep you on track – you can follow its instructions or use Ciallos rather like a joker in a playing card pack, when you need it.

As you work with the Moon and plot her daily path over years you will become naturally in tune with the prevailing energies.

I have briefly listed the moons and the kind of magick you can perform either on the full moon itself or the day that precedes or follows it, and on page 216 I have given a basic full moon ceremony to use for your special moons. You may not wish to celebrate every full moon this way, just the significant ones in your year. The names are a synthesis of lunar names I have gathered and used over the years. You will see the echo of these themes throughout the seasons (see Chapter 13).

Moons of the Coligny Calender

Samnios, Seed Fall

Native American name: Hunter's Moon, Trading Moon

Full moon date: October/November (April/May in the southern hemisphere)

Ritual: Making an end to what is not fruitful, drawing up realistic plans for the coming year

Dumannios, the Coming of Deep Darkness

Native American name: First Snows or Frost on the Grass Moon

Full moon date: November/December (May/June in the southern hemisphere)

Ritual: Bringing light into the darkness, seeking inner as well as outer illumination and inspiration

Riuros, the Time of the Long Coldness

Native American name: When Wolves Huddle Close Moon

Full moon date: December/January (June/July in the southern hemisphere)

Ritual: Material security, the home and family

Angantios, Staying at Home

Native American name: Gnawing on Bones Moon

Full moon date: January/February (July/August in the southern hemisphere)

Ritual: Acceptance of life as it is, seeking joy in what one has, not fretting for what one has not

Ogronios, the Time of Shining Ice

Native American name: When the Geese First Lay Moon

Full moon date: February/March (August/September in the southern hemisphere)

Ritual: The stirring of new hope and trust, releasing potential that has been frozen

Cutios, the Time of the Winds

Native American name: Purification or Eagle Moon

Full moon date: March/April (September/October in the southern hemisphere)

Ritual: Change, clearing away stagnation and inertia

Glamonios, Growing Green Shoots

Native American name: Frog or Blossom Moon

Full moon date: April/May (October/November in the southern hemisphere)

Ritual: New horizons and opportunities, fertility

Simiuisonnos, Bright Time or the Time of Dancing

Native American name: Flowering or Full Leaf Moon

Full moon date: May/June (November/December in the southern hemisphere)

Ritual: Joy, permanent relationships, maximising opportunities

Equos, the Time of the Horse

Native American name: Strawberry Moon When the Buffalo Are Calling

Full moon date: June/July (December/January in the southern hemisphere)

Ritual: Travel, moves of all kinds, house or career expansion

Elembiuos, Claim Time

Native American name: Ripe Corn Moon, Moon When the Young Geese Take Wing

Full moon date: July/August (January/February in the southern hemisphere)

Ritual: Justice, promotion, recognition and financial gain

Edrinios, the Time of Arbitration

Native American name: Harvest Moon, Dark Butterfly Moon

Full moon date: August/September (February/March in the southern hemisphere)

Ritual: Reaping what has been sown, abundance, assessing life and resources with a view to shedding what cannot be used

Cantios, the Song Moon

Native American name: Nut Moon, Moon When the Birds Fly South

Full moon date: September/October (March/April in the southern hemisphere)

Ritual: Final burst of energy for tasks undone, salvaging relationships and missed opportunities

A full moon ritual for energy

Use this ritual to bring specific lunar energies into your life. It should be carried out on the evening of the full moon or as close as you can.

I choose Cantios, my favourite full moon of the year, when calling for help to finish things I have left undone, but you can use the same method and much of the ritual for any of the full moons. You can also use this ritual without focusing on a specific full moon, for bringing plans to fruition or for an extra surge of energy when you need it to overcome an obstacle or seize an opportunity.

🎇 Light a row of three silver candles, two of the same size for the waxing and waning phases and one much larger in the centre for the full moon.

🎇 Light three sticks of jasmine or mimosa incense.

🎇 Take a branch from a willow or any other tree or plant that grows near water, and on it hang three silver baubles; one should be very large. If you have no baubles, make discs from silver foil. Silver is the colour and metal of the Moon. Add nine tiny, silver-coloured bells, hung with thread.

🎇 If the full moon is visible, use a hand mirror, silver if possible, to direct its light toward the tree or plant, saying:

Isis, mother of the Moon, your power this night bring to me soon. Your silver radiance on me shine, your fertile light now strengthen mine. Full moon, full glory, fill my heart, your loving wisdom to me impart. Mother Isis, your child I call, uplift and guide me lest I fall.

(You can, instead of Isis, choose your own Moon goddess if you prefer or just invoke the Moon mother.)

🎇 Now with silver thread or ribbons, bind the tree and the baubles with nine loose knots, saying:

I bind your tree with tasks undone, Maiden, Mother, not yet Crone. I bind your strength my race not won, I take the power and it is done.

❧ Pull all your knots undone, one after the other, and shake the tree so the bells ring and the energy is released.

❧ Leave the candles to burn down in a safe place.

Leave the branch or plant still hung with silver baubles and bells throughout the week of the full moon and use the week to focus on your specific Moon theme. Sit, if you can, for a few minutes each night by silver candlelight and see yourself surrounded by an orb of silver light. Maximise the possibilities in your everyday world.

You can adapt the words to suit the different months and, if you wish, rest an appropriate symbol in the branch, tied on with silver ribbon, for example, a toy horse during the month Equos, for travel and the expansion of horizons, mental as well as physical.

The cycle of the Moon

As I mentioned earlier in the chapter, as well as the months, the phases of the Moon offer scope for different kinds of magick during the individual monthly moon cycles. However, problems in interpretation of these energies can arise because astronomy and astrology are no longer regarded as the same thing. For example, to our ancestors, the astrological Dark of the Moon was the same as the astronomical dark – the first two and a half days of the cycle when the Moon is not visible at any hour of the day or night. To this were added the preceding three days of the old moon, when it did not rise until the early hours of the morning. So when books of magick speak of the new moon, they may mean the time when the crescent first appears in the sky. But if you prefer, you can, as some modern practitioners do, count the Dark of the Moon only as those three last waning days and start new moon magick from the literal calendar day. It's a bit like deciding exactly when a chicken comes to life: you don't actually see it until the chicken pops out of the egg but you know it's alive even when it's invisible, inside the shell.

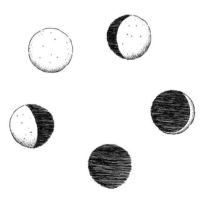

I prefer to wait for the crescent because to me those last days of the old moon are still very precious. I can remember waking before it was light in Spain and seeing that last waning crescent with its accompanying star, shining like a jewel in the warm sky. The answer, as always, is to do what you feel is best for you.

Working with the phases

There are eight astronomical phases of the Moon, but magick generally focuses on three that are considered to be particularly significant.

The waxing moon: As the Moon is increasing in size, it is said to be waxing. The light increases, appearing to spread from right to left, and this phase lasts right until the moment that the Moon becomes completely visible – the full moon. The waxing phase is the time for magick for increase or to attract good things. The more the Moon increases in size, the more powerful become its energies to attract abundance.

The full moon: The full moon phase, when the whole of the Moon is visible, is the time for the most potent magick, but it lasts for only 24 hours – although, as I have said, most practitioners allow a day on either side.

The waning moon: From the second following the 24 hours of the full moon, the Moon is waning. The light decreases as the Moon shrinks from right to left and the energies too start to wane until the Moon is no longer visible at all. The wane is the time for banishing and for decreasing influences. The more it decreases, the more the potency decreases, so the pull that keeps any destructive influences in you is also decreasing. You can, however, use the waning moon like an emptying bath and wash away all the bad things into the cosmos or the earth as the energies swirl away, to be restored and reformed into positivity.

Moon phases and you

Like the Moon, you and everything around you – children, pets, plants and, of course, crystals – will become more dynamic and charged as the Moon increases. This is especially noticeable with moonstones and topaz. Then, as the Moon wanes, everything loses energy and enthusiasm.

It's the spirit and body's way of telling you to slow down and regenerate. I am convinced that a great deal of the stress, premenstrual tension and irritability that we all suffer is because we are running counter to those energies. Of course, you can't ring into work and say that you are not coming in because the Moon is seriously waning, but you can cut down on non-essential tasks. I, for example, would certainly not take children to pleasure parks on the waning moon where they will be whirled upside down on dangerous rides and tears and fights may occur. Instead, save the Action Man/Superwoman stuff for the full moon and go for a wander instead in woods and gardens and by gently flowing streams.

Tuning magically into the lunar phases

The cycle from new moon to new moon lasts 29.5 days but because the Moon has an irregular orbit, the time of its rising and setting will vary each day. For this reason, phases can vary in length by a day or so each month. The best way to understand the Moon is as our ancestors did, by studying in the sky. Use an almanac or a diary that contains Moon phases or consult your daily paper to identify the phases to start you off on the right day. The weather section of your paper also gives you precise timings and there is usually a chart so you can adjust for time zones and summer time differences.

Each day, look to see whether the Moon is in the sky or, if it is cloudy, calculate where it ought to be. On clear nights you will see how it rises diagonally. You can use a tree in your garden or the roof of a house or even a tall fence to note the position at a specific time of the night and month. Each month it will be slightly different, because of that irregular orbit. Don't be fooled in the waning phase – in the later part, you may see in the early morning yesterday's Moon that has not yet set.

Children love keeping a 'Moon watch', and you may like to buy a sky globe or map or lunar software for your computer so that you can all track its progress.

Most importantly, note what effect the Moon has on your emotions. Does it make you feel like lighting a candle, making love, dancing in the garden, cleaning out a cupboard, having an argument – or doing absolutely nothing? If you monitor these feelings for three or four months or so, you will find your own Moon pattern emerging. Soon you will be able to understand why you feel the way you do (and we all know that it will seem quite irrational sometimes!). Most importantly, you will be able to maximise your best moon times for action. Make full moon water by catching the full moonlight in a silver-coloured bowl; drink it or add it to your bath.

In addition, if you want to understand the mechanics as opposed to the workings of the Moon, read a book on astronomy rather than astrology to learn about orbits and the eight phases.

You might also, even if you do not read horoscopes, keep an eye for when the Moon enters your birth sign – this happens for about two and a half days each month – and monitor the effects over a period of several months. Does it make you more jittery, less cautious (which may or may not be a good thing), more intuitive, more family-orientated, reverting to out-moded patterns of reaction? Again, you can maximise positive effects if you are aware of them, like anticipating a wave and riding it, rather than being submerged by the surge of power.

Rituals and Moon phases

If possible, always work out of doors or near an open window so that you feel connected to the lunar energies. However, do not feel that you must freeze if the weather is cold: in spite of the superstitions, it is not unlucky to look at the Moon through glass. I have suggested a ritual for each phase and listed the best kinds of magick for each time.

The waxing moon

This is the time for new beginnings and long-term goals and you can repeat the same spell during each waxing moon period for projects that will take months or even a year or more to bring to fruition. The closer to the full moon, the more intense the energies will be, and a spell lasting over three days, up to and including the full moon, is excellent for an urgent project or one with a necessarily short time scale.

The waxing moon is good for spells to improve health, the gradual increase of prosperity, for attracting good luck, for fertility magick, for finding friendship, new love and romance, for job hunting, for making plans for the future and increasing psychic awareness.

The Virgin Goddesses ruled the waxing moon.

A waxing moon fertility spell

I get asked for fertility spells perhaps more than any other kind, as the modern world with everything running 24 hours a day, including lighting and heating, throws our bodies out of sync. Certainly, people no longer make love in tune with the rising energies of the Earth. While physiological problems need medical input, fertility spells practised over a few months are good for women who come off the Pill and feel anxious if they do not become pregnant in the first two or three months. They will counter the anxiety that builds up and blocks the natural rhythms. It has been scientifically shown that pleasurable sex increases the chances of conception.

But for men and women who do have difficulty conceiving, who use IVF or artificial insemination, fertility spells do seem to help to create spiritual and mental cycles and conception may prove easier. It is certainly worth trying as I know a number of people for whom fertility spells have worked – and even where they do not, they have restored joy to lovemaking.

This ritual should be carried out when the crescent moon is visible in the sky and if you live near the sea, you may be able to coincide your lovemaking with the high tide (a secluded beach is brilliant if the weather is good, although I have known people do this hundreds of miles from the sea). But if the tide is out of sync, then you still have lunar energies aplenty. You could even plan an overnight stay in a hotel with a room overlooking the shore so you can hear the sound of the waves.

※ Take an egg and carefully with a needle make a hole in it to drain out all the fluid. You can cook this and eat it or feed this to an animal to avoid waste. If you do not want to use a real egg, you can buy painted wooden or even agate ones in two halves that slot together.

※ Cut your shell in half and in one half place either a moonstone or a tiny crystal egg.

※ Place both halves open on your window ledge.

※ Make love when you wish.

※ On the night the full moon is in the sky, take a tiny paper knife and gently prick the crystal still inside the shell saying:

God to Goddess, thee to me, grant increase, if 'tis right to be.

※ Make love in the full moonlight if it is shining or at any time that night even if it is not, so that you can see the egg on the window ledge or if you are outdoors on a nearby rock.

※ As you reach orgasm, repeat, silently if your partner is nervous of magick:

God to Goddess, thee to me, grant increase, if 'tis right to be.

※ Leave your egg in the moonlight.

※ The next morning, place the two halves together and wrap the egg with the crystal inside, together with the knife, in a white silk scarf in a drawer in your bedroom.

※ Repeat, using a fresh eggshell each month. You may find your menstrual cycle moves slowly to synchronise with the Moon. If possible, make love when you wish, rather than by the chart, for a month or so.

The full moon

If you look in your Moon diary, you will see the exact time the full moon rises in your area. That is the most powerful moment of all and if you can time the climax of a spell for that time you will touch the stars. The time between rising and setting is also very potent and can do wonders for lovemaking that has become routine.

Full moon magick is good for any immediate need, for a sudden boost of power or courage, for a change of career, location or for travel, psychic protection, healing acute medical conditions, for a large sum of money needed urgently, the consummation of love or for making a permanent love commitment, for fidelity spells, especially if a relationship is looking shaky, for justice, ambition and promotion.

The full moon is ruled by the lunar Mother Goddesses.

A ritual for drawing down the Moon

There are many versions of this goddess-focused ritual and it can be used to draw power into yourself and, if you wish, to channel wisdom from a higher source (see also the Charge of the Goddess and the Charge of the God on pages 83 and 86). You can use it either for a specific purpose or for increasing your spiritual awareness and it can be used by both men and women.

You may wish during this ritual to focus on a specific lunar goddess form in her full moon aspect. The most famous one still central to modern Wicca is Diana, Roman goddess of the Moon, the hunt and fertility. Though, like her Greek counterpart, Artemis, she was worshipped originally as the maiden aspect of the Moon, in time she came to represent the full moon also.

Sometimes the Triple Lunar Goddess of modern Wicca is represented by the classical deities, Diana (the Greek Artemis), Selene and Hecate, being maiden, mother and wise woman or crone.

Isis, the Egyptian goddess who was both Moon Goddess and mother of the Sun, is also a potent focus. If you are going to use a specific goddess form, study images of her in the days before the ritual or if you have a favourite statue hold it for a few minutes before bedtime. I have a wooden figure of the Moon Mother Goddess sold to me by a Moroccan guy who said she was a patroness of his village. Whether that was a sales pitch or not, I still associate her with palm trees and a brilliant Moon in a cloudless sky. However, you may prefer to tune directly into the physical light of the silver Moon as a source of power.

You can carry out this ritual either alone or with a group. Though traditionally it is the High Priestess who draws down the Moon into herself and then channels wisdom, each member can absorb the power in his or her own way and experience the connection between the individual divine spark and the collective Divinity. The ritual I have given can easily be adapted for either a lone practitioner or a group. If there is no Moon visible because of adverse weather conditions, you can use mirrors and candles to draw down the power.

❀ Surround what is to be your circle with silver candles. In the centre, place a mirror flat on a table or the altar so that the Moon is reflected within it. Have a single, large, silver candle near the centre of the circle so it can also shine within the mirror. If you cannot position the mirror so that the Moon is seen within it, place additional silver candles close to create a light within it (before the ritual experiment with white candles that you can use around the home afterwards).

❀ If you are working in a group, each person in the ritual should stand in front of (but not too close to) their personal candle.

❀ Light the central candle and then take a lighted taper from it to the northernmost candle and light it, saying:

Thus do we light the circle of the Moon.

(If you are working in a group, pass the taper to the person standing at the candle, who will light it and say the words.)

❀ Continue in this way, re-lighting the taper if necessary from the central candle, until the entire circle of candles is alight.

❀ Now focus on the mirror and the light of the Moon or candle and say:

Goddess of the Moon, [name one or more], Silver Mother,
come to full increase, enter now those who seek your
inspiration and healing light.

❀ Chant:

Come down, O Mother, fill the sky with thy orb, come now,
come, come within.

This may develop into a song or a slow rhythmic circle dance around the mirror, as you whisper the words on the wind.

❀ Project the moonlight, actual or visualised, so that it fills the mirror and creates a brilliant sphere of light around, over and beyond the candles, so that you (or the group) are within the sphere of the Moon.

❧ As the power builds, circle and chant:

> *Within the Moon, within the power, within the Moon,*
> *now at this hour, we are the Moon.*

❧ At this point there is silence and stillness. Then, one by one if you are in a group, speak words of wisdom, inspired by the light.

❧ When this is done, sit quiet in the light of the Moon or candle.

❧ Working widdershins from the last candle to be lit, the candles can be extinguished slowly, saying at each one:

> *May the light remain within as the circle is uncast without.*

❧ Leave the central candle burning as you write and burn wishes in it, written with a silver pen on dark paper.

❧ Finally, light a small, silver candle on a cake and if you are working in a group, wish everyone present a happy Moonday. It is said that the first birthday candles were lit on moon-shaped cakes on the festival of the lunar goddess Artemis and as they were blown out, wishes were sent to her that they might be answered.

The waning moon

This is for banishing magick and for removing pain, sickness and obstacles to success and happiness. It will lessen negative influences, addictions, compulsions, negative thoughts, grief, guilt, anxiety, the envy and malice of others and destructive anger that is best let go. It can also be used for gently ending relationships and stages where there are regrets but still goodwill. A gradual binding spell to divert a person from a place or person can be effective, though binding spells are often done with the power of the full moon. The Crone Goddess rules the waning moon.

A banishing ritual

The ebb tide is very good for carrying away what is no longer wanted, but if you do not live near the sea, you can use any downward-flowing water, even a drain.

❀ Take either a dying flower or a long frond of seaweed to represent whatever it is you wish to banish.

❀ Draw a square around it, in the sand or in the earth or using chalk on a paved area. Say:

These are the limits of your power, these are the limits of your sway,
thus you lose your thrall, away, now, away.

❀ Rub out the square, saying:

See, even this your power is gone, leave my life,
your day is done.

❀ Cast the symbol on to the ebb tide. You may need to wade out to make sure it does not come back to shore. Alternatively, cast it into flowing water with a final:

Away, no more stay.

❀ Do something, however small, to make yourself happy for the rest of the day, so that it has happy memories.

You may need to repeat the spell for a number of waning moons if the matter or person has a strong hold.

If the compulsion or person returns before the next waning moon, try this short ritual.

❀ Run a bath and add a drop or two of eucalyptus or pine and lavender.

❀ On a tiny square bar of soap, write a symbol to represent the problem, draw a cross through it and leave it to melt in the water while you enjoy your bath.

❀ Get out of the bath when you are refreshed and when the soap has completely melted, pull out the plug, saying:

Sorrow grievous, flow to sea, never more to trouble me.

❀ Do something positive while the soap is melting. If you do not have time for a bath, you can melt your soap in a bowl or bucket and pour it down a drain.

CHAPTER 12
Planets and Angels

Different days of the week and hours of the day and night are associated with specific energies and each particular time is ruled by a planet and an archangel. Though these were primarily centred on ceremonial magick, they can also be used to give focus and potency to informal spells. The planetary and angelic hours can also be applied to the everyday sphere, for example by choosing the appropriate day and even hour for beginning a money-making scheme or a first meeting with a potential business partner or lover. You can further amplify the salient qualities and strengths of these times by using oils, incenses, coloured candles and crystals linked with the specific planets and angels. There are also strong connections between the planet and angel of the day, though angelic magick tends to be used, not surprisingly, for rituals with a more spiritual and ecological or global focus. As you discover particular combinations that work well, you can add them to your Book of Shadows.

Planetary magical days of the week

Though I have written primarily about the significance of the different days, I have also listed the effects of the planetary hours.

The planets have had a special place in both ritual magick and astrology, since the Ancient Babylonians and Chaldeans first observed them wandering across the sky (the word 'planet' derives from the Greek *planetes,* meaning 'wanderer') against the fixed constellations of the zodiac.

The ancients knew of only five planets – Mercury, Venus, Mars, Jupiter and Saturn. Uranus, Neptune and Pluto were discovered only after the invention of the telescope and so have not assumed the importance in magick that they have in astrology. What is more, the first astronomers also counted the Sun and the Moon as planets and credited them with certain qualities that have become woven into the Western astrological and magical traditions.

Astrologers believe that the positions of the planets in the zodiac at the time of an individual's birth can influence and indicate that person's fate. In magick, the planetary strengths can be applied to any purpose under the 'As above, so below' principle that stresses the interconnectedness of the whole universe.

You can create your own spells by using the associations, much as you create recipes by knowing the qualities and blending power of individual ingredients. And just as in cookery, those spells or recipes where you break away from the set formula are often the most successful. For example, if you wanted to do well in an interview for a job, you might burn a wish in a candle of the colour blue – for careers – on Thursday, the day of Jupiter, who is associated with employment and worldly success and all matters of increase; for extra potency, the candle could be surrounded with small blue sodalite or lapis lazuli, Jupiter's special crystals. You could also burn cedar, one of Jupiter's incenses or sandalwood oil.

If you needed more general career success, you could make or buy an amulet of tin, the metal of Jupiter, perhaps a coin from a museum shop that you charged with power every Thursday by sprinkling it with salt, passing it through cedar incense, a blue candle flame and the fragrance of burning sandalwood oil.

If your projected job was to do with communication, technology or the media which are ruled by Mercury, you could carry out the spell on two consecutive days, beginning with the communicative power of Mercury on his hour, the third after sunset on a Wednesday (see page 235). You could light yellow candles and use a Mercurian crystal, such as yellow jasper or a yellow-banded agate, and burn dill incense and fennel essential oil. On the second day of the spell, the Thursday, carry out the spell again at the third hour after sunset, which on this day is Jupiter's evening hour, to add his authority and opportunities for expansion.

Planetary days and their applications

In this section I have listed the particular strengths of each planet, together with their most powerful times. Remember that, in addition, the sign you are born under will exert its influences on you at all times.

☉ The Sun

Sunday, the day of the Sun, is for spells for personal fulfilment and ambition, power and success, for increasing the flow of the life force, asserting or strengthening your identity and individuality, for innovation of all kinds and new beginnings. It is potent also for energy, joy, health prosperity, spiritual awareness, self-confidence, for bringing wealth and prosperity if there is poverty and failure, for breaking a run of bad luck, and for all matters concerning fathers. I have listed various solar deities in Chapter 4. Though there are powerful Sun goddesses, the Sun's focus is mainly male/animus/yang in both men and women.

Sun hour spells bring a surge of energy and vitality and so are excellent for personal empowerment and renewal.

Element: Fire

Colour: Gold

Crystals: Amber, carnelian, diamond, clear crystal quartz, tiger's eye, topaz

Incenses: Cloves, cinnamon, frankincense

Trees: Bay, birch, laurel

Herbs and oils: Juniper, rosemary, saffron, St John's wort

Metal: Gold

The Sun rules Leo, 23 July–23 August, and is most powerful for those born under this sign.

☽ The Moon

Monday, the day of the Moon, is for spells concerning the home, family matters and the influence of the family, especially the mother, children and animals. Its prime focus is fertility and all the ebbs and flows of the human body, mind and psyche. It is also potent for protection, especially while travelling, for psychic development, clairvoyance, secrets and meaningful dreams, all sea and garden rituals and for herb magick and healing.

Although there are Moon Gods, lunar energies are primarily yin/female/anima in both men and women.

Moon hour spells are good for bringing unconscious powers to the fore and thus also for gaining magical insights and for bringing wishes into actuality.

Element: Water

Colour: Silver or white (although some magical traditions that use the Triple Goddess in ritual dress show the Maiden in white, the Mother in red and the Crone in black)

Crystals: Moonstone, mother of pearl, pearl, selenite, opal

Incenses: Jasmine, myrrh, mimosa

Trees: Willow, alder

Herbs and oils: Chamomile, lotus, poppy, wintergreen

Metal: Silver

The Moon rules Cancer, 22 June–22 July, and its spells are particularly potent during that period and for all who are born under Cancer.

♂ Mars

Tuesday, the day of Mars, is good for spells for courage, taking the initiative at home, independence and separateness from others, and change. It also represents aggression, competitiveness and anger, all qualities that can be used positively for altruistic purpose, for example, standing out against injustice and protecting the vulnerable and loved ones under threat. This is the lifeblood planet and so can be used to overcome seemingly impossible odds, to defeat opposition, to survive and thrive. It is also for physical health and vitality and so its rituals are always dynamic.

Mars rules passion and the consummation of love. Like Fire magick, the energy of Mars is very powerful and so spells should always be for positive purpose and with a circle that can afterwards be closed down.

Mars was the Roman Warrior God, and legendary father of Romulus and Remus, the founders of Rome. As god of both agriculture and war, he represented the ideal Roman, first as a farmer and then as a conqueror and so the agricultural Fire festivals are linked with his power. He is the Roman equivalent of the Greek Ares and the Viking Tyr, the altruistic Warrior God who sacrificed his sword arm to save the other deities (the word Tuesday derives from his name).

The hour of Mars is especially good for psychic self-defence and for courage in a crisis.

Element: Fire

Colour: Red

Crystals: Garnet, bloodstone, ruby, jasper

Incenses: Dragon's blood, ginger, mint, thyme

Trees: Cypress, holly, pine

Herbs and oils: Basil, coriander, garlic, pepper, tarragon

Metal: Iron or steel

Mars rules Aries, March–20 April, and is the co-ruler of Scorpio, 24 October–22 November. In magick, it is most potent during these two Sun sign periods and for those born under Aries and Scorpio.

☿ Mercury

Wednesday, the day of Mercury, is good for spells to assist money-making ventures, for clear communication, persuasion, adaptability and versatility, for improving memory and sharpening logic, for learning, examinations and tests, for mastering new technology, for short-distance or brief breaks, and for conventional methods of healing, especially surgery. It is also potent for business negotiations, overcoming debts, repelling envy, malice and spite and those who would deceive. For this reason, Mercury spells must always be used with honest intent. Wednesday is also traditionally associated with divination.

Mercury, the planet nearest the Sun, completes its orbit in only 88 days and so is named after the fleet-footed messenger god who, like his Greek predecessor, Hermes, carried the healing caduceus. He is also linked with the Anglo-Saxon god, Woden, after whom Wednesday is named.

Mercury hour spells are good for finding a quick way out of difficulties and for melting rigid opinions in others.

Element: Air

Colour: Yellow

Crystals: Agate, citrine, falcon's eye, jasper, malachite, onyx

Incenses: Lavender, lemongrass, mace

Trees: Hazel, ash

Herbs and oils: Dill, fennel, parsley, valerian

Mercury rules Gemini, 22 May–21 June, and also Virgo, 24 August–22 September. In magick it is most potent during those periods and particularly so for those born under Gemini and Virgo.

♃ Jupiter

Thursday, the day of Jupiter, is good for all forms of increase and expansion, whether improving fortune or career prospects or bringing promotion, power, ambition and joy through fulfilment of objectives. Jupiter's influence may be personal or more usually socially orientated; it is also potent for leadership, for conscious wisdom, creativity, for extending one's influence in the wider world, for idealism, matters of justice and the law, authority and altruism. Jupiter increases what already exists, so can bring greater prosperity and abundance or success and good fortune. It rules marriage, permanent relationships (both business and personal), fidelity, loyalty and male potency in both the human and animal kingdom.

Ironically, Jupiter can lead to excesses, including greed, addictions and obsessions, so it can also be used for banishing these.

Jupiter, known as the Sky Father, was the supreme Roman god, ruler of the universe. Like Zeus, his Greek counterpart, Jupiter controlled the thunderbolts, which were carried by his eagle, the noblest of the birds. However, he ruled not despotically, but as the chief of a triumvirate of gods: the other two were Juno, his consort, and Minerva, goddess of wisdom, who made up the feminine principle of deeper, more instinctual wisdom.

Use the hour of Jupiter to profit from an opportunity to upgrade your life.

Element: Air

Colour: Blue/purple

Crystals: Azurite, lapis lazuli, sodalite, turquoise

Incenses: Agrimony, cedar, sandalwood, sage

Trees: Beech, oak

Herbs and oils: Borage, cinquefoil, coltsfoot, hyssop, mistletoe

Metal: Tin

Jupiter rules Sagittarius, 23 November–21 December, and is co-ruler of Pisces, 19 February–20 March. Jupiter spells are therefore especially potent in the period of Sagittarius and Pisces and at all times to those born under these Sun signs.

♀ Venus

Friday, the day of Venus, is associated with love and all forms of love magick, especially to attract love. Because Venus rules harmony and peace, however, if the success of a love spell depends on ruining another person's happiness and security, it tends not to work without repercussions on the spell-caster.

Venus is also invoked for beauty, the arts, crafts and music, relationships, friendships, blossoming sexuality, the acquisition of beautiful possessions and the slow but sure growth of prosperity, for Venus rules all matters of growth. Like the Moon, she can be invoked for horticulture and the environment; because she can be associated with excesses of unwise love and romance, spells can be created in her name to reduce the influence of destructive lovers and possessiveness. Also like the Moon, the spells of Venus are potent for fertility and for matters of women's health.

Venus is sometimes known as the morning or evening star and at her brightest she is the most brilliant object in the sky besides the Sun and Moon. For this reason, in many cultures she took the name of the goddess of beauty. She was Ishtar to the Babylonians, Aphrodite to the Greeks and her Viking counterparts are the goddess Frigg, the Mother Goddess, and Freyja, maiden goddess of beauty and love, after one or both of whom Friday is named.

Spells at the hour of Venus are especially good for new love and the growth of self-love, for if we do not love ourselves we cannot love others creatively.

Element: Earth

Colour: Green, pink

Crystals: Amethyst, emerald, jade, moss agate, rose quartz

Incenses: Geranium, rose, strawberry, vervain

Trees: Almond, apple, birch

Herbs and oils: Feverfew, mugwort, pennyroyal, verbena, yarrow

Metal: Copper

Venus rules Taurus, 21 April–21 May, and also Libra, 23 September–23 October. Venus spells are especially potent during these Sun sign periods and for those born under Taurus and Libra.

♄ Saturn

Saturday, the day of Saturn, is potent for spells concerned with unfinished business, and with endings that lead to beginnings. It is therefore a good day for all slow-moving matters and for accepting limitations, as well as for overcoming obstacles that are long-standing or need careful handling. It also aids lifting depression or doubts, meditation, long-term psychic protection, locating lost objects, animals and people and regaining self-control whether over bad habits or emotions. It is also the planet of mystical experiences and of exploring the unconscious depths of the individual and collective psyche and for past-life work.

Saturn can be used to slow down the outward flow of money and to encourage repayment by those who owe you favours or money. It helps banish pain and illness and brings acceptance of what cannot be changed.

Saturn is the shadow side of Jupiter, and offers the reality factor, the constraints of fate, time and space, but also turns challenge into opportunity, effort and perseverance. He represents the joy of Jupiter tempered by experience, the expansiveness of Jupiter held in check by caution. Saturn was the Roman form of Cronus, Greek god of time, who was deposed by his son Jupiter, after he had refused to allow natural change and progression. But even this led to joy, because Saturn was sent to Italy where he taught the farmers agriculture and engineering and he established a Golden Age of peace and plenty.

Saturn hours are especially good for bringing patience and for dealing with long-terms obstacles and difficulties.

Element: Earth

Colour: Black/grey

Crystals: Haematite, jet, lodestone, obsidian, smoky quartz

Incenses: Aconite, cypress, patchouli

Trees: Blackthorn, yew

Herbs and oils: Aspen, bistort, comfrey, horsetail, Solomon's seal

Metal: Lead or pewter

Saturn rules Capricorn, 22 December–20 January, and is co-ruler of Aquarius, 21 January–18 February.

These Sun periods are most potent for Saturn spells and for those born under these signs at all times.

Magical hours

The hours of the day are also influenced by the planets. To choose the best time for a spell, you should consult first pages 227–32 on the planetary days and then page 235 where I explain the planetary hours. For example, if you were carrying out a love spell in which you wanted rapid results, perhaps for a special meeting, you could work on a Friday, Venus's day, on both her hours – sunrise and the third hour after sunset. If you wanted courage in love, you would use a Mars hour on a Friday. If you needed to communicate your feelings, but found it difficult, you could add the energies of a Mercury hour to a Friday love spell. If you wanted a banishing spell for shedding excess weight, you could use the last days of the waning moon cycle when it is in the sky during the morning before it sets. The banishing lunar energies should take away the compulsion to binge that is keeping you from a healthy lifestyle and if you use them at the hour of Venus, this would increase your inner beauty and help to bring you to a state of self-love. Remember that the beginning of the hour is always the most potent.

The times of sunrise and sunset are different each day. Calculate the precise timings from true sunrise, which is the first hour of the magical day. Alternatively, for a less formal spell, you can make an approximation. Any good diary will have the sunrise and sunset for each day, but choose one also with the moonrises and moonsets. You will need a calculator if you decide to use the exact planetary hours. You can calculate a week or even a month ahead if there is a period in which you intend to do a lot of magical work. In this way you can maximise the energies of specific hours and choose a good time for anything from asking for a rise at work to sorting out the budget with a reluctant partner. Enter the planetary and angelic hours in your diary or the appropriate section in your Book of Shadows. These calculations can also keep bored children amused on rainy afternoons – just tell them stories about the angels and planets first. Children also adapt quickly to angelic time – after all, it's far more fun if you change sad old bedtime into St Michael's hour and have a bedtime story by the light of his golden candle.

To calculate the magical hours, you need to divide the time from sunrise to sunset and then the time between sunset and sunrise by 12. At the height of summer, the days are much longer than the nights, so each 'day' hour will be longer than the 'night' hours. At the spring and autumn equinoxes, when day and night are equal, day and night hours will be of the same length.

As a short-cut, when you need instant magick, you can use the times of sunrise, noon, sunset and midnight and the day of the week energies, with approximations of hours if you wish. Combine the day energies with the power of solar magick, which tends to be more immediate than lunar. So if you are seeking a new beginning, go for dawn. For full power or realising your potential, carry out your rituals at noon, the height of the Sun, and for banishing spells, try sunset. You will know instinctively if it's a solar or lunar issue and whether you need a blast of Sun power or clarity, or more subtle Moon bindings or unravellings.

The planetary hours

Sunrise to sunset

The first 'hour' of each day, starting at sunrise, is ruled by its day planet. The planetary order has a regular pattern.

Hour	Sunday	Monday	Tuesday	Wednesday	Thursday	Friday	Saturday
1	Sun	Moon	Mars	Mercury	Jupiter	Venus	Saturn
2	Venus	Saturn	Sun	Moon	Mars	Mercury	Jupiter
3	Mercury	Jupiter	Venus	Saturn	Sun	Moon	Mars
4	Moon	Mars	Mercury	Jupiter	Venus	Saturn	Sun
5	Saturn	Sun	Moon	Mars	Mercury	Jupiter	Venus
6	Jupiter	Venus	Saturn	Sun	Moon	Mars	Mercury
7	Mars	Mercury	Jupiter	Venus	Saturn	Sun	Moon
8	Sun	Moon	Mars	Mercury	Jupiter	Venus	Saturn
9	Venus	Saturn	Sun	Moon	Mars	Mercury	Jupiter
10	Mercury	Jupiter	Venus	Saturn	Sun	Moon	Mars
11	Moon	Mars	Mercury	Jupiter	Venus	Saturn	Sun
12	Saturn	Sun	Moon	Mars	Mercury	Jupiter	Venus

Sunset

Hour	Sunday	Monday	Tuesday	Wednesday	Thursday	Friday	Saturday
1	Jupiter	Venus	Saturn	Sun	Moon	Mars	Mercury
2	Mars	Mercury	Jupiter	Venus	Saturn	Sun	Moon
3	Sun	Moon	Mars	Mercury	Jupiter	Venus	Saturn
4	Venus	Saturn	Sun	Moon	Mars	Mercury	Jupiter
5	Mercury	Jupiter	Venus	Saturn	Sun	Moon	Mars
6	Moon	Mars	Mercury	Jupiter	Venus	Saturn	Sun
7	Saturn	Sun	Moon	Mars	Mercury	Jupiter	Venus
8	Jupiter	Venus	Saturn	Sun	Moon	Mars	Mercury
9	Mars	Mercury	Jupiter	Venus	Saturn	Sun	Moon
10	Sun	Moon	Mars	Mercury	Jupiter	Venus	Saturn
11	Venus	Saturn	Sun	Moon	Mars	Mercury	Jupiter
12	Mercury	Jupiter	Venus	Saturn	Sun	Moon	Mars

Angelic correspondences

You can, if you wish, use angelic rulers instead of planetary ones for the magical hours, or combine the energies of both. In practice, if your magick has a spiritual focus or is concerned with healing or global or ecological matters, angels work better than planets. If you have calculated your daily planetary hours, your angels will correspond exactly.

As with the planets, each archangel rules the first hour after sunrise of his own day. Though many people do regard the Archangels as male, they are androgynous and so I have called them 'he' merely for convenience.

Many magicians from the Middle Ages onwards have used angels as part of formal rituals and they have long been a potent form of psychic protection both for guarding the four corners of the ritual circle and as personal guides in less formal magick.

Below I have given the association for each of the daily and hourly angels. Since angels are a very personal form of empowerment and protection, I have not made the descriptions too precise, however. To learn more about them, see the section in Further Reading on page 297, or try entering angels on your web browser. Images can be downloaded and form a focus for meditations, through which you can invoke each angel using your own higher self or consciousness. In this way, the protective angel draws on your own spiritual powers.

Archangels and their days of the week

Michael

Michael is the archangel who rules the Sun (see also page 227). Michael's day is **Sunday**.

Michael, the Initiator, brings illumination and inspiration in many spheres of life, through the efforts of our individual creative spirit. Michael is the guardian of all who stand alone with their unique vision for bettering the world and are not prepared to compromise their ideals for humanity, purely for money or fame. This archangel can be invoked in ritual for all creative ventures, for original ideas and individuality, contact with the Divinity and the Spirit Guides, for reviving barren land despoiled by industrialisation, and for cleansing air pollution.

Colour: Gold

Crystals: Citrine and pure crystal quartz

Incenses or oils: Frankincense and orange

Gabriel

Gabriel is the archangel who rules the Moon (see page 228). Gabriel's day is **Monday**.

Gabriel, the Integrator, brings increased spiritual awareness, mystical experiences, astral travel and significant dreams, as well as connection with the world soul and mind through the unconscious mind, especially in prayer and meditation and in beautiful, natural places close to water. He brings deepening spirituality within the family and work environment. He can be invoked for protection against inclement weather, for travel across water, for taking away sorrow and for diminishing self-destructive tendencies and replacing them with the gentle growth of new hope. Gabriel also rules rituals to protect water creatures and to cleanse polluted seas, lakes and rivers.

Colour: Silver

Crystal: Moonstone and opal

Incenses or oils: Myrrh and jasmine

Samael

Samael is the archangel who rules the planet Mars (see page 229). Samael's day is **Tuesday**.

He is sometimes called the Severity of God and as such is an angel of cleansing and of righteous anger. One of the seven regents of the world and said to be served by two million angels, he is also called the Dark Angel who in the guise of the serpent tempted Eve. This is a very ancient concept in which kings and rulers were constantly tested to prove worthy of their sacred trust and so he is not an angel to invoke lightly.

Samael is also the avenger who offers protection to the weak and vulnerable and cleanses doubts and weakness, replacing them with spiritual courage to stand against what is corrupt, especially those who abuse power. He can be invoked for rituals to relieve those in war-torn lands, minorities who are being oppressed and endangered species

Colour: Red

Crystals: Garnet and bloodstone

Incenses or oils: Allspice and dragon's blood

Raphael

Raphael is the archangel of the planet Mercury (see page 230). Raphael's day is **Wednesday**.

Raphael, the Harmoniser, offers healing of all kinds, protects children, bringing guidance and sustenance to all who are lost whether physically, emotionally or spiritually. He can be invoked in all health matters, for spiritual knowledge and insight and for alleviating the worries of daily lives that keeps us bound to the Earth. Most importantly he shows us how to teach others our spiritual insights. He heals technological and chemical pollution and the adverse effects of modern living.

Colour: Yellow

Crystals: Citrine and yellow jasper

Incenses or oils: Lavender and clover

Sachiel

Sachiel is the archangel of the planet Jupiter (see page 230). Sachiel's day is **Thursday**.

Sachiel, the Divine Benefactor, is the angel of charity who says that only by giving freely to others will our own needs be met. He works constantly to help others and to improve the lives of humankind. He can therefore be invoked for all rituals to bring better harvests, both physical and emotional, and for increasing abundance and prosperity, not just for a minority but the good of all. He restores run-down areas or cities where unemployment has been lost, blending new skills with traditional knowledge.

Colour: Blue

Crystals: Lapis lazuli and turquoise

Incenses or oils: Sandalwood and sage

Anael

Anael is the archangel who rules over Venus (see page 231). Anael's day is **Friday**.

Anael, the Regenerator, is one of the seven angels of creation; he is Prince of Archangels and controls kings and kingdoms. His is pure, altruistic love, love of one's fellow beings and of all creatures in the universe. He can be invoked for all matters of forgiveness, both towards ourselves for what is past and towards others that we may be free from their thrall.

Anael brings harmony to places and people. He restores natural balance, healing rainforests, bringing wildlife habitats to the city and greenery everywhere. For his fertility is that of the whole Earth, rich in fruit, flowers, people and creatures of all kinds, whether living in the wild or in sanctuaries.

Colour: Green

Crystals: Jade and rose quartz

Incenses or oils: Valerian and rose

Cassiel

Cassiel is the archangel of Saturn (see page 232). Cassiel's day is **Saturday**.

Though Cassiel, the Conservator, is the angel of solitude and temperance, he was traditionally invoked for investment and speculation. In a sense, this is not incompatible, for true speculation is based not on random selection, but on deliberation and an almost intuitive scanning of any situation. He brings moderation in actions and dealings and development of inner stillness and contemplation.

Cassiel can form a focus for rituals for the reversal of bad fortune and for conserving resources and places in their natural state. Invoke him for conserving history and tradition as a legacy for future generations.

Colour: Purple

Crystals: Obsidian and jet

Incenses or oils: Cypress and thyme

Archangels and their hours

Like the planets, archangels influence particular hours as well as days.

Sunrise to sunset

Hour	Sunday	Monday	Tuesday	Wednesday	Thursday	Friday	Saturday
1	Michael	Gabriel	Samael	Raphael	Sachiel	Anael	Cassiel
2	Anael	Cassiel	Michael	Gabriel	Samael	Raphael	Sachiel
3	Raphael	Sachiel	Anael	Cassiel	Michael	Gabriel	Samael
4	Gabriel	Samael	Raphael	Sachiel	Anael	Cassiel	Michael
5	Cassiel	Michael	Gabriel	Samael	Raphael	Sachiel	Anael
6	Sachiel	Anael	Cassiel	Michael	Gabriel	Samael	Raphael

7	Samael	Raphael	Sachiel	Anael	Cassiel	Michael	Gabriel
8	Michael	Gabriel	Samael	Raphael	Sachiel	Anael	Cassiel
9	Anael	Cassiel	Michael	Gabriel	Samael	Raphael	Sachiel
10	Raphael	Sachiel	Anael	Cassiel	Michael	Gabriel	Samael
11	Gabriel	Samael	Raphael	Sachiel	Anael	Cassiel	Michael
12	Cassiel	Michael	Gabriel	Samael	Raphael	Sachiel	Anael

Sunset to sunrise

Hour	Sunday	Monday	Tuesday	Wednesday	Thursday	Friday	Saturday
1	Sachiel	Anael	Cassiel	Michael	Gabriel	Samael	Raphael
2	Samael	Raphael	Sachiel	Anael	Cassiel	Michael	Gabriel
3	Michael	Gabriel	Samael	Raphael	Sachiel	Anael	Cassiel
4	Anael	Cassiel	Michael	Gabriel	Samael	Raphael	Sachiel
5	Raphael	Sachiel	Anael	Cassiel	Michael	Gabriel	Samael
6	Gabriel	Samael	Raphael	Sachiel	Anael	Cassiel	Michael
7	Cassiel	Michael	Gabriel	Samael	Raphael	Sachiel	Anael
8	Sachiel	Anael	Cassiel	Michael	Gabriel	Samael	Raphael
9	Samael	Raphael	Sachiel	Anael	Cassiel	Michael	Gabriel
10	Michael	Gabriel	Samael	Raphael	Sachiel	Anael	Cassiel
11	Anael	Cassiel	Michael	Gabriel	Samael	Raphael	Sachiel
12	Raphael	Sachiel	Anael	Cassiel	Michael	Gabriel	Samael

A ritual with seven angels

This would be a suitable ritual for welcoming a new baby or child into a family whether in birth, by adoption or through the joining of two existing families. It may also be used for sending a teenager out into the world. You can also adapt the ritual to welcome adults into a family or help them to move on to a new phase or place.

You might like to use a seven-branched candlestick, like the Jewish menorah, and light a candle on seven consecutive hours throughout the day. You could carry it out on the baby's christening or naming day or on a quiet day with the teenager. Alternatively, you could perform the ritual for seven days at the same hour of the day on the week before the christening or departure and make this a special family orientated hour.

It does not matter in which order you invoke the angels. Start at the hour that suits you best. If you keep to the same hour, you will work with the energies of each of the archangels over a seven-day period.

Alexandra, a friend who carried out the ritual for her son Sam who was going away to college, began on the first hour at sunset on Wednesday, which meant the ritual used the energies of the archangel Michael. The final ritual on the Tuesday was Sam's leaving party. Sam joined in the final candle-lighting just before his party and later said that when he was lonely or scared at college, he remembered the candles and felt protected.

If you cannot obtain candles of the right colour, use white. If you cannot find the right angelic fragrance, substitute lavender or sandalwood – these are all-purpose. For angelic crystals, use any of the colours associated with the angel, if the specific ones you want are not available. The crystals need only be tiny.

I have set this out as a seven-day ritual but if you are instead holding the ritual on seven consecutive hours, then consult the tables above for the order of angels, as this will be different. You can start at any day or hour as long as you use the fragrances and candles or their substitutes of the ruling angel.

✤ Take your seven angel candles and place them in holders.

✤ Light a golden candle as the hour begins and then light your frankincense incense.

✤ Take a small, clear crystal quartz for Michael and pass it through the candle flame, saying:

> *Flame high, O power of illumination, enter might*
> *of Michael's sword, inspiration, life-bringer.*

✤ Pass the crystal through the smoke of the incense, saying:

> *Enter through this fragrance the clear vision of Michael,*
> *fire of the Sun, light-bringer.*

✤ Hold the crystal high in the air and circle it deosil, over the child, if present. If they are absent or would be self-conscious, use a photograph or personal item belonging to the child, saying:

> *Endow, O Michael, – [name the child] that he/she may have*
> *the powers of originality and the creativity to make the world*
> *a better place by his/her presence here.*

✤ Place the crystal in a clear dish in front of the candles and blow out the candle, sending the light to the person. Leave the incense to burn through and spend the rest of the hour in a pleasurable way with the focus of the ritual or in a family-orientated activity.

❧ On the second day at the same hour, light the Michael candle and the silver Gabriel candle, plus some myrrh incense.

❧ Take a moonstone, or other crystal of Gabriel, and pass it through the flame of the silver candle, saying:

Flame high, O mystical guardian, with thy mighty sceptre, ruler of the waters of the Moon and the oceans, bringer of dreams.

❧ Pass the crystal through the incense, saying:

Enter through this fragrance, the compassion and understanding of Gabriel, truth-bringer and clarion of hope.

❧ Hold the crystal high in the air over the child or their symbol and circle it deosil, saying:

Endow, O Gabriel, – [name the child] that he/she may speak always wise words and gentle counsel, drawn from the depths of the universal well of wisdom.

❧ Place this crystal in the dish with the crystal quartz and blow out first the Michael and then the Gabriel candle, sending the light to the child. Leave the incense to burn. Again, spend a quiet but joyful hour.

❧ On the third day at the same hour, light the first two candles and then the red Samael candle and some dragon's blood incense.

❧ Take a bloodstone and pass it through the Samael candle, saying:

Flame high, O protective spirit, dispelling danger and darkness, warrior of flame, bringer of faith.

❧ Pass the crystal next through the incense, saying:

Enter through this fragrance, the courage and determination of Samael, defender of the weak and oppressed.

❧ Hold the crystal high in the air over the child or symbol, and circle it deosil, saying:

Endow, O Samael, – [name the child] that he/she may never falter from a challenge and fear none who seek to oppress or intimidate with harsh words or unjust deed.

❧ Place this crystal in the bowl with the others and blow out the candles, ending with the Samael candle, sending the light to the child and leaving the incense to burn through.

❧ On the fourth day at the same hour, light the first three candles and then the yellow Raphael candle and lavender incense.

❦ Take a citrine and pass it through the Raphael candle, saying:

Flame high, great messenger, with thy pilgrim's staff, bringing safety to travellers far from home, O guide and keeper of all.

❦ Pass the crystal next through the incense, saying:

Enter through this fragrance, the healing and nurturing powers of Raphael, teacher and uplifter of the spirit.

❦ Hold the crystal over the child or symbol and circle it deosil, saying:

Endow, O Raphael, `– [name the child] that he/she may pass between the dimensions and be as at home in the world of spirit as of matter.

❦ Place the crystal in the bowl with the others and blow out the candles, ending with the Raphael candle, sending the light to the child and allowing the incense to burn through. Again, spend time in a positive family way.

❦ On the fifth day at the same hour, light the four candles, then the blue candle of Sachiel and some sandalwood incense.

❦ Take a lapis lazuli and pass it through the blue candle flame, saying:

Flame high, lord of all abundance, bringing increase of all that is good and noble and joy-giving.

❦ Pass the crystal next through the incense, saying;

Enter through this fragrance, the benign and all-encompassing powers of Sachiel, bringer of knowledge and understanding of the universe and its creatures.

❦ Hold the crystal high over the child or symbol and say:

Endow, O Sachiel, – [name the child] that he/she may know prosperity of spirit as well as of material blessings, and share willingly with others the fruits of good fortune won by endeavour and application.

❦ Place the crystal in the dish and blow out the candles, ending with the Sachiel candle, sending its light to the child and leaving the incense to burn through.

❦ On the sixth day at the same hour, light the five other candles and the green Anael candle and some rose incense.

❦ Take a rose quartz crystal and pass it over the green candle, saying:

Flame high, gentle peace-bringer, spreading harmony and goodwill even where there is division.

❅ Pass the crystal next through the incense, saying:

Enter through this fragrance, the love and fertility of Anael,
bringer of reconciliation and connections between souls
as well as mind and body.

❅ Hold the crystal high over the child or symbol and circle it deosil, saying:

Endow, O Anael, – [name the child] that he/she may love all
creatures, man, woman, child, bird, animal, plant and all
sacred places, which is the whole world.

❅ Blow out the candles, the last being the Anael candle, and send the light to the child. Leave the incense to burn through.

❅ Finally, on the seventh day at the same hour, light a purple candle and cypress incense for Cassiel.

❅ Take an obsidian crystal and pass it through the purple candle flame, saying:

Flame high, you who bring silence and contemplation to a
noisy world, spreading stillness and detachment in which
the spirit may thrive.

❅ Pass the crystal next through the incense, saying:

Enter through this fragrance the patience and perseverance
of Cassiel, bringer of wise caution and preserver of all that is
of worth in our heritage.

❅ Hold the crystal high over the child or symbol, saying:

Endow, O Cassiel, – [name the child] that he/she may turn
obstacle into challenge and maximise opportunities within
the constraints of what is possible, rather than lamenting what
is not, and build on the foundations of the old world
a new and better place.

❅ This time, leave all the candles and the incense to burn through and if the child is present express in your own words, even to a tiny baby, how much you treasure them in your life and how they have enriched your being. Give the crystals to the child.

CHAPTER 13
Seasons and Festivals

It was the day before Hallowe'en and my caravan site was closing for the winter season. As always, I had left the packing and cleaning to the last evening, reluctant to believe that as Samhain, the Celtic name for Hallowe'en, recalls, it really was summer's end. Then the worst storms in the UK since the 1987 hurricane blew up and suddenly there was total darkness. Fortunately I have a number of candles, but the light was not great enough to continue working (at least that was my excuse). All round was total blackness with only the sound of the wind and crashing sea and the centuries slipped away. Time without the clock was now measured by the burning down of the candles and took on another dimension. Though it had been barely five o'clock when the power cut occurred, it was already dark.

It truly was time out of time and the rhythms of the modern world that had ruled even my country haven suddenly ceased to exist. It was not possible to read, work, watch television, listen to music or, most importantly, keep an eye on the clock in order to know when to switch to the next period of activity or to meet external demands. I could not drive home because the roads were closed.

Suddenly, seasonal magick made a great deal of sense, for if you do live by natural light, then in winter, with its long and cold nights, your body will slow down and your priorities will become food, rest and warmth, needs expressed magically in the ancient festivals of winter.

Living by the seasons

It may be that our very early ancestors mainly made love in the late spring/early summer when the energies of the Earth were rising and the days getting longer and warmer. In this way, the newly pregnant mother could benefit from an abundance of fresh food in the summer and autumn and give birth at a time when she would naturally be resting for the winter with the dark nights. This would enable her to spend time with the infant before returning to the fields or to tend the herds in spring. This pattern is reflected in the old myths of the Virgin

Goddess, who became pregnant at the spring equinox and gave birth to the new Sun on the mid-winter solstice that became christianised as our Christmas.

So in these earlier and by no means idyllic times, everything – Earth, cattle, corn, humans and animals – was in harmony, not only physically, but spiritually. Fertility spells and the rituals marking the passing of the year were a natural part of popular folk magick and of the everyday world and with the celebration of the harvest, so blessings were called down on every hearth and home.

Nowadays, even if you live in rural areas, it is very easy to miss the passing of the seasons. With artificial lighting, central heating, cars and the availability of once seasonal and localised foods now flown around the world to meet an all-year-round demand, we can lose touch with our own rhythms and the natural fluctuations of our spiritual as well as bodily energies. However, as you work with the seasonal divisions of the Wheel of the Year (see below), so you will harmonise into your own natural cycle. Of course we can't stay at home all winter, but we can rearrange our priorities so that slower activities centred on self or family come to the fore. We may even, perhaps, try to spend at least a day a month when we live by the sky and not the clock, and sleep and wake with the light.

SAD, or Seasonal Affective Disorder, the recently recognised condition that seems to cause depression and inertia through lack of sunlight, may occur because we need to operate at full peak in the modern world at a time when our body clock is telling us to rest in our cave. Even in warmer lands, the absence of light can indicate a time for talking quietly with friends by candlelight, rather than seeking bright lights and music. On my visits to Andalucia, I have observed that, especially in country places, older people keep much more to the cycles that have determined the rural way of life for many centuries.

The Wheel of the Year

The Wheel of the Year, or Eightfold Wheel, is a magical and spiritual division of the year that may date back to the first agricultural societies. It was formalised by the Celts, although some historians believe that it was predated by an earlier threefold division that celebrated the beginning of winter, mid-winter and midsummer, and was perhaps linked to the movement of the herds.

The Wheel of the Year co-exists with the wider seasonal divisions of the year and incorporates the four solar festivals; these fall on the solstices and the equinoxes, the astronomical marker points of the ebbs and flows of cosmic energies. Between each of these solar festivals, which are known to witches as the Lesser Sabbats, is one of the four great Fire festivals that are major rites in the Wiccan and neo-pagan calendar, as they were to the Celts.

It is interesting to note that the Wheel of the Year is mirrored almost exactly in the Medicine Wheel, or Circle of Power, that is central to all the magick of the Native American Indians. The spokes of the Medicine Wheel link the celestial, human and natural cycles. The Medicine Wheel was made of stones and could be created wherever a tribe camped. Some were 90 feet in diameter, but research suggests that some were much smaller and were placed around ceremonial tepees to be used not only by the shaman but also by anyone seeking a spiritual path. Depicted around the wheels are *totem*, or power, animals, representing each birth month and season, the four main directions and winds. The totems vary according to each tribe's mythology. There are more than 500 different systems in North America alone.

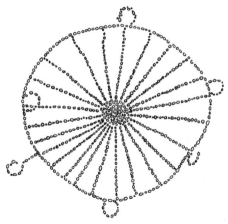

In the southern hemisphere, as I explained on page 42, practitioners can re-time the magical associations so that, for example, the mid-winter solstice falls in mid-June, rather than December. However, some parts of the world do not have four seasons. For example, parts of Australia and other lands in the southern hemisphere have just two, the wet and the dry, and others have three or six seasons. In parts of the US too, there are not such definite seasonal variations, while in Northern areas of Scandinavia and Canada, it may still be snowing and icy on May Day, so the Swedes, for example, have their equivalent of maypole dancing round their midsummer tree.

In practice, wherever you are, you can either carry out the symbolic rituals at the times I have suggested or adapt them to your own clime. You may, indeed, find that if your ancestors came from another land or continent, your seasonal energies resonate more with theirs. Even if you live in Sydney or Florida, it may be that come November you instinctively hibernate; in this case, you may find the Celtic pattern right for you no matter what the barometer says.

Because the solstices and equinoxes are astronomical measures – that is they depend on the movement of the planets and stars – the dates will vary by a day or two depending on the year.

I have written in several of my books about the folk and religious lore behind seasonal festivals and there are many other good books on this subject (see Further Reading, page 298). In this chapter I mainly focus on the way they amplify the positive energies of the universe and provide a personal connection to the ebbs and flows of the cosmic cycle of existence. The rituals can be either private or group celebrations of power. They will also vary because they originate from many different myths, so that different gods and goddesses may appear in a variety of aspects. This may give rise to what seem to be contradictions, but in the coming together of myths this is inevitable and the god and goddess forms are a powerful metaphor for the energies of each era. One theme common to all, however, is the belief in a cycle, or wheel, of birth, maturity, death and rebirth, which underpins nature and, some believe, all creation.

The energies of the eight major festivals of the Eightfold Year reflect global as well as personal concerns, and our ancestors linked their own fortunes with those of the herds, the soil, the trees and the crops. This is a very valid principle of white magick and one that I have returned to many times in this book. If our spells focus, for example, on increasing general abundance at the time of the harvest, our own needs will be met as part of the cosmic process of regeneration.

What is more, the responsibility felt and still expressed in ritual by some indigenous peoples, for the coming of the rains or the annual rebirth of the Sun, is not merely an unlearned response as some anthropologists suggest. It acknowledges the interconnectedness of universal and personal life forces and the responsibility humans have for care of the Earth. As an ancient Malaysian proverb says: 'We have not inherited the Earth from our forefathers, but borrowed it from our descendants'.

Using the seasons in magick

You can add extra depth and significance to your rituals by carrying them out using the associated candles, crystals, herbs and incenses when the particular seasonal energies are at their height. Such seasonal empowerments will bring the related qualities into your life, to be stored for times when you need their strengths in your everyday world, perhaps at a time of change or crisis. After a year or so of tuning into the seasonal cycle, you will build up a repository of energies for every occasion, like an inner harvest ready for whenever you need them.

On the other hand, if an urgent need suddenly arises in your life, you can at any time of the year repeat the seasonal ritual most representative of the necessary strengths you require, to amplify the powers within you.

You can enter the Wheel of the Year at any point. Some people begin at the Celtic New Year in November, but it may be easier in modern life to begin as I have with the rituals of the early spring, when stirrings of new life first appear. The Celtic day is calculated from sunset to sunset and so the festivals began on the eve, usually the most important time in the festival, and continued for three days. The first we shall work with is the festival of Imbolc (meaning 'in the belly of the mother', and also known as Oimelc 'ewe's milk').

The festival of Imbolc

Time: Sunset 31 January–sunset 2 February (31 July–2 August in the southern hemisphere)

Focus: New growth, melting the ice, bringing light into the darkness, the return of the Maiden Goddess

This was the festival of early spring when ewe's milk was first available after the long, cold winter and the first shoots might be seen in the still-frozen fields. One of the Celtic names for the pagan festival was Brigantia, named after Brighid, the Celtic Triple Goddess, here in her maiden aspect ending the rule of the old hag of winter. She was christianised as St Bridget of Kildare, whose day is 1 February. Brigantia was also the name of a Gallic Earth goddess.

Blazing torches were carried deosil around the still-frozen fields and sacred fires were lit on hilltops to attract the new Sun. It is said that Brighid went around the fields with her white wand of fire, melting the snows and stirring new life, so it is primarily a festival of light. In both pagan and Christian traditions it has involved the lighting of candles and torches, to restore warmth and light into the world.

The maiden goddess Brighid in myth mated with Lugh the young god of light and so, traditionally, a virgin was chosen to mate with the chief of the tribe to ensure the coming of new life to the land. It is said that, like Lugh, he embraced Cailleach, the old hag of winter who was thus transformed in his arms into the Maiden Goddess.

In medieval times, a girl representing Brighid would be brought to the door of the main house or farmstead of a village with cows and a cauldron, symbols of plenty. Her straw bridal bed would be created close to the fire, adorned with ribbons and blessed with honey. Milk, the first available after the winter, was central to the festival as a symbol of renewed fertility. It was poured on the bed of straw. Workers from the farms and villages would approach the bride bed, and in return for a coin, a posy of flowers or tiny gift would receive her kiss, bestowing blessing on their trade and homes.

In churches, the candles that were to be used for the coming year in ceremony were purified on the feast of Candlemas on 1 February. Each person was given a blessed candle that acted as protector of the home against storms, fire and flood and defended cattle and crops against evil.

The energies of this seasonal festival are good for the regeneration of any areas devastated by neglect or pollution, for melting rigid attitudes that may have led to conflicts between counties or ethnic groups, and the isolation and alienation of disadvantaged groups through prejudice. They are especially helpful for the welfare of infants, small children and animals.

On a personal level, these gentle rituals can bring mental, emotional and spiritual regeneration, especially if you have been hurt or lack confidence. If you carry them out, by Easter you will be filled with new optimism and a sense of direction and hopefully any new relationships, whether for love or friendship, initiated at Imbolc will be slowly but gradually developing.

Traditionally, those celebrating this festival would light candles and place them at each window of their houses on 31 January or Candlemas Night, 1 February, and leave them to burn down completely. For safety reasons, nowadays, however, many people use the type of electric candle sets that are popular in windows in Swedish homes before Christmas. A single, large, white candle was also lit in or near the family hearth as a centrepiece for the family feast on the same evening to welcome back the Maiden energies and to bring blessings on home and family. The traditional Brighid straw and beribboned crosses were woven and passed though the candle flame, thereafter serving as amulets to keep homes, animals and barns from harm. These crosses, whose four arms extend at different points around a square centre, are still dedicated to St Brighid and are still kept in homes for protection.

Associations

As before, if you wish to carry out a similar ritual, choose candles, crystals, incenses, etc. of the correct associations to strengthen your ceremony.

Candle colours: White, cream and pink or any pale colour – these are associated with innocence and gentleness

Crystals: Garnet and bloodstones, also amethysts, rose quartz and gentle moonstones for awakening fertility and feelings

Symbols: Ice, milk, seeds, first snowdrops or very early-budding leaves or flowers

Flowers, herbs, oils and incenses: Angelica, basil, benzoin, celandine, heather and myrrh

A ritual to release the frozen life force

Work after dusk on the eve of 31 January or on the following evening, 1 February, and perhaps incorporate the ritual into your Candlemas party. With close supervision, even children can join in the ritual. Place the candles in a deep holders and make the miniature straw bed perhaps in a deep metal bowl or even the family hearth, if it is no longer used for fires.

- On a table, your altar or the hearth, create a small bride bed of straw or dried grasses, decorated with coloured ribbons and any early flowers. Near it place a tiny fabric doll or any small doll to represent the Maiden Goddess.

- Encircle the bed with seeds and newly budding flowers or greenery and behind it, at a safe distance to avoid the danger of fire, place a single, tall, white 'bride' candle.

- On a tray in front of the bride bed, place an earthenware jug of milk, a small dish of honey and a dish containing an ice cube or small amount of ice. Round these, again being careful to avoid fire risk, set a circle of small pink and pastel candles.

❧ Light first your 'bride' candle, saying:

> *Bride, bride, enter your bower, your reign begins at this hour.*
> *The old hag her sway is done, winter's gone, new spring has won.*

❧ Place the doll in the bed and then light the candles surrounding the jug deosil, saying:

> *The maiden's wand of fire does melt the snow,*
> *Ice depart and spring flowers grow.*

❧ Drop the ice or ice cubes into the jug of milk, stirring it deosil with a wooden spoon or birch twig, repeating the chant.

❧ Add a teaspoon of honey to the milk and again stir your jug deosil, saying:

> *Flow, life anew, through bud and flower, the thrall*
> *of winter has no power;*
> *Flow, love and joy and growth and light, ice and*
> *snow begone from sight.*

❧ Leave the ice to melt while you and any others present can place coins, flowers and ribbons on the bride bed, making wishes for the coming spring, for the land, the creatures, for others and for yourselves.

❧ When the ice is melted, stir the jug and very carefully pour a single drop on the bride bed, saying;

> *See, bride, I bring the first milk, symbol of nourishment and fertility,*
> *honey from the warm South, heralding fertility and abundance and*
> *above all the life force now released that can transform wish into*
> *reality and sustain us through the days of cold and wet still to come.*
> *For we have seen the spring and so I send you light, that light may be*
> *shed throughout the world.*

❧ Blow your tiny candles out widdershins, naming for each a blessing that you ask for the world.

❧ Leave the 'bride' candle to burn through and the bride bed in place for the rest of the festival.

If you are working in a coven, you can create a real, full-sized bride bed and choose the youngest member to be the bride. I once carried out the ritual on television, in which all the crew came to kiss the bride, played by Becky, the presenter, and ask her blessing. In spite of their over-enthusiasm and the male presenter Carl's generosity in spreading honey on all who came near, the festival was well and truly a celebration of the return of life.

Ostara, the spring equinox

Time: From sunset on or about 20 March for three days (from sunset on or about 21 September in the southern hemisphere)

Focus: The triumph of light over darkness, resurrection, new beginnings and opportunities; spring cleaning and casting out what is no longer of worth; fertility and conception, the winds of change

At the spring equinox, the Sun rises precisely in the East and sets precisely in the West, giving exactly 12 hours of daylight and so heralds the longer days and shorter nights. As is so often the case, myth and religion are intertwined in the sources of their festivals that share the same dates. In the old Celtic tradition, Lugh, the god of light overcame his twin, the god of darkness, and at Easter, the Christian spring festival most closely associated with the spring equinox, the resurrection of Christ is associated with the restoration of light to the world. The first eggs of spring were painted and offered on the shrine of Eostre, the Anglo-Saxon goddess of the spring. Her Norse counterpart was Ostara, the maiden aspect of Frigg, the Mother Goddess, to whom the hare was sacred (this is the origin of the Easter rabbit). At the spring equinox, bonfires were lit and the corn dolly of the previous harvest (or in Christian times a Judas figure) was burned on the Easter fires. The ashes were scattered on the field for fertility.

Wake at dawn on Equinox morn or Easter Sunday and, it is said, you can see the Sun or in the Christian tradition, angels, dancing in a stream or river. The Green Man is another central figure that features in rituals at this time in southern and eastern Europe and especially among Romany communities. The Green Man, or Green George, as he is sometimes known, was the spirit of plants, trees and vegetables, fruit and vegetation, the male spring deity, consort of the Earth Mother and an early forerunner of both Robin Hood and St George.

The Mother Goddess in her maiden aspect mated with the ascended Sun God or, in popular folk tradition the Green Man, so that the conceived infant would be reborn as the new Sun at the next winter solstice, thus ensuring the Wheel of the Year continued to turn. In the Christian church, 25 March is the Feast of the Annunciation of the Blessed Virgin Mary when Gabriel told her she was with child.

The energies of this festival are good for cleansing the seas and air of pollution, for new peace-making initiatives of all kinds, for beginning reforestation and regeneration projects, the reclamation of wildlife habitats and work to restore the indigenous trees and wildlife to an area. They will also support major attitude changes towards international, national and local issues.

On a personal level, this is the time for clearing emotional and spiritual clutter and wiping the slate clean; for life changes, new beginnings, sowing the seeds for new projects that will bear fruit in the future, for herb gardening, for all matters of fertility and for putting new ideas into practice. Matters concerning children and young people and new flowering love are specially favoured.

Associations

Candle colours: Yellow and green for the clear light from the East and the budding vegetation

Symbols: Eggs, any spring flowers or leaves in bud, a pot of sprouting seeds, pottery or china rabbits, feathers

Crystals: Aquamarine, jade, tourmaline, fluorite

Flowers, herbs, oils and incenses: Celandine, cinquefoil, crocus, daffodil, honeysuckle, primroses, sage, tansy, thyme and violets

A spring equinox cleaning ritual

Use this ritual to welcome the winds of positive change. You can perform it on any of the three days of the rising equinox energies that precede the equinox. Alternatively, it can be adapted for cleansing away negativity and sorrows at any time. I give an alternative version in my book *Psychic Protection Lifts the Spirit* (see page 301).

You can join with family or friends in a communal spring cleaning of a collective living area or workspace. Alternatively, you can use it alone to help you to clear out not only physical clutter but also emotional and spiritual stagnation in those areas of your life and relationships that would benefit from the winds of change.

This spell is another that I performed on TV and though it involved a lot of laughter and dancing – as all good rituals should – many deep sorrows and anxieties were anonymously placed in the cauldron. Our ancestors probably took such folk magick a lot less seriously and so were able to tune into the natural joyous energies of the season.

Begin your ritual in the morning. Open the windows and doors of the place in which you are carrying out the ritual. Alternatively, work in a yard or on a patio.

✤ Place your cauldron – a large pot, wide-necked vase or jug will do – on the floor.

✤ Each of those taking part in the ritual should now write or draw on a piece of paper a representation of every redundant issue or bar to happiness and fulfilment that they wish to blow away on the winds of change.

✤ Draw a cross through the words or image, then tear it into pieces and drop it in the pot, saying:

It is done, it is gone, no more to trouble me. Banished be.

✤ When all the papers are in the cauldron, you (or the whole group) tip the paper into the centre of the floor and scatter dried lavender on top, chanting:

Out with sorrow, out with pain, joyous things alone remain.

✤ Then take your broom, a traditional besom if possible, and hold it horizontally. If you are working with others, everyone should take the brush-head of the person to their right and the broom-handle of the person to the left, holding them horizontally at a comfortable height for all of you.

✤ Dance nine times deosil round the paper and lavender, swirling faster and faster, and chanting:

Three times three, the power I /we raise,
Bringing with it happier days.

✤ Then sweep the paper and lavender out of the back door. If you are working out of doors, sweep it through out of the back gate into a gutter (you can clear up afterwards). As you sweep, say:

Dust to dust, away you must. New life bring, welcome spring.

✤ After the ritual is over, try to leave enough time in the remainder of your day to go to the top of a hill. Take a kite (made from a biodegradable fabric if possible) and in your mind, tie any lingering doubts, fears and concerns to the kite's tail and let it fly away. If you don't have a kite, use a feather for each of your worries and throw them into the air. Hopefully, a child will find the kite, cleansed by the winds, and it will bring joy.

I know of a group of women who carried out a similar sweeping spell in the warehouse where they worked, using wood shavings for the negativity, and then swept out right through the yard into the packing bins which were later taken away by lorry. They commented that afterwards everyone was much more energetic and positive and the internal fighting and backbiting, which had been quite serious, melted away.

A ritual to wash away negativity

Infusions can be made, using lemon, peppermint, pine or tea tree oil, to wash away negative feelings. Use 12 drops of essential oil to a bucket of hot water. Alternatively, add two peppermint tea bags to a cup of boiling water and leave to infuse for five minutes. Use your essential oil infusion to scrub or mop floors, yards, balconies, doorsteps or patios.

✿ Work in circles widdershins, saying:

> *One for joy, two for gladness,*
> *Three and four to banish sadness,*
> *Five and six flee useless anger,*
> *Seven, eight, nine, linger no longer.*
> *Nine, eight, seven, six, five, four, three, two, one,*
> *Darker days now begone.*

✿ Alternatively, strain and use the cooled peppermint liquid to sprinkle around rooms, to inject the freshness of spring emotionally and spiritually.

✿ Afterwards, place a vase of spring flowers, growing daffodils or hyacinth bulbs on a table in the centre of the room to increase the life force.

Beltain, the festival of fire

This Celtic festival of summer is also called Bel-fire, the festival of Belenus, Celtic god of light.

Time: Sunset 30 April–sunset 2 May (31 October–2 November in the southern hemisphere)

Focus: The fertility of the Earth, creatures, crops, people and animals; the instinctive energies that can be manifest as passion whether in sexual terms or for any cause; the interconnectedness of all existence and the mutual dependency of one life form on another

Beltain, which has survived as our modern May Day festival, marked the beginning of the Celtic summer when cattle were released from

barns and driven between twin fires to cleanse them and to invoke fertility as they were released into the fields.

Sundown on May Eve heralded the signal for Druids to kindle the great Beltain fires from nine different kinds of wood by turning an oaken spindle in an oaken sockets. This was carried out on top of the nearest beacon hill, for example Tara Hill, County Meath, in Ireland, home of the Tuatha de Danaan, the hero gods of old Ireland. Every village would have its Beltain fire, which was attributed with both fertility and healing powers.

Winter was finally dead at midnight on May Eve, when Cailleac Bhuer, the old hag of winter, cast her staff under a holly bush and was turned to stone. She would be restored six months later on Hallowe'en.

Young men and girls made love in the woods and fields on May Eve to bring fertility to the land as well as themselves; they gathered flowers and blossoms from the magical hawthorn tree to decorate houses and to make into may baskets which were left as gifts on doorsteps. This custom lasted well into Victorian times and is recalled in Rudyard Kilping's poem *Oak, Ash and Thorn*, which begins:

> *Do not tell the priest our plight,*
> *For he would think it a sin,*
> *For we have been in the woods all night,*
> *Bringing summer in.*

This echoes the woodland wedding of the Goddess, the first May Queen, whose name came from Maia, the Greek goddess of flowers, whose festival occurred at this time and who also gave her name to the month of May. She married Jack o' Green, the god of vegetation – another form of the Green Man – and the deity of the green crops as yet unripened. He became Robin Hood to her Maid Marian. Once

257

again, there is also a Christian connection here: the name Marian is a form of the name Mary, and St Bridget was called Mary of the Gaels.

The maypole, which we still recognise today, once symbolised the ancient cosmic tree and was the focus of fertility dances whose origins are unknown. Red, blue, green, yellow and white ribbons, representing the union of Earth and Sky, winter and summer, Water and Fire, were entwined and the spiralling dance stirred up the life force and fertility of the Earth. The maypole formed a central phallic symbol that could be 40 foot high and echoed the rising potency of the Sun, or Corn, God and the growing corn. Fires were lit and it was believed that the height the young men could leap over the fires would indicate the height the corn would grow and, since for safety reasons this deed was performed without clothes, the festival was one of joyous, unbridled sexuality.

In modern times, this festival has a global significance and survival issues are to the fore. These may concern endangered species or the fight for the rights of indigenous peoples, for freedom of speech, action and belief everywhere. Also involved are the struggle to discover more natural forms of medicine and Earth-friendly products with fewer side effects, and all matters of the countryside.

On a personal level, Beltane is a festival potent for fertility magick of all kinds, whether to conceive a child or aid financial or business ventures to bear fruit. It is good for an improvement in health and an increase in energy as the Sun's light and warmth also gain intensity, and for enthusiasm and creative ventures of all kinds. It will assist the consummation of love matches, travel and job moves and all matters concerning young adults, especially those making commitments.

Associations

Candle colours: Dark green, silver and red

Symbols: Fresh greenery, especially hawthorn; any flowers that are native to your region, placed in baskets; dew gathered on May morning (girls should bathe their faces in it), coloured ribbons, twigs from the three trees sacred to the festival (oak, ash and thorn) or any other woods from your own area

Crystals: Clear crystal quartz, golden tiger's eye, rutilated quartz and topaz

Flowers, herbs, oils and incenses: Almond, angelica, ash, cowslip, frankincense, hawthorn, lilac, marigold and roses for love

A Beltain ritual for fertility and Earth energies

Such a ritual can be used to encourage creativity and growth of all kinds. It may be performed either alone or in a group, with everyone present joining in the chants.

Use as many kinds of wood as possible in the kindling for your fire. Traditionally the magical trees were oak, ash, thorn, willow, birch, rowan, alder, holly and yew, but you can use wood indigenous to your region. An arboretum will offer a variety of fallen twigs.

❦ Light a small fire. (This may be either a small bonfire out of doors, or a fire in a hearth indoors. Barbecue pits are easily adapted.) If you are working in a group, each person can ignite the fire at a different place. If you cannot light a fire, choose a really large, fat, dark green candle as your focus. Place it on a wide, deep fireproof tray, secured in sand.

❦ If you are in a group, stand in a circle around it, with each person holding a taper. The first person lights their taper, then the flame is passed from one taper to the next until the person holding the final taper lights the central candle. Each person can say the chant, with one voice after another joining in.

❦ As you build and light your fire or candle, say:

Fire of Bel, fire of the summer Sun and the ascending light,
flame in my heart, my soul, my loins, that my life and light
may be kindled and flare upwards to greet the summer Sun.

❦ Take a twig, if possible oak, ash or thorn, and circle the fire or candle deosil, saying:

Fires of healing, fertile fires, bring what is needed, not desired.
Heal the planet, bless the corn. Lord of Light, we greet your dawn.

❦ Carefully light the twig and allow it to smoulder and then hold it momentarily upwards, saying:

Fire of Bel, join with my fire and with all fires in all places on
this day at this hour, rise in a web of glorious flame to empower
the Sun, to be empowered and to flame within my heart forever.

❦ Cast the twig into the flames, then leap high in the air, crying:

Ascend and bring fertility, power and creativity.

I do not suggest you try to emulate our ancestors and leap across the flames, as presumably the casualty rate was horrendously high.

❦ If you are using a candle, each person can in turn hold the end of the twig in the flame until it smoulders, then rest it on the tray and allow it to burn slowly down or go out.

❧ End the ritual by taking scarlet ribbons and spiralling round the fire or candle, waving them like flames, as you chant. Finally throw them into the air, away from the flame.

❧ Allow the fire or candle to burn down. Afterwards, make up small posies of flowers to leave on the doorsteps of people who you know would appreciate them – perhaps the ill or lonely.

Litha, the summer solstice

Time: Three days beginning from sunset around 20 June (20 December in the southern hemisphere)

Focus: Full potency, illumination, mysteries revealed; healing, the height of joy, fulfilment, the need to seize the moment

The summer solstice has been celebrated in cultures as far apart as Russia and North America, where Sun dances were an assertion of power and courage and in a new form still bring healing to the nations and the Earth.

The height of the festival is the first light falling on the morning of the solstice, like a shaft of gold across standing stones and stone circles, linking the dimensions. Many circles throughout Europe and Scandinavia, such as Stonehenge in Wiltshire, are aligned to the summer solstice sunrise, as are a number of stone medicine wheels in America and Canada. These places, built on centres of great power, have accumulated not only the power of the thousands of midsummer suns that have shone on this day since their creation, but the hopes and prayers of those who have and still gather at such places. These include priests, Druids, healers, warriors, monarchs and ordinary men and women who connect with fusion of Sky and Earth energies, the sacred and ceremonial marriage of god and goddess on this most magical of days.

There is a long-standing pagan tradition of lighting bonfires on beacon hills to strengthen the power of the Sun before it began its decline. On Midsummer Day, fire wheels were rolled down the hillsides, flaming tar barrels were swung on chains and blazing torches tossed in the air. In Sweden, they still hold a midsummer weekend with a midsummer tree, or pole, decorated with greenery and flowers forming the centrepiece of music and revels. There is feasting in towns as well as the countryside in what is a national event and thousands of people gather as they have for centuries at focal points such as the Island of Oland on the Stockholm archipelago.

St John's wort, the golden herb of midsummer and symbol of the summer solstice, was said to offer fertility and powers to attract love if picked at midnight on 23 June, the eve of St John's Day, or the eve of the actual solstice. Hopeful lovers would carry it or place it under a pillow.

The power of the summer solstice can be harnessed for tackling seemingly insoluble problems and bringing light and life and hope to those who are depressed or who have been unable through circumstances such as poverty to fulfil their potential. It can help to tackle global warming, famine and disease, and to prevent oppression of people and cruelty in intensive farming methods where livestock suffer for human greed.

On a personal level, summer solstice rituals are for courage, male potency and fertility, for achievement, success, confidence, health and happiness, for fulfilling potential and providing ever-expanding opportunities both physical, mental and spiritual. These spells are especially potent for maturing adults approaching middle age.

Associations

Candle colours: Gold, orange or red to mirror the Sun at its height

Symbols: Brightly-coloured flowers, oak boughs, golden fern pollen that is said to reveal buried treasure wherever it falls

Crystals: Amber, carnelian, citrine, golden beryl, sunstone

Flowers, herbs, oils and incenses: Chamomile, dill, elder, fennel, frankincense, lavender, St John's wort and vervain

A summer solstice stone ritual

This ritual can be used to absorb the courage, power and joy of the season. You can carry out this ritual at any time during the three-day period. You might like to perform it at dusk on the eve of the solstice or at one of the other traditional times, such as midnight, the dawn of the solstice day or noon. Alternatively, you may prefer to watch the actual solstice sunrise from a hill or an open place or even close to one of the sacred sites at dawn.

❀ Take eight large, long, rounded stones, one for each spoke on the Wheel of the Year.

❀ Arrange them around the edges of a circle. The eight points correspond with the mid-winter solstice in the North, Imbolc in the North-east, the spring equinox in the East, Beltain in the South-east, the summer solstice in the South, Lughnassadh in the South-west, the autumn equinox in the West, and Samhain in the North-west. (In the southern hemisphere, they will all move six months so that the summer solstice is in the North, etc.)

❀ In front of each stone, place a yellow beeswax or gold candle and set a large gold candle in the centre of the circle. If you have a cauldron or large pot, you can set the central candle in that. Surround the central candle with flowers and herbs of midsummer, if possible freshly picked from an outside source, and any greenery.

❀ If you are working in a group, members can stand around the circle, one at each of the points of the year, with the rest of the coven standing in the North, in a line, facing the South. If you are alone, you may wish to adapt the ritual so the stones and candles are smaller. Place the central candle on your altar, which will on this occasion be standing in the North, facing the South, and move round the altar in a circle.

❀ Enter the circle at the mid-winter solstice (North), the position of the birth of the Sun, and light the central candle, saying:

> *Sun, sacred centre of warmth, light, light and fertility,*
> *I greet you on this your time of glory.*

❀ Behind the candle, light a semicircle of frankincense sticks, saying:

> *Sun who has been from the beginning, King, God, Father, orb of*
> *inspiration, I greet you now at this your time of glory.*

❀ Face the North and light the mid-winter candle, saying:

> *The Sun is born anew, see light grows, light flames to illuminate*
> *the darkness and promises renewal as the Wheel turns too.*

❧ Move round the Wheel to face the North-east. Light the Imbolc candle, saying:

> *The Sun increases and the maiden flames the white fields.*
> *You claim her as your own and so the year turns and life*
> *and light wax as day returns.*

❧ Move next to the East and, facing this direction, light the spring equinox candle, saying:

> *Once more you overcome the darkness; the throne of light*
> *is yours to ascend and longer days are won.*

❧ Move to the South-east and, facing this direction, light the Beltain candle, saying:

> *Your warmth brings green growth once more to the*
> *barren Earth. I kindle fires to draw your healing strength*
> *and the corn will grow high.*

❧ Move to the South, face the direction of the summer solstice, light the candle and say:

> *The Sun is at its height and all nature filled with power.*
> *The Lord and Lady of the Universe, Sky and Earth,*
> *are joined on this day.*

❧ Around the summer solstice candle, scatter a circle of dried or fresh dill, St John's wort, vervain and clover (trefoil) – these are the herbs that bloom at this time and were used to exorcise harm and bring protection to home and people. If you cannot get any of them, use rosemary or any of the herbs of the Sun (see pages 110–21.

❧ As you scatter the herbs, say one of the variations of the old midsummer chant that can be found in folk legend in Europe. My favourite is:

> *Trefoil, vervain, John's wort, dill,*
> *Drive off darkness at your will.*
> *Trefoil, vervain, John's wort, dill,*
> *May the summer sunshine fill*
> *All with life and hope – and keep*
> *Hearth and home safe while I sleep.*

❧ Scoop up some of the herbs in a tiny purse or drawstring bag. Keep it and place it beneath your pillow before sleep. You will, it is said, dream of the person who can make you happy and also, if you add some golden pollen to the sachet, of ways of increasing your wealth.

❀ Light the final three candles in turn, saying:

> *Wheel turn, though light from henceforth falls,*
> *Turn year, till spring and new life calls.*

❀ Leave your solstice wheel of candles to burn down.

❀ The following day, when daylight comes again, plant golden flowers and spend the day in the open air if at all possible, enjoying every moment of light until you witness the Sun setting in the West.

Lughnassadh, the festival of the corn harvest

This festival accords with many of Wiccan principles, especially the Threefold Law.

Time: Sunset 31 July–sunset 2 August (31 January–2 February in the southern hemisphere)

Focus: Willing sacrifice for the greater good, natural justice and karma, trusting the cosmos to provide by giving without seeking immediate return; also spiritual transformation, renewal of the life force by absorbing the powers of the spirit of the corn through food and drink

This is the festival of the corn harvest, called Lammas or Loafmass, when on 1 August the first loaf is baked from the harvested wheat. It corresponds to the Christian harvest festival when in some churches corn is still offered on the altar, but the concept of offering up the first fruits to the deities in return for abundance throughout the year is a very ancient one.

The Lammas loaf, made in the pagan tradition from the last sheaf of corn to be cut down, was regarded as sacred by very early agricultural societies onwards. Before Christian times, it was believed to contain the spirit of the corn; the barley fermented by the autumn equinox was the blood of the Corn God, or the spirit of the crops, who in popular folk song was called John Barleycorn. This is probably the origin of the Wiccan cakes and ale ceremony. This last sheaf was cut by a number of people casting their sickles simultaneously, so no one would know who killed the Corn God, though he offered himself willingly so that there would be abundant future harvests.

As well as being used to make the harvest loaf, some of the corn was woven into corn dollies, symbol of the Earth Mother, decorated with the scarlet ribbons of Frigg, the Norse Mother Goddess. These corn dollies would be hung over domestic hearths throughout winter. Some were made into the shape of a Corn Mother or a cornucopia, or horn of plenty, and others were tied into knots that bound in the power and protection. This art continues today in rural places.

The old name for this month in the Celtic Coligny calendar was Claim-time, when debts would be collected and contracts were arranged. Trial marriages for a year and a day were frequently set up at Lammas, by young couples simply joining hands through a holed stone – they could renew the contract annually if they wished.

Lammas evolved over the centuries into an occasion for craft fairs and festivals, with people travelling from miles around to sell their wares. There were also parades by the trade guilds, and hiring fairs where workers were found to help in the fields for the summer weeks.

Nowadays, the festival energies are good for fighting injustice for oppressed people or creatures, especially for making sure that workers in Third World countries are not exploited financially; for teaching new skills so that people in poor lands and deprived areas may have a chance to create their own prosperity, and for all acts of unpublicised charity.

On a personal level, Lughnassadh is potent for rituals concerning justice, rights, contracts, business affairs, regularising finances and seeking advancement in career; for personal and legal commitments and partnerships of all kinds; also for learning new skills and trades and for mature people in their forties and fifties.

Associations

Candle colours: Dark orange and yellow candles, to reflect the coming of autumn, and purple for justice

Symbols: Ears of corn, corn dollies, anything made of straw; bread, cereals of all kinds

Crystals: Brown agate, desert rose, fossilised wood, leopardskin jasper

Flowers, herbs, oils and incenses: Cedarwood, cornflowers, chamomile, cinnamon, fenugreek, ginger, myrtle, rosewood and sunflowers

A Lughnassadh ritual for renewing the sacred exchange with the Earth

You can work around dusk, either alone or in a group or perhaps invite a friend or family member to share the ritual.

🎇 Bake or buy a round loaf of wholegrain bread and a small bottle of barley wine, organic ale or a fresh fruit juice.

🎇 Place the bread in a straw basket and surround it with ears of grain or dried grasses and pour the wine, ale or juice into a pottery jug.

🎇 Light first a large, orange candle on a very large, fireproof tray and place it so that light falls on the food and drink.

🎇 Burn gentle chamomile, cedarwood or rosewood oil or incense, saying:

Spirit of the corn, I thank you for your bounty
for giving your life for the life of the land and the people.
I offer in return my crafts and skills.

🎇 Take an ear of grain, straw, or a dried grass and pass it through the oil vapour or incense smoke and then begin to weave a knot, saying:

I offer... [make a pledge, however small, of some way you
can use your abilities for the good of the family/workplace/
community or any project dear to your heart].

🎇 Now take a second grass and pass it through the candle flame, then weave it into the first, forming a second knot, this time asking for something you or your loved ones need.

🎇 Place your miniature corn knot in a straw basket, continuing to make a double knot of pledges and needs, until you have exhausted your ingenuity. Pass each through the incense and the candle. (If you are working with others you can take it in turns to make and name your corn knots and place them in the basket. If you have a joint goal as a coven, you can work on a large knot to represent the collective energies and needs, by making individual knots and binding them together with red ribbon.)

🎇 Then take the bread and raise it above the candle, saying:

I give thanks for this the willing gift and offer the first fruits
to the Earth Mother who transforms and restores
all in the ever-turning Wheel.

✿ Crumble some bread either on to the ground if you are working out of doors or into a large wooden or ceramic dish.

✿ Break the bread in its dish and offer it to anyone present before eating yourself.

✿ Take the wine or ale and raise it above the candle, saying:

> _We give thanks and offer this free-flowing life force_
> _to the Earth Mother who reforms and renews all_
> _in the ever-turning circle of the year._

✿ Pour some of the wine either on to the ground or into the dish with the crumbled bread and pour the wine into a glass. (If you are working in a group, pour it into individual glasses and hand them round before serving yourself.)

✿ After drinking, blow out the candle and say as a rising chorus:

> _Power to the Sun._

✿ On the final word, blow out the candle.

✿ Bury your crumbled bread and wine in a hole in the garden or a large plant pot, saying:

> _Grow anew, come forth in the spring and_
> _keep your promise as I will mine._

✿ If you poured the offerings directly on to the ground, plant flowers close by.

Keep your dish of knots. Take them out one by one and as you fulfil your pledges cast each into flowing water or from the top of a hill on a very windy day. Before long, your needs should be met, in a way that should bring you new opportunities, though perhaps not exactly as you planned.

Mabon, the autumn equinox

Time: For three days from sunset on or around 21 September (21 March in the southern hemisphere)

Focus: A time of abundance, reaping the bounty of the Earth and of celebration for life and its gifts; welcoming the waning, darker part of the year, the god in the Underworld or within the womb of the Earth Mother; for letting go and if necessary grieving for what is not fulfilled

The autumn equinox, or time of gathering, was traditionally celebrated as the wild or green harvest, a time of celebration for the fruits and vegetables of the earth and the Earth Mother. This equinox is the second time of the balance between day and night in the Wheel of the Year, and sees Lugh, the god of light, defeated by his twin and alter-ego, Goronwy, the god of darkness. Goronwy was associated with the Horned God as Lugh was with the Green Man, god of vegetation.

Mabon, or Maponus, was another form of Lugh, and was regarded as the son of the Earth Mother and known as the liberator–prisoner. The Corn God lies fallow in the womb of the Mother. But because his sacrifice was willing, Death has no dominion over him and he grows stronger.

This is the time of the second harvest of vegetables, fruit and remaining crops, the harvest home that pre-dates Christianity. On the day when equal night and day heralded winter, the feast formed a sympathetic magical gesture to ensure that there would be enough food during the winter, by displaying and then eating in celebration the finest fruits of the harvest. Druids traditionally climb to the top of a hill to take leave of the summer Sun as the nights will get longer. Michaelmas, the day of St Michael, the Archangel of the Sun, is celebrated on 29 September. St Michael was patron saint of high places and replaced the pagan Sun deities in Christianity.

Today, global rituals concentrate on positive steps to ensure enough food, shelter and resources for vulnerable communities and individuals, relief of flood and famine, protection of endangered water creatures, dolphin, whales and fish whose death involves great suffering; they also look for peace especially where initiatives are already in motion.

On a personal level, autumn equinox rituals are potent for the completion of tasks, for abundance in all aspects of your life, including security for the future which may involve issues of employment or the need to consolidate finances; reconciliation, the setting down of unresolved anger and quarrels; all matters concerning retirement and older people, especially those who are turning their experience to new fields; the resolution of chronic health problems and all Water magick.

Associations

Candle colours: Blue for the autumn rain and green for the Earth Mother

Symbols: Ripe fruit and vegetables, autumn leaves, berries and nuts

Crystals: Blue lace agate, aventurine, malachite, laboradite

Flowers, herbs, oils and incenses: Chrysanthemum, geranium, lemon, parsley, pine, sage and Solomon's seal

A falling leaf ritual

This ritual of the autumn equinox may be performed to shed fears and regrets and welcome the coming of winter. Anyone who has seen a profusion of swirling brilliant red, yellow, orange and vibrant brown leaves will understand that this is a time of great energy as the light battles but finally submits to the darker days.

As the winds blew at the spring equinox, bringing new life, now they and the autumn rains carry away all that is fulfilled and unfulfilled, leaving room for the quieter contemplation of a time when the Sun still shines and the fruits of the harvest are all around. In this way we can say goodbye to the summer with joy.

❈ Collect a basket of autumn leaves or any dying greenery and surround it with the fruits, vegetables, seeds, and nuts of the harvest.

❈ Place blue and green candles alternately at the four quarters, beginning with green in the West, marking out a square that holds both the joys and sorrows of the year that has passed. Make the square large enough so you can work within it.

❈ Light first the blue candle of the North, followed by the green candle in the East and the blue candle in the South, saying:

> *The light is born, increases, flames and flares, and with it*
> *our lives increase, intensify, we plough and plant, create*
> *and tend, travel far and seek our destinies.*

❈ Light finally the green candle of autumn and the West, the Celtic direction of endings and the direction of the Otherworld, to which souls go for rest and regeneration, saying:

> *The harvest is gathered and the fruits of our endeavours*
> *made great by the bounty of Mother Nature.*

✤ Take now a large bowl (or your cauldron) filled with water and place it to the West of the leaves and the circle of the harvest fruits.

✤ Take a leaf to symbolise an ending, an unfulfilled hope or plan and another for one that was achieved or a problem now resolved; name first the sorrow and then the gain and drop the leaves into the bowl of water, saying:

> *What is lost and what is gained are balanced and one*
> *and the same, as the waters of life flow on.*

✤ Eat a nut or seed or a sliver of fruit, saying:

> *I take with thanks the abundance of the harvest and*
> *I bid farewell to the summer with joy and not with sadness.*

✤ Continue to name and float leaves and eat nuts and seeds until your repository of regrets is empty.

✤ Move the candles closer to the container of water and look into the water and see, either in your mind's vision, or on the surface images in the light and shadows. If you wish, drop blue and green wax from the candles on to the surface of the water to create images that may suggest ways in which you can make the darker days ahead rich and fulfilling.

✤ When next you go out of doors, scatter your unused leaves into the air, saying:

> *Fly free, fly joyous, not in sorrow, to return renewed in the spring.*

Use the remaining fruit and vegetables for a meal for family and friends.

Samhain, the festival of wisdom

Time: Sunset 31 October–sunset 2 November (30 April–2 May in the southern hemisphere)

Focus: Ancient wisdom, moving between the dimensions, the intersection between past and future and so a present that is not limited by time and space; welcoming the ancestors, confronting and overcoming fears of ageing and mortality

This festival, recalled in the modern world as Hallowe'en, or All Hallows Eve, marked the beginning of the Celtic year that officially began at sunset on 1 November. It was an occasion for welcoming home family ghosts to the family hearth where their favourite food would be left. This custom continues today in Mexico and to some extent in strongly Catholic countries, such as France and Spain, and in France, All Saints' Day, 1 November, is a public holiday. In earlier times, people in many lands would put garlic on West-facing windows and open the shutters to allow the good family dead to enter. It was also the time when the cattle were brought from the hills for the winter and either put in byres or slaughtered for meat, having been driven between twin fires to purify them. These fires also served to drive away bad spirits who were believed to lurk at the transition of the year. Food was stored for the winter and so it is a time of housekeeping, spiritually as well as physically and mentally.

Fears of the unknown and evil have become focused around this festival: our ancestors projected their anxieties on to bad witches and malevolent faeries who might be kept away by a Jack o' Lantern, a candle in a pumpkin or turnip. The name derives from a legendary Jack who escaped from Hell and was ever after forced to walk in limbo carrying a hot coal.

In the myth of the Wheel of the Year, the descended god now guards the gate to the Otherworld and on this festival he holds sway. In some myths, the Goddess enters the Underworld to be reunited with him and returns to Earth on the third day to prepare for the birth of the new Sun, the ascended god, at mid-winter.

The year too is dying and will be also reborn on the mid-winter solstice, so there is a cross-over of energies as the new year begins on the wane of the tide at a period of decline and darkness. Just as the Celtic day began at sunset, with the darkest part of the night still to come, the Celtic year begins in darkness.

This is a time for charities and initiatives to aid the family, the elderly, the sick and dying, to encourage experience to be valued in a culture that worships youth; also for the preservation of ancient sacred sites and the cultural heritage of the world, including the wisdom of indigenous peoples.

On a personal level, rituals are potent for family concerns, especially those about older members of the family or any who are sick or need constant care; for psychic protection, overcoming fears, for laying old ghosts, psychological as well as psychic, and for marking the natural transition between one stage of life and the next, for remembering the family dead and linking the young to the traditions of the past; also for increasing divinatory skills.

Associations

Candle colours: Black, navy blue or deep purple, for letting go of fear, and orange for the joy of immortality that is promised at this time

Symbols: The pumpkin, or Jack o' Lantern, apples – these are symbols of health and feature in Hallowe'en love divination, a custom dating from Druidic times – photographs and journals of deceased family members, to form a focus for happy memories, favourite foods, flowers and symbols of deceased relatives

Crystals: Smoky quartz, apache tears (obsidian), very dark amethysts, boji stones

Flowers, herbs, oils and incenses: Any seasonal yellow flowers – Mexicans scatter yellow flowers from the cemeteries to the homes on 1 and 2 November, their Days of the Dead – cypress, dittany, garlic, marjoram, mugwort, nutmeg, rue

A Samhain ritual to move beyond the constraints of linear time

Unusually, this is a solitary ritual, so that you can make connection with your personal ancestors, though you may wish to share it with close family members. Perform it on Hallowe'en Eve, as it gets dark.

❧ Light an orange candle.

❧ Cut the top off a pumpkin or large turnip, to make a lid, and scrape out the inside and place the flesh in a bowl in front of the candle.

❧ When the skin is quite empty, do not draw a scary face with grinning teeth, but instead make eight large, regular, round holes in it to let in the light.

❧ Place a small, orange nightlight or tiny candle inside and leave off the lid.

❧ Beginning anywhere in the circle of holes, look into each hole in turn, asking a question about your future life path and saying:

Jack o' Lantern burning bright, let me pass through time this night,
Seeing not a future set, but possibilities that yet
I can seize as paths unfold, Jack, guide me to new joys untold.

❦ Shut your eyes, open them, blink and write down the first image that comes either in your mind's eye or in the circle of light.

❦ Continue until you have explored each of the eight windows of the future and have eight images. You can either interpret the images as referring to the eight time points of the Wheel of the Year, beginning with Samhain, or integrate them into a story about eight steps on your unfolding path throughout the coming year.

❦ Cook and eat the pumpkin or turnip flesh to absorb the magic.

❦ Leave the candle to burn down as you make plans for the future.

Alban Arthuran, the mid-winter solstice

Time: For three days from sunset on or around 20 December (20 June in the southern hemisphere)

Focus: Rebirth, the return of light, the triumph of life over death, spiritual awakening, light in the midst of darkness, faith that the Wheel will turn and the life cycle begin anew

The mid-winter solstice pre-dates organised religion. When early humans saw the Sun at its lowest point and the vegetation dead or dying, they feared that light and life would never return. So they lit great bonfires from yule logs, hung torches from trees and decorated caves and homes with evergreens to persuade the other trees to grow again. So this really is a time of faith and hope and also an awareness once more of the responsibility of individuals to ensure by ritual and by giving hospitality to family, neighbours and strangers that at this lowest point (the yoke or yule of the year) life would be rekindled. This is a long way from the present commercial and consumer emphasis that has overtaken our Christian festival of Christmas.

The name Alban Arthuran means 'light of Arthur', named after King Arthur who in legend bore the title Sun King. His round table represented the great solar Wheel of the Year.

The common theme of the festival that spans many ages and cultures is that the Mother Goddess, under one of her many names, gives birth to the Sun itself, the Sun God. It is the same theme as the Virgin Mary giving birth to the Son of God in a cave or stable at the darkest hour of the year. The virgin birth features in several cultures and traditionally a candle (or other flame) is left burning all night on this longest of nights, to persuade the newborn Sun to rise again on Christmas Eve to light Mary on her way. The feasting of Christmas was another magical gesture to ensure there would be food again in the spring and good harvests the following year.

Globally, this is a time for rituals of renewed faith in the face of despair and cynicism; for work to provide homes and shelter for people, birds and animals, more efficient and humane welfare services; the regeneration of famine or war-torn lands; rekindling goodness even in wrongdoers, improving conditions in all institutions; also individual charitable endeavours.

On a personal level, the mid-winter solstice is a good time for matters concerning the home and practical family matters, for money spells as well as abundance in less material ways; for relieving depression and anxieties for all matters where improvement, relief or success will come after patience and perseverance; also potent for rituals concerning the very old, unborn children, mothers-to-be, nursing or new mothers and newborn infants.

Associations

Candle colours: White, scarlet, brilliant green and gold

Symbols: Evergreens, Christmas trees adorned with lights, oak, ash or pine, brightly coloured baubles, gold, holly, ivy and mistletoe, nuts

Crystals: Any precious stones, especially rubies, diamonds and emeralds, amazonite, garnets, zircons, spinels; you can also substitute glass nuggets in rich red, green and white

Flowers, herbs, oils and incenses: Bay, cedar, holly, juniper, mistletoe, orange, rosemary, and frankincense and myrrh in golden-coloured holders

A mid-winter ritual to celebrate the rebirth of the Sun

This ritual should be performed on the solstice eve. To prepare, decorate a bough of evergreen with red and gold baubles and bows of ribbon and surround it with a circle of five long-burning, pure white candles or a single candle with five wicks. The first candle will need to burn for 24 hours, the second for about 18 hours, the third about 12 hours, the fourth and fifth for shorter periods, although you can always replace a candle by lighting another.

We are keeping to the Celtic time and so our ritual will end with the beginning of the new day at sunset on the actual day of the solstice.

However, if you prefer, you can celebrate 24 hours later or at a weekend where you can be at home for a longer period. Some families move the ritual to the Christian festival and begin on Christmas Eve. Alternatively, you can work for a shorter period, combining the stages and using fewer candles.

This is a ritual you can share with family and friends or with your coven, or practise alone, as an antidote to the bustle and sometimes frayed tempers of Christmas.

❧ Just before dusk, extinguish all lights except a tiny one so you can see what you are doing, saying:

> The light is gone from the old Sun, but we know it will return,
> pure and true, and with it the rebirth of our hopes.

❧ Sit for a few minutes in the darkness, avoiding conscious thought, merging with the energies.

❧ At dusk, light your first white candle, saying:

> The light returns; we offer our light to join with those
> kindled around the world that the darkness may be no more.

❧ Leave the candle burning and spend an evening away from all the frantic preparations that will be there tomorrow; share a meal, listen to seasonal music, talk about Christmas past, its highlights and disasters.

❧ When it is midnight or just before you are ready to go to bed, light the next candle, saying:

> The light increases, as the new Sun streams forth within the cave,
> soon to herald the new day; we offer this light, joining with our
> ancestors and those as yet unborn to call forth radiance.

🎄 Leave the candles in a safe place and when you awaken, even if it is not fully day, light the third candle, replacing and re-lighting the others if they are almost burned down, saying:

The Sun comes forth from the cave, in joy and glory and promise;
we join our light with the rays of the new morning.

🎄 Spend the morning out of doors, if possible, collecting greenery, or making tiny clay figures of the Nativity figures, *santons* as they are called in France, to create a personalised nativity, including figures to represent your family and friends.

🎄 At noon, light the fourth candle, again after replacing any that are burned through, saying:

I rejoice that the light surrounds us; the Sun lives and thrives
and multiplies in a thousand cascading sunbeams.

🎄 If possible, enjoy a festive meal with family and friends and make a phone call or perhaps take a small present to someone who is alone at Christmas and might appreciate a visit; if they will not be offended, invite them to join your family table.

🎄 Finally at dusk, light the last candle, saying:

Ever burn bright and warm on fields and sea and sky and
all the creatures born of the Mother. We give thanks.

🎄 At bedtime, extinguish your remaining candles, making wishes and saying:

Go in happiness, bring joy and peace and plenty to all in need.
Blessings on this Yule and on you all.

CHAPTER 14

Magick for You

Creating your own spells

Spells for global causes, such as cleansing the oceans, regenerating areas of high unemployment and bringing peace to warring factions are important, and, as I have said, by focusing on wider aims you can attract abundance or harmony into your own life under the Threefold Law of magick. But sometimes you may feel you want to concentrate on a specific personal dream or need. And as I have also said many times in the book, if you are worried or unfulfilled in your own life, you are hardly going to have energy to spare to worry about rainforests. So in this chapter I have listed 12 of my own favourite rituals for a variety of purposes that can easily be adapted for your own opportunities or dilemmas.

You can also create your own spells very simply for any personal need, using the relevant colours, crystals, oils, incenses and herbs listed throughout the book. Having arranged any candles, crystals or incenses that can help to strengthen your own inner powers, you must first focus on your wish or need by stating what it is you want, perhaps in the form of a chant or power mantra, gradually increasing its speed and intensity. At first this may seem strange but as you can get caught up in the rhythm, some people find they like to dance or drum; then, finally, you can send the accumulated energies out into the cosmos. This can be done in a variety of ways, for example by leaping in the air if you are dancing, giving a final shout if you are chanting, blowing out a candle or casting your symbol into fast-flowing water. You can also bury it or burn it in a candle flame or on a bonfire. If you are banishing something from your life, you can write it in chalk and rub it out or cut it up and dispose of the pieces.

You can use absolutely anything as a symbol for magick: a flower, a leaf, a feather, words or images written or drawn on paper, candles to represent people or objects, Tarot cards, photographs, related miniature versions of the desired acquisition – a key for a new home, a toy car for transport, a postcard for a holiday destination.

At the end of your spell you may like to finish the ritual by saying something like 'The wish is mine', or 'The power is won', or 'The spell is done', or even 'So let it be, god and goddess willing'. Many practitioners add 'If it is right for me'. Wiccans often say at the end of the ritual, 'So mote it be'.

For a complete guide to making your own spells, see the step-by-step spell template that I have arranged on pages 287–89.

A three-day candle spell for reconciliation

✿ On the first night, light two pink candles (pink is the colour of Venus in her gentle aspect), one for yourself and the other for the person from whom you are estranged.

✿ Set the candles apart at opposite ends of the table and into the one you designate for the absent person, speak the words you would like to say if he or she were present, whether regrets or forgiveness or both.

✿ Then, into your own candle, recall aloud the good qualities of the other person.

✿ Blow out your own candle, sending a message of love to wherever the other person is.

✿ Blow out his or her candle, absorbing positive feelings from all the good times you shared.

✿ On the second night, set the candles so that each has moved a quarter of the way across the table towards the other.

✿ Again light the candles in turn, this time speaking into the other person's candle thanks for the kindnesses shown to you in the past; into your own candle, express what you miss most about the relationship and would like to rekindle.

✿ As you blow out your candle, send positive wishes for the other person's happiness and absorb the light from his or her candle as healing of unfair or harsh words spoken in anger.

✿ On the final evening, place the candles so that they are almost touching and as you light your candle, express your hopes for happy times together once more.

✿ Into the second candle, make promises to try to be more tolerant and understanding in future, even if you think the disagreement or estrangement was not your fault.

❀ This time, leave the candles to burn down and sit in the candlelight, looking at old photographs, reading poetry or listening to music you both enjoyed.

❀ When the candles have burned down, plan a simple non-confrontational gesture of friendship – sending a postcard of a place you both visited, an e-mail recounting mutually pleasurable news about a joint friend or family member, or a small bunch of favourite flowers. Even if the gesture of reconciliation is refused, you have freed yourself of bitterness, though you may need to repeat the ritual several times if the hurt is deep.

A spell for increasing self-confidence

Sometimes people around us – perhaps a critical relative, a spiteful ex-lover or a thoughtless colleague – can damage our self-esteem. We look at media ideals of loveliness and feel we are far from the image of perfection created by a society that worships youth. But if we can only believe in ourselves and love ourselves, hey presto, we radiate our own unique beauty and others are drawn to us, because of this powerful but indefinable personal magnetism. This spell is designed to boost that self-belief.

❀ Around your bathroom, light purple candles, placed safely so that they cast pools of light on the water when you fill the bath.

❀ Let the water run and then turn off the taps and add five drops of rose essential oil and five of ylang-ylang, dropping them into the pools of light.

❀ Place a rose quartz or amethyst crystal in the water to strengthen self-love and approval.

❀ Lie in the water and swirl the light pools in turn, making an affirmation for each one, for example:

I exist, I am unique, I am of worth, I have many gifts
[name them], I value myself, I love myself, I am complete
in myself, I treasure what I have and what I am,
as I am right now.

❀ Continue to swirl the light, visualising it flowing within you, making you a body of light and loveliness.

❀ Finally, make a wish for yourself in each light pool.

❀ When you are ready, wrap yourself in a soft towel or robe and take out the plug, saying:

Doubts and sorrow, flow from me, what I wish, I can be.

✿ Look at yourself in the mirror framed by light and you will see how your inner radiance creates true beauty that cannot fade.

✿ Carry the candles into your bedroom or living room and spend the rest of the evening reading a special book, listening to music or just dreaming of golden tomorrows as you gaze into the light.

A spell to repel spite, gossip or psychic attack

Traditionally, witch bottles filled with rusty nails, sour red wine (or even urine) and sprigs of rosemary were buried under the doorstep of a house as an age-old method of keeping away spite.

✿ Take a dark bottle with a cork and into it pour sour milk, old red wine and some dried rosemary, saying:

Viciousness and venom, malevolence and malice,
feelings turned sour, envy and spiked tongues, begone.

✿ Close the bottle with a cork and shake it over a sink, saying:

Curdle and coil, serpents of spite, hiss and miss me,
spit where you will do no harm.

✿ Uncork the bottle and run it under the cold tap until the mixture has flowed away and the bottle and sink are clean.

✿ Add a few drops of tea tree oil to the bottle and pour some into the sink drain and rinse the bottle again. Saying:

Anger cease, go in peace.

Note that you have neither attacked anyone nor even returned the spite. You will probably find that the other person may be more positive on the next encounter. If you are suffering from an emotional vampire who drains you emotionally, add powdered garlic to the mix. It really works.

A binding spell for protecting children against bullying

✿ Create a featureless image of clay to represent your child (or anyone you wish to protect – this could be your partner who is being bullied at work by an over-critical boss).

✿ Cover the image with tiny, clear quartz crystals – these are empowering as well as protective.

✿ Set a ring of pink candles around the image.

✿ Gently breathe in the light and blow it out around the image, creating a protective pink sphere as you exhale.

❧ When you have done this, extinguish the candles one by one, sending the light into the clay, saying:

> _Stand symbol for my child [or partner]. Protect him/her with love and light from all who would do harm._

❧ Wrap the image in soft cotton wool or pink cloth and with a pink ribbon tie the cloth with three knots, saying:

> _I bind thee in security, from all who would bring harm to thee, cocooned in peace and harmony._

❧ Keep the image very safely in a drawer with soft, fluffy clothes. If the problem still persists when the clay crumbles, make another image and carry out the spell again, if necessary using golden candles for stronger protection.

A rainy day spell to banish sorrow or a bad habit

❧ On a large piece of dark paper, with either white chalk or washable paint, write or draw what it is you wish to lose.

❧ Draw a square round the word or image to mark the limitations of its power, followed by a diagonal cross through the words or image.

❧ Put the paper on paving stones as it begins to rain and standing in the rain watch the words or image blur and disappear.

❧ When the paper has disintegrated, say:

> _It is gone, it is done. Nought left of pain, I thank the rain._

❧ Scoop up the soaked paper and dispose of it in an outside bin.

A spell to attract the right person into your life

I have used this spell for people who wish to call a current lover who is being over-reticent, but people have told me after I demonstrated it on television that it works just as well for an unknown lover; so I have modified it.

❧ Take a map either of your local area or country or a world map if you want a lover from afar.

❧ Scatter five roses across the map, saying:

> _Near or far, o'er land and sea, a lover true I call to me._

❧ Light a pure white candle and taking a sixth rose (six being the number of Venus and love), pluck from it in turn five petals and burn each in the candle flame, saying:

Burn a pathway to my door, five rose petals now are four,
Four to three in candle fire, bringing closer my desire.
From three to two I burn the rose, love no hesitation shows,
From two to one till there is none, the spell is done, come, lover, come.

❦ Place the map and the roses, the candle and a vase with the rose from which you plucked the petals, in a safe place near an uncurtained window until the candle has burned down.

❦ Then put all the roses in the vase in your bedroom and when they die repeat the spell if necessary.

A knot ritual for making a wish come true

❦ Name your wish.

❦ Take nine scarves or nine pieces of cord, each about the length of a bootlace.

❦ Place them on a table and slowly tie a loose knot in each so you secure the nine together in a circle, saying with increasing intensity:

By the knot of one, the spell's begun,
By the knot of two, this dream come true.
By the knot of three, the power's in me,
By the knot of four, I make it more.
By the knot of five, the spell's alive,
By the knot of six , my fate's not fixed.
By the knot of seven, my cause is leaven,
By the knot of eight, my aim is straight.
By the knot of nine, the wish is mine.

❦ Toss your scarves or knotted cords into the air and spiral round, waving them and chanting,

My power renewed, the dream is true,
The wish is free, so shall it be.

❦ Gradually, slow down and reduce your chant to a whisper until you are quite still.

❦ Sit and make a nine-day plan for making your wish materialise and each morning untie one of your knots as you repeat the chant.

A fertility spell

❈ When the crescent moon is in the sky, take a hen's egg and paint or colour it with permanent marker pens and decorate it with Mother Goddess symbols, such as spirals, butterflies, bees and birds.

❈ Place it on the window ledge of your bedroom and leave it there until the night of the full moon.

❈ On this night, prick the egg gently with a silver pin or paper knife.

❈ The next day, early in the morning, sprinkle it with a few drops of almond or pure olive oil for added fertility.

❈ Place the egg in one half of a coconut shell (the coconut is the most potent fertility fruit) or a tiny straw basket, and set your little boat sailing on a river or the outgoing tide. If you cannot sail it, bury your egg and coconut shell beneath a willow or alder tree and water the soil with Moon water (water that has been collected when the full moon shines on it).

❈ Make love whenever you wish during the month, but if possible on the night of the full moon.

This spell will not overcome gynaecological problems, but can relieve anxiety and stress, which seem to block fertility.

A spell to attract money

❈ During the waxing moon phase, prepare a circle of six green prosperity candles on a tray made of brass or any shiny metal. Use small, broad-based candles so that the wax can flow on to the tray.

❈ Heap nine coins in the circle.

❈ Light the candles, starting in the North, saying:

> _Light of increase, shower on me money and security._
> _Bring, I ask, prosperity._

❈ Leaving the coins in the centre, push the candles so that they are almost touching and the wax flows on to the coins. Allow the candles to burn down.

❈ When the wax has hardened, cut a disc containing the coins and sprinkle dried basil on the wax for added prosperity.

❈ Leave your coin amulet where it can catch any light, day and night, from the waxing to the full moon and when the Moon begins to wane, keep it wrapped in silk in a drawer. If necessary, repeat the spell when the crescent moon is in the sky, turning it over three time on the crescent.

A spell to pass an examination or a test or succeed in an interview

✤ Take three small dishes of dried sage, rosemary and thyme, the herbs of memory and concentration.

✤ Choose a book, a manual or notes you have made, to symbolise what you need to know or remember.

✤ Scatter in turn a circle of each herb round the book, beginning with sage as the innermost circle, then rosemary and finally thyme, saying:

> *Sage, rosemary, thyme, let this knowledge now be mine,*
> *In the circles three, memory increased be.*

✤ Gather the three circles of herbs into a small purse or sachet. Keep it with you while you study and place it under your pillow at night so you may learn while you sleep. You can also take it to an examination.

A spell to get a job

✤ Find or write an advertisement for a job you have seen in the newspaper or employment agency or for one you would like. If you are creating a hypothetical position, be specific about salary, location, etc. The more focused you are, the more powerful the energies you generate from within, but keep a weather eye on reality, so that you are not asking the impossible of the cosmos.

✤ Light a really big, deep blue candle (blue is the colour of Jupiter and excellent for job-hunting) and place it in a holder on a broad metal tray.

✤ Read the advertisement several times so you memorise it and then form it into a taper and slowly burn it in the candle flame, allowing the ash to fall on the tray.

✤ When the paper is burned, gather the ash in a small box or bag. (If it goes out, don't worry – just 're-light it, showing your persistence and determination to get the job.)

✤ Bury it beneath a power tree, such as the oak or ash, if possible on land near to your chosen place of employment. If you cannot find a tree, bury the ash in a pot of mint (mint is a powerful energiser).

A spell for when you wish to travel

✤ Find four dandelion clocks with full, white seedheads, and carry them in a small neck or waist pouch to the top of a hill.

✤ Using a compass, find the direction of your chosen destination and, facing it, say:

> North, South, East, West, take me where I love the best
> – [name the place].

✤ Spin round nine times deosil, saying:

> Far from home, may I roam, Far to fly, o'er sea or sky.

✤ Now open your purse and blow the dandelions clocks, one for each direction, beginning with your chosen one, saying:

> Fly far, fly free, 'cross land and sea, With you I go, Let it be so.

✤ Finally, run or walk fast down the hill, reciting the name of your chosen destination as a mantra.

✤ When you get home, make a step, however small, towards planning your trip.

A spell for moving house

Whether you are stuck at the buying or selling stage, this spell can get the energies moving to conclude the deal. If you are trying to sell your house, use a door key from your present property, but if you are trying to buy a house, use a brand new key.

✤ Find an estate agent's picture of your present house or the one you wish to buy. On top of it, place four frankincense or fern incense sticks, to represent the sides of an invisible square. Inside this square, place the key.

✤ Light the four incense sticks, saying for each:

> May the winds of change blow away stagnation.

✤ Take the incense set in the centre top of the square and pass it three times deosil round the key and picture, saying:

> Thus I remove one wall and, with its power
> transformed, move forward.

✤ Plunge the incense stick into a bowl of cold water. The end will harden so that you can write on paper with it like a pencil. Without thinking, let words form from your magic pencil, advising the next step you should take to bring closer the house move.

❀ Repeat this for the other three sticks until you have written four steps with the four incense sticks. You will find that the solutions you wrote offer new avenues that you had not considered.

❀ Place the key and picture near an open window or door where the air can circulate round them.

❀ Each evening, place your key and picture on the table and light a single frankincense stick to keep the energies moving, wafting it round in three circles deosil, saying:

> *May the winds of change blow away stagnation.*

If you hit another impasse, repeat the ritual.

A sea ritual for the return of what is lost

This is based on a very old custom; wives of sailors would keep a bottle of sea water and then tip it back into the waves just before their husbands were due home. If you cannot go to the shore, use any pond, lake, river or stream. The spell can be used for finding lost or stolen objects, pets, or even straying partners, though with the latter you may decide not to bother.

❀ Go to the seashore just before high tide and, in a bottle, collect some sea water, saying:

> *Lady Ocean, Mother Sea, I take of yours, not willingly,*
> *but as a token of what I lack, I ask your help*
> *to bring him/her/it back.*

❀ Wait until the tide turns and tip the water back into the sea, saying:

> *Lady Ocean, Mother Sea, I return what is yours,*
> *send mine back to me.*

❀ Cast flowers on the water, sending a silent message to the person you have lost or whoever now has your missing item, asking for its safe return – if it is right to be.

Spell Template

This guide can be used to help you create spells for every occasion.

It lists all the materials, tools and stages that may be included in a spell but you will not need to use every item every time – some you will only use for formal rituals.

Preparation

🎄 Choose the subject matter of your spell, bearing in mind the Threefold Law.

🎄 Note down the purpose of the spell and the order in which you intend to work. Decide whether it will be divided into phases, such as invoking the four elements, raising and releasing the power (see pages 40–1) or merge into one.

🎄 Plan what you are going to say and write it down. (You may of course let the words come to you spontaneously.)

🎄 Choose the time for your spell. Check the following influences:

  The seasons (see page 245)

  The equinoxes (see pages 253–67)

  The phase of the Moon (see page 218)

  The day of the week (see pages 227–39)

  The hour (see pages 235 and 239–40)

🎄 Check any time limits (for example, 'May this spell hold sway until the Moon has ebbed away') and ensure that you can adhere to them.

🎄 Choose the place for your spell. If you are working out of doors, and it is a spell that will last over several days, bear in mind any possible changes in the weather. Make sure you have enough room for the circle you intend to cast. Set up your altar in advance, if you can (see page 46).

❋ Choose candles for the altar (see page 89), to mark the quadrants of the circle (see page 90) and to represent people (see page 93). Check they are the right colour (see page 94). Choose elemental candles (see page 91).

❋ Inscribe your candles (see page 194).

❋ Anoint your candles (see page 195).

❋ Choose your associated symbols that will act as a focus for the spell (see page 191).

❋ Choose your elemental tools (see page 184).

❋ Choose your herbs (see page 110). Decide if you are going to empower them before or during the ceremony and write down the words if necessary. Make any sachets or poppets you intend to use.

❋ Choose your oils (see page 128).

❋ Choose your incenses (see page 139).

❋ Choose your crystals (see page153).

❋ Choose your ritual substances (see page 191).

❋ Consecrate the ritual substances (see pages 161 and 163).

The ceremony

※ Cast your circle (see page 49).

※ Invoke the elements (see page 198) and angels (see page 200).

※ Focus on the symbol of the spell and declare your intentions (see page 38).

※ Endow the symbol with magical energies, chanting if appropriate (see page 39).

※ Raise the power to absorb energy from the cosmos, creating a cone of power (see page 40).

※ Release the power, sending it out into the cosmos (see page 41).

※ Close the energies down (see page 209).

※ Uncast the circle (see page 52).

※ Ground the energies (see page 41).

After the ceremony

※ Dispose of materials – some may need to be left out in the light of the Moon, or buried or thrown to the winds; others may be kept, wrapped in silk, or sent to the person for whom the spell is intended.

※ Blow out all the candles, unless they are to be left to burn down. If this is the case, make sure there is no risk of fire.

※ Cleanse and recharge your tools (see pages 196–97).

Glossary

Akasha: The fifth and greatest element, formed by the combination of the ancient elements of Earth, Air, Fire and Water that were considered in classical times and by alchemists to be the components of all life and matter. Also sometimes called Spirit or Ether.

Akashic records: The collective memory bank on the spirit plane said to hold the experiences of all people, past, present and future.

Alban Arthuran: The festival of the mid-winter solstice, named after King Arthur, the legendary Sun King, which takes place on or about 21 December in the northern hemisphere.

Alpha waves: Brain waves, cultivated in psychic work, that are associated with a very relaxed state of mind in which it is possible for intuitive faculties to find expression.

Amulet: A charm carried on a person or placed in a house to offer protection against danger and illness. When charged with healing energies, it becomes a talisman and can attract health and good fortune.

Anima: The term coined by Carl Gustav Jung to represent the female power within men as well as women.

Animus: Jung's term for the male power within women and men.

Ankh: An Egyptian symbol of eternal life.

Archangels: Higher orders of angels, celestial beings featuring in the cosmologies of the three major religions of the Western world, Christianity, Judaism, and Islam, as well as many other world religions.

Athame: A double-edged knife used in formal ritual magick.

Auric field/aura: The personal energy field around all animate life, visible to clairvoyants.

Beltain: The Celtic festival of summer, beginning on 30 April and lasting for three days.

Bicarmel mind: A way of thinking that uses both hemispheres of the mind, the logical and the intuitive, rather than the left (logical) hemisphere predominating as is normal in adults.

Book of Shadows: A book of reference containing magical spells, herbs, flowers, incenses and moon phases, etc.

Caduceus: The staff of the classical messenger of the gods (Hermes to the Greeks and Mercury to the Romans), shaped like two snakes, entwined in a double circle.

Cardinal: Principal, as in the four cardinal directions set round a circle – North, South, East, and West. Also a term applied to the astrological signs of Aries, Cancer, Libra and Capricorn, because when the Sun moved into these signs it marked the start of a new season. Those born under a cardinal sign manifest this quality as a desire to initiate and to take command of people and situations.

Cauldron of Undry: A magical cauldron, one of the original four Celtic treasures, that could provide an endless supply of nourishment and had great healing and restorative powers. Believed by some scholars to be the inspiration for the Holy Grail.

Censer: A container for granular incense that is burned on charcoal. Also called a thurible.

Chalice: A cup or goblet made of glass, crystal, pottery or metal, traditionally silver, used in ceremonies to represent the Water element and to hold wine, juice or water.

Charge: A declaration of the power and benevolence of the Goddess (or god) in Wicca, similar to the Creed in other religions. It is spoken usually in the first person and is sometimes believed to be the words of the Goddess channelled through the speaker.

Ch'i: The invisible life force, the flow of positive energy through everything, promoting growth, health and vitality.

Clairaudience: A natural psychic ability to hear sounds beyond the range of the physical sounds and the physical ear, sometimes from other dimensions. Mediums often communicate with spirits by hearing their voices and so can convey messages to relatives or friends in whom the ability is not so developed.

Coven: A meeting of any group, numbering from two to 13 practitioners, who meet together to perform magick.

Deosil: Clockwise, or, literally 'in the direction of the Sun'. The direction used in creating a circle, in all forms of attracting magic and for giving healing energies. *See also* Widdershins.

Devas: The angelic beings who watch and direct the natural world. In formal magick, one Deva rules over each segment of a magical circle and one of the four elements of Fire, Water, Air and Earth. Also known as the Devic Lords of the Watchtower.

Dhoop: An incense stick like a slender rope, from India.

The Divinity: Generic term for the ultimate source of goodness, light and creation.

Djinn: An invisible, shapeshifting creature of fire and air, originating in the Middle East. In Islamic tradition, djinns live in a parallel universe and so are invisible, created, it is said, before mortals from smokeless fire.

Druids: Celtic high priests and wise men (and women) who preserved a common culture, religion, history, laws, scholarship, healing, magic and science amongst the disparate Celtic tribes. There is historical evidence of Druids in Ireland, England, Wales and Gaul and it would seem that they also held sway in the Celtic settlements of Spain, Italy, Galatia and the Danube valley, although under a different name.

Eightfold Wheel of the Year: An ancient magical and spiritual division of the year, formalised by the Celts, though possibly dating back to the first agricultural societies.

Elementals: The forces or energies that in nature and magick give shape to living things and bring thoughts and desires into actuality.

Equinox: The two times of the year when day and night are equal – namely, the spring equinox around 21 March (21 September in the southern hemisphere) and the autumn equinox around 22 September (22 March in the southern hemisphere). In Celtic myth these were the times when the twin gods of light and darkness fought each other for control.

Esbat: A monthly coven meeting traditionally held 13 times a year during each full moon.

Evil eye: A way of transmitting negativity to another person, not as a deliberate curse, but through feelings of envy, jealousy or resentment.

Evocation: The summoning-up of angels (and sometimes demons) in order to bind them to perform tasks.

Fixed: In astrology, a term applied to the signs of Leo, Taurus, Aquarius and Scorpio because the Sun enters them in the middle of a season. Those born under these signs exhibit stability and a tendency to continue in a predetermined path. *See also* Cardinal, Mutable.

The Goddess: The archetype or source energy of the feminine ultimate power or principle. All the named goddesses are aspects of particular qualities of the Goddess in different cultures.

Grail: The chalice that Christ used at the Last Supper, in which His blood was collected after the crucifixion.

Grail guardians: Nine maidens, sometimes associated with the guardians of sacred wells or with the nine priestesses of the Isle of Avalon who included Morgan le Fay, Arthur's half-sister, and Vivien, the Lady of the Lake in Arthurian tradition who accompanied Arthur on his funeral barge. In some Grail legends, the Knights Templar were the traditional guardians of various holy relics, including the Grail Cup, that were brought back from the Crusades.

Grail treasures: The main elemental ritual items in magick, associated with the treasures of the Celts, and having parallels in Christianity.

Handfastings: A popular marriage rite among Wiccans, named after the focal point of the rite in which a couple's right hands are loosely joined by a cord to symbol the uniting of the two people, body, mind and soul.

Hedge witches: Lone witches; the name comes from the practice of village wise women surrounding their homes with a hedge of hawthorn, a magical tree that afforded privacy from the curious.

The Horned God: The male principle in Wicca, Lord of the Hunt, the Herds, Winter and the Underworld. Known to the Celts as Cernunnos, the generic name for 'horned one'.

Imbolc: The Celtic festival of early spring. A Fire festival, christianised as Candlemas on 1 February. Also known as Oimelc.

Immanent: Usually refers to a god or the Goddess; indicating that they are manifest within the object of their creation, as the divine spark within people. *See also* Transcendent.

Inner-plane teaching: Contacting through meditation or rituals the cosmic memory bank or Akashic records in order to tap into the great existing magical systems and wisdom without external formal teaching.

Invocation: The process by which the wisdom and benign powers of the natural world and of higher planes of consciousness, associated with the evolved self and divine power, are drawn into oneself. Medieval magicians would invoke spirits to take over their bodies – dangerous and mind-blowing.

Karma: The concept that the good and bad deeds and thoughts accumulated in an individual lifetime may either progress us forwards to spiritual perfection or mean we need to learn lessons in subsequent lives in order to right our mistakes.

Litha: The Celtic festival of light, held around the midsummer solstice on 21 June.

Lughnassadh: The Celtic festival of the first corn harvest, held from 31 July to 2 August in the northern hemisphere. Christianised as Lammas ('loaf mass'), the day on which loaves of bread were baked from the first grain harvest and placed on the altar to symbolise the first fruits.

Mabon: The second Celtic harvest festival of the autumn equinox, around 22 September.

Medicine Wheel: A concept central to all Native American magick. The wheels link the celestial, human and natural cycles. Also known as the Circle of Power.

Morphic resonance: The spreading of goodwill and positivity, through magick and good deeds, to increase the benign energies of the Earth and cosmos.

Mother Goddess: The giver of all life and fertility and mother of the animals, worshipped by hunter–gatherer societies since paleolithic times. In the shamanic religions in Siberia and Lapland, the Mother of the Herds is still a central icon of power. During the neolithic period, the Mother Goddess was the bringer of fertility to the land as well as to animals and humans. Gradually, she came to be seen as the wife of the great Sky Gods. She survives in the form of Mary in the Christian religion.

Mutable: The mutable signs of the zodiac are Sagittarius, Gemini, Virgo and Pisces, as when the Sun enters them the seasons are about to change. Those born under them are correspondingly versatile and ready to compromise.

Oimelc: *See* Imbolc.

Ostara: The Celtic festival of the spring equinox.

Pentacle: A ritual item, symbol of the Earth, consisting of a flat, round disc, engraved with a pentagram.

Pentagram: A five-pointed diagram, one of the most sacred geometric forms in magick. Each of the five points represents one of the five elemental powers. The uppermost, single point is symbolic of Spirit, or *Akasha*.

Poppet: A featureless doll made of cloth that is filled with herbs and used in healing or as a talisman to attract love or fertility. It may also be made of clay and used as a focus for positive magick to being health or happiness to the person represented by it.

Power hand: The hand you write with, used to transmit assertive and creative energies. *See also* Receptive hand.

Quarters: The four segments of a magical circle. Each is associated with specific archangels, colours, crystals, herbs, incenses, ritual tools, etc.

Receptive hand: The hand you do not write with. Used for receiving energies. *See also* Power hand.

Rede: A rule or moral code. The Wiccan Rede states: 'An [If] it harm none, do what you will', and so ensures all magick has a positive intent.

Sabbat: One of eight special days of the year on which Wiccan celebrations are held – the solstices, the equinoxes and the Celtic Fire festivals.

Samhain: The Celtic Fire festival of the new year, celebrated at the end of summer.

Scrying: Seeing magical images in a reflective medium, such as a crystal ball, mirror or a natural moving source of inspiration, such as fire, water or clouds. The word 'scry' comes from the Anglo-Saxon word *descry*, which means 'to perceive dimly'.

Shamanism: Possibly the oldest spiritual practice in the world, continued today in communities as far apart as India, Australia, Japan and China, Siberia and Mongolia, in Africa, among the Bedouins in the Middle East and in North, Central and South America.

Sky-clad: Naked.

Sky Gods: The powerful patriarchal gods of the classical and Viking world, for example Zeus of the Greeks, Jupiter of the Romans, Odin of the Vikings and Thunor of the Anglo-Saxons. They gained supremacy over the Earth Mother who appears as their wife–consort, full of human foibles.

Solstice: One of the main astronomical points of the year. The summer solstice (21 June, or 21 December in the southern hemisphere) marks the Sun at its height and greatest power. The winter solstice (21 December or 21 June) is the shortest day when the Sun is at its weakest and it was feared by early humans that the Sun would die.

Spirit guides: Guardians from another dimension who advise and protect humans. They may be deceased relatives, wise teachers, for example Native Americans, angels or evolved essences who never assumed mortal form.

Talisman: A charm or amulet that has been charged with specific healing or magical energies to make it powerful and to attract health, wealth or luck. It tends to become more powerful the more it is used.

Tarot: A pack of 78 highly illustrated cards often used in rituals to represent people or qualities that are being sought in a spell.

Threefold Law: A law in Wicca that states that whatever you do or send to others, good or bad, will be returned to you threefold – a great incentive to positive thought and action.

Thurible: *See* Censer.

Transcendent: Term used of god forms to express the belief that their existence extends beyond and is separate from creation. *See also* Immanent.

Triple Goddess: A concept of a deity found in many cultures. May represent the three main phases of the Moon – maiden, mother and crone – or, as in Celtic tradition especially, three sisters.

Tulpa: A thought form created by medieval occultists seeking mastery over the elemental beings that they fashioned by their incantations. In extreme cases a tulpa might destroy its creator – hence the warnings of the Threefold Law.

Wheel of the Year: *See* Eightfold Wheel of the Year.

Wicca: A contemporary, neo-pagan religion that regards the divine life source as a part of nature, not a force beyond creation. This divine source of life is manifest as the god and goddess within everything living, male and female, animal, bird, tree and flower. Sometimes regarded as the oldest religion on the world.

Wiccan Rede: *See* Rede.

Widdershins: Anti-clockwise, moonwise, or against the Sun. The direction used in closing a circle, banishing or removing pain and in banishing magick generally. *See also* Deosil.

Yin and yang: The complementary components of everything in life, according to ancient Chinese philosophy. Yang is the original Sun concept of light, power, masculinity, assertiveness, logic and action. It controls heaven and all things positive. It is balanced by Yin, the original Moon concept of darkness, receptivity, femininity, intuition, acceptance and inaction. Yin controls the Earth and all things negative.

Further Reading

Alchemy

Holyard, E J, *Alchemy*, 1990, Dover Publications

Jung, Carl Gustav, *Alchemical Studies*, 1983, Princetown University Press

Amulets and talismans

Gonzalez-Wipler, Migene, *Complete Guide to Amulets and Talismans*, 1991, Llewellyn

Thomas, Willam, and Pavitt, Kate, *The Book of Talismans, Amulets and Zodiacal Gems*, 1998, Kessinger

Annual almanacs

Llewellyn's Almanac, Llewellyn

Llewellyn's Pocket Planner and Ephemeris, Llewellyn

Old Moore's Almanack, Foulsham

Tybol Astrological Almanac, 27 Heversham Avenue, Fulwood, Preston PR2 9TD

Angels, faeries and nature spirits

Bloom, William, *Working with Angels, Faeries and Nature Spirits*, 1998, Piatkus

Burnham, Sophie, *A Book of Angels*, 1990, Ballantine

Candle magick

Buckland, Ray, *Advanced Candle Magic*, 1996, Llewellyn, St Paul, Minnesota

Eason, Cassandra, *Candle Power*, 1999, Blandford

Heath, Maya, *Ceridwen's Handbook of Incense, Oils and Candles: Being a Guide to the Magical and Spiritual Uses of Oils, Incense, Candles and the Like*, 1996, Words of Wisdom International Inc.

Pajeon, Kala and Pajeon, Ketz, *The Candle Magic Workbook*, 1991, Citadel Carol, New York

Candle-making and uses

Guy, Gary V, *Easy-to-make Candles*, 1980, Dover Publications

Innes, Miranda, *The Book of Candles*, 1991, Dorling Kindersley

Larkin, Chris, *The Book of Candlemaking: Creating Scent, Beauty and Light*, 1998, Sterling Publications, New York

Celtic spirituality

Anderson, Rosemarie, *Celtic Oracles*, 1999, Piatkus

Ellis-Berresford, Peter, *The Druids*, 1994, Constable Robinson

Green, Miranda, *Dictionary of Celtic Myth and Legend*, 1992, Thames & Hudson

Matthews, Caitlín and John, *The Encyclopaedia of Celtic Wisdom*, 1994, Element

Nichols, Ross, *The Book of Druidry*, 1990, Aquarian/Thorsons

Chakras

Dale, Cyndi, *New Chakra Healing, The Revolutionary 32-Center Energy System*, 1996, Llewellyn

Karagulla, Shafica and Van Gelder Kunz, Dora, *Chakras and the Human Energy Field*, 1994, Theosophical University Press

Colour healing and magick

Buckland, Ray, *Practical Color Magic*, 1996, Llewellyn, St Paul, Minnesota

Klotsche, Charles, *Color Medicine: The Secrets of Color/Vibrational Healing*, 1993, Light Technology Publications

Sun, Howard and Dorothy, *Colour Your Life*, Piatkus, 1999

Crystals

Bourgault, Luc, *The American Indian Secrets of Crystal Healing*, 1997, Quantum

Cunningham, Scott, *Encyclopaedia of Crystal, Gem and Metal Magic*, 1991, Llewellyn, St Paul, Minnesota

Eason, Cassandra, *Crystals Talk to the Woman Within*, 2000, Quantum

Dowsing and black streams

Bailey, Arthur, *Anyone can Dowse for Better Health*, 1999, Quantum

Lonegren, Sig, *Spiritual Dowsing, Gothic Images*, 1986, Druids

Flowers, trees and plants

Graves, Robert, *The White Goddess*, 1988, Faber and Faber (in my opinion the best book on the tree alphabet and tree lore)

Tompkins and Bird, *The Secret Life of Plants*, 1974, Avon Books, New York

Flower remedies

Barnard, Julian, *A Guide to the Bach Flower Remedies*, 1992, C W Daniel & Co.

Harvey, Clare G, and Cochrane, Amanda, *The Encyclopaedia of Flower Remedies*, 1995, Thorsons/HarperCollins

Korte, Andreas, *Orchids, Gemstones and the Healing Energies*, 1993, Bauer Verlag

Goddesses

Budapest, Z, *The Holy Book of Women's Mysteries*, 1990, Harper Row, New York

Farrar, Janet and Stewart, *The Witches' Goddess, The Feminine Principle of Divinity*, 1987, Phoenix Publishing Inc., New York

Gadon, Elinor, *The Once and Future Goddess*, 1990, Aquarian/Thorsons

Starhawk, *The Spiral Dance*, 1999, Harper Row, San Francisco

Healing

Brennan, Barbara Ann, *Hands of Light: A Guide to Healing Through the Human Energy Field*, 1987, Bantam Publishers

Eden, Donna, *Energy Medicine*, 1999, Piatkus

Herbalism

Cunningham, Scott, *The Encyclopaedia of Herbs*, 1997, Llewellyn, St Paul, Minnesota

Lipp, Frank J, *Herbalism*, 1996, Macmillan

History of witchcraft

Adler, Margot, *Drawing Down the Moon*, 1997, Penguin, USA

Briggs, Robin, *Witches and Neighbours, The Social and Cultural Context of European Witchcraft*, 1996, HarperCollins

Crowley, Vivienne, *Wicca, The Old Religion on the New Age*, 1989, Aquarian/ Thorsons

Guiley, Rosemary Ellen, *The Encyclopaedia of Witches and Witchcraft*, 1989, Facts on File, New York

Murray, Margaret, *The God of the Witches*, 1992, Oxford University Press

Incenses and oils

Cunningham, Scott, *The Complete Book of Oils, Incenses and Brews*, 1991, Llewellyn, St Paul, Minnesota

Dunwich, Gerena, *The Wicca Garden, A Witch's Guide to Magical and Enchanted Herbs and Plants*, 1996, Citadel, Carol, New York

Magick and ritual

Eason, Cassandra, *The Complete Guide to Magic and Ritual*, 1999, Piatkus

Eason, Cassandra, *Every Woman a Witch*, 1996, Quantum

Fortune, Dion, *Applied Magick*, 2000, Samuel Weiser, New York

Fortune, Dion, *Moon Magick* (fiction), 1985, Aquarian

Fortune, Dion, *The Sea Priestess* (fiction), 2000, Samuel Weiser, New York

Valiente, Doreen, *Natural Magic*, 1985, Phoenix Publishing Inc., New York

Native Americans

Meadows, Kenneth, *Earth Medicine*, 1996, Element

Wallace, Black Elk, and Lyon, William, *Black Elk: The Sacred Ways of a Lakota*, 1990, Harper and Row, New York

Psychic phenomena

Sheldrake, Rupert, *Dogs that Know When Their Owners Are Coming Home and Other Unexplained Powers of Animals: An Investigation*, 1999, Crown Publishing

Psychic protection

Eason, Cassandra, *Psychic Protection Lifts the Spirit*, 2000, Quantum

Fortune, Dion, *Psychic Self-Defence*, 1988, Aquarian

Seasonal magick, old festivals and mythology

Cooper, JC, Aquarian *Dictionary of Festivals*, 1990, Aquarian/ Thorsons

Green, Marian, *A Calendar of Festivals*, 1991, Element

Stewart, Bob, *Where Is St George? Pagan Imagery in English Folksong*, 1988, Blandford

Walker, Barbara, *The Woman's Encyclopaedia of Myths and Secrets*, 1983, Pandora

Willis, Roy, *World Mythology*, 1993, Piatkus

Shamanism

Castenada, Carlos, *Journey to Ixtlan*, 1972, Penguin

Devereux, Paul, *Shamanism and the Mystery Lines*, 2000, Quantum

Wahoo, Dhyani, *Voices of Our Ancestors*, 1987, Shambhala

Theosophy

Blavatsky, Helena, *The Key to Theosophy*, 1991, Theosophical University Press

Blavatsky, Helena, *The Secret Doctrine: The Synthesis of Science, Religion and Philosophy*, 1992, Theosophical University Press

Western magical tradition and the Golden Dawn

Matthews, Caitlin and John, *The Western Way: A Practical Guide to the Western Mystical Tradition*, 1986, Arkana

Regardie, Israel, *The Golden Dawn: A Complete Course in Practical Ceremonial Magic*, 1989, Llewellyn, St Paul, Minnesota

Wicca and witchcraft

Buckland, Raymond, *Buckland's Complete Guide to Witchcraft*, 1997, Llewellyn

Cunningham, Scott, *Living Wicca, A Guide for the Solitary Practitioner*, 1994, Llewellyn

Steele, Tony, *Water Witches*, 1998, Capall Bann Publishing

Useful Contacts

Cassandra Eason's web site can be found at:
www.cassandraeason.co.uk

Candle suppliers and candle-making equipment

Australia
Price's Candles Ltd
18 Gibson Avenue, Padstow, NSW 2211

Canada
Lyndon House International Inc.
12605A–127 Avenue, Edmonton, Alberta, T5L 3ES

UK
Price's Candles Ltd
10 York Road, London, SE11 3RU

USA
Wax Wonder
221 North Main Street, Versailles, Kentucky 40383

Collectibles

Australia
G &M Treasures
PO Box 133, Kippas, ACT 2615
(Fantasy figures, pewter figurines)

UK
The Faerie Shoppe
105 High Street, Marlborough, Wiltshire
3 Montpelier Walk, Cheltenham, Gloucestershire
6 Lower Borough Walk, Bath, Avon
(All things faerie)

Snapdragon
12 South Park, Sevenoaks, Kent, TN13 1AW
(All kinds of faerie collectibles, dragons, etc.)

USA
Light as a Feather
Eric Torgeson, 216 Palisade Drive, Eureka Springs, Arizona 72631
(Hand-sculptured glass faeries)

Joyce Wiseman
PO Box 333, Comptche, CA 95427
(Mermaids, faerie dolls, mermaid and faerie cards)

Crystals, amulets, magical supplies, etc.

Australia
The Mystic Trader
125 Flinders Lane, Melbourne 3000
(Mail order as well as personal service)

Mysterys
Level 1, 314–322 Darling Street, Balmain, New South Wales
(Wiccan Supplies by mail order)

South Africa
The Wellstead
1 Wellington Avenue, Wynberg, Cape 7300
(Mail order)

UK
Futhark
18 Halifax Road, Todmorden, Lancashire, OL14 5AD
(Occult, magical and alchemical supplies of all kinds by mail order)

Mandragora
Essex House, Thame, Oxfordshire, OX9 3LS
(Mail order)

Mysteries
7 Monmouth Street, London, WC2H 9DA
(Shop and mail order for absolutely everything for the New Age, plus good advice)

Pentagram
11 Cheapside, Wakefield, West Yorkshire, WF1 2SD
(International mail order and personal service for everything for the New Age, Wicca and the occult)

USA
The Crystal Cave
415 West Foothill Blvd, Claremont, CA 91711
(Mail order suppliers stocking a huge variety of crystals and stones, including unusual ones)

Eye of the Cat
3314 East Broadway, Long Beach, CA 90803
(Mail order crystals and other New Age commodities)

Open Door Metaphysical Shoppe
428 North Buchanan Circle, Suite 16, Pacheco, CA 94553
(Mail order New Age supplies)

Spirit Search Emporium
Sun Angel Innovations, 3939 West Windmills Blvd, 2060 Chandler,
Arizona 85226

Druids

UK
The Order of Bards, Ovates and Druids
PO Box 1333, Lewes, East Sussex, BN7 1DX
(Worldwide contacts and training programme)

Earth energies

Australia
Dowsers Society of New South Wales
c/o Mrs E Miksevicius, 126 Fiddens Wharf Road, Killara, NSW 2031

Southern Tasmania Dowsing Association
PO Box 101, Moonah, Tasmania, Australia 7009

UK
British Society of Dowsers
Sycamore Barn, Hastingleigh, Ashford, Kent, TN25 5HW

Findhorn Foundation
The Park, Forres, Scotland, IV36 OTS
(Workshops and courses that teach about meditation, consciousness
and nature spirits)

USA
The American Society of Dowsers
Dowsers Hall, Danville, Vermont, 05828-0024

Flower and tree essences

Australia
The Australian Flower Remedy Society
PO Box 531 Spit Junction, New South Wales 2007

Sabian, PO Box 527, Kew, Victoria, Australia 3101
or The Sabian Centre, 11 Selbourne Road, Kew, Victoria 31031

UK
Bach Flower Remedies
Healing Herbs Ltd, PO Box 65, Hereford HR2 0UW

USA
Alaskan Flower Essence Project
PO Box 1329, Homer AL99603

Desert Alchemy
PO Box 44189, Tucson, Arizona, AZ 85733

Pacific Essences
PO Box 8317, Victoria,V8W 3R9

Herbs and oils – professional organisations

Australia
The National Association of Herbalists
PO Box 65, Kingsgrove, NSW 2208

UK
The National Herbalists' Association
56 Longbrook Street, Exeter, Devon, EX4 6AH

The International Society of Professional Aromatherapists
Hinckley and District Hospital and Health Centre (Head Office),
The Annexe, Mount Road, Hinckley, Leicestershire, LE10 1AG

The Herb Society
PO Box 599, London, SW11 4BW
(Information on herbs)

Herbs and oils – suppliers

UK
G Baldwin and Co.
171–173 Walworth Road, London, SE17 1RW
(Largest range of herbs and herbal products in the UK with extensive
mail order)

Gerard House
736 Christchurch Road, Bournemouth, BH7 6BZ
(Dried herbs by mail order)

Neals Yard Remedies
15 Neal's Yard, London, WC2H 9DP
(Oils by mail order)

USA
The American Herbalists Guild
PO Box 1683, Soquel, CA 95073

Joan Teresa Power Products
PO Box 442, Mars Hill, NC 28754
(Unusual herbs, plants, oils, incenses, etc. by mail order)

The Sage Garden
PO Box144, Payette, ID 83661
(Herbs, oils, amulets and incenses by mail order)

Meditation and visualisation music

Australia
New World Productions
PO Box 244, WBO, Red Hill, Queensland 4059

UK
New World Cassettes
Freepost, Paradise Farm, Westhall, Halesworth, Suffolk IP19 8RH
(Music by mail order; free catalogue)

Stress Busters
Beechwood Music, Littleton House, Littleton Road, Ashford,
Middlesex, TW15 1UU
(Music of pan pipes, rainforest, surf and whales)

USA
Raven Recordings
744 Broad Street, Room 1815, Newark, New Jersey 07102
(Meditation music, videos and tapes by Gabrielle Roth, an expert on
the subject)

Paganism

Australia
Novocastrian Pagan Information Centre
Laren, PO Box 129, Stockton, New South Wales 2295

The Pagan Alliance PO Box 823, Bathurst, New South Wales 2795
(An umbrella movement for pagan organisations)

UK
The Pagan Federation
PO Box 7097, London, WC1N 3XX

Shamanism

UK
Eagle's Wing Centre for Contemporary Shamanism
PO Box 7475, London, WC1N 3XX

Faculty of Shamanics
Kenneth and Beryl Meadows, PO Box 300, Potters Bar, Hertfordshire,
EN6 4LE

USA
Dance of the Deer Foundation
Center for Shamanic Studies, PO Box 699, Soquel, CA 95073

Spiritual healing

Australia
Australian Spiritualist Association
PO Box 248, Canterbury, New South Wales 2193

Canada
National Federation of Spiritual Healers (Canada), Toronto, Ontario

Spiritualist Church of Canada
1835 Laurence Ave East, Scarborough, Ontario, M1TR 2Y3

UK
British Alliance of Healing Associations
Mrs Jo Wallace, 3 Sandy Lane, Gisleham, Lowestoft, Suffolk,
NR 33 8EQ.

National Federation of Spiritual Healers
Old Manor Farm Studio, Church Street, Sunbury on Thames,
Middlesex, TW16 6RG

USA
World of Light
PO Box 425, Wappingers Falls, NY 12590
(List of healers)

Wicca and Goddess organisations

UK
Fellowship of Isis
Lady Olivia Robertson, Clonegal Castle, Enniscorthy, Co. Wexford,
Eire
(Worldwide network of Goddess worshippers)

USA
Circle Sanctuary
PO Box 219, Mount Horeb, WI 53572
(Contacts with 700 pagan groups, networks, etc.)

Covenant of the Goddess
PO Box 1226, Berkeley, California, 94704

The Witches' Voice Inc.
PO Box 4924, Clearwater, Florida
(A resource organisation with worldwide links)

Index of Spells

Ceremonial rituals

Index